Theory Construction in Nursing

Theory Construction in Nursing
An adaptation model

Sister Callista Roy

Chair and Associate Professor
Department of Nursing
Mount St. Mary's College

Adjunct Associate Professor
School of Nursing
University of Portland

Sharon L. Roberts

Associate Professor
Department of Nursing
California State University, Long Beach

PRENTICE-HALL, INC., *Englewood Cliffs, N.J. 07632*

Library of Congress Cataloging in Publication Data

Roy, Callista.
  Theory construction in nursing.

  Includes bibliographies and index.
  1. Nursing—Philosophy. 2. Theory (Philosophy)
3. Adaptation (Physiology) 4. Adjustment (Psychology)
I. Roberts, Sharon L., joint author.
II. Title.
RT84.5.R69   610.75'01   80-24418
ISBN 0-13-913657-6

©1981 by Prentice-Hall, Inc., Englewood Cliffs, N.J. 07632

Editorial/production supervision by Karen J. Clemments
Interior design by Karen J. Clemments
Cover design by Edsal Enterprises
Manufacturing buyer: John Hall

Printed in the United States of America

10 9 8 7 6 5 4 3 2

PRENTICE-HALL INTERNATIONAL, INC., *London*
PRENTICE-HALL OF AUSTRALIA PTY. LIMITED, *Sydney*
PRENTICE-HALL OF CANADA, LTD., *Toronto*
PRENTICE-HALL OF INDIA PRIVATE LIMITED, *New Delhi*
PRENTICE-HALL OF JAPAN, INC., *Tokyo*
PRENTICE-HALL OF SOUTHEAST ASIA PTE. LTD., *Singapore*
WHITEHALL BOOKS LIMITED, *Wellington, New Zealand*

To Sister Rebecca Doan

> President, Mount St. Mary's College,
> Founder and Chair, Department of Nursing:
> my teacher, my friend
> S.C.R.

To Jim and Brad Wille

> my nephews and friends
> S.L.R.

Contributing authors

Betty J. Hill, R.N., Ph.D.

Associate Professor
Northern Michigan University
Marquette, Michigan

Carolyn S. Roberts, R.N., Ph.D.

Associate Professor
Faculty of Nursing
The University of Western Ontario
London, Canada

Dorothy McLeod, R.N., Ph.D.

Professor
College of Nursing
Arizona State University
Tempe, Arizona

Contents

III Theory of Adaptive Modes:
Physiological Needs 71

6 **Exercise and rest** 72

7 **Nutrition** 93

8 **Elimination** 112

Preface

One important aspect of the development of any scientific field is theory development. Concepts describe the phenomena of the discipline. Then concepts are linked in propositions and finally propositions are linked in theoretical formulations. These theoretical formulations are used to explain and predict the phenomena involved. When quantum theory was introduced into physics many physical phenomena became understandable. This understanding could be turned into prescriptions for the practice of engineering. Nursing has entered a time when theories are being developed to explain the phenomena of nursing. From this understanding will come prescriptions for nursing practice.

One model of nursing that can lead to theory development is the adaptation model. A number of authors have written on the various forms of this model. One form, the Roy Adaptation Model, has become increasingly well known. It has been adopted as the basis for nursing curricula in numerous schools in this country and Canada, and is receiving increasing attention abroad. An earlier text, *Introduction to Nursing: An Adaptation Model*, developed the model for the beginning student and practitioner using the model for the first time. Yet it was recognized that the model needed to be developed in depth on the theoretical level. Based on the need for theory development in nursing and the need for a theoretical approach based on the Roy Adaptation Model, this book discusses theory construction in nursing and uses the elements of the Roy Adaptation Model to construct nursing theory.[1]

All nursing students study theory development in nursing. On the associate degree and diploma level this study is included within the nursing practice courses. On the baccalaureate level, it is likely to be a major part of specific courses in research and professional trends. Masters and doctoral students take courses in nursing theory and theory development. Scholars in nursing are vitally interested in theory construction in nursing and in defining a science of nursing. Instructors in associate degree and diploma programs, students on the baccalaureate, masters, and doctoral level, and scholars in nursing need materials on theory construction in nursing. The numerous schools using the Roy Adaptation Model need further theoretical material on this model. Yet textbook material on theory construction in nursing is limited. Certainly, there has been limited theoretical treatment of the Roy Adaptation Model. This book is therefore offered as a contribution to the growing scientific discipline of nursing and also as a response to specific needs within nursing education and academia.

Part I of the book focuses on theory construction in nursing. It discusses the types, procedures, uses, and evaluation of theory construction, then examines where nursing is in its theory development. Finally, one example of formal theory construction is given.[2] Part II of the book introduces the Roy Adaptation Model. It then begins the process of theory construction by proposing a general theory of the adaptive system. Parts III and IV develop individual theories of each adaptive mode—physiological needs, self concept, role function and interdependence.

These two sections reflect different levels of theoretical development of the adaptive modes. It was originally intended that for each basic need, a system would be constructed which showed the parts involved. In dealing with the physiological mode we hesitated to use biological systems since this is the specific domain of medical science. Thus, in keeping with the goal of developing theory for nursing science, the regulator is used as the overall system of the physiological needs. The propositions[3] for the regulator system

---

1. A model is broader than a theory and, as will be clear from the discussion in Chapter 2, the model is basic to the theorizing done, but we are not claiming that the concept of nursing presented by Sister Callista Roy is a theory.

2. This example, Chapter 3, presupposes some understanding of the Roy adaptation model. The reader who is unfamiliar with the model may want to read Chapter 4 before reading Chapter 3 or to refer to other works by Roy listed in the references.

3. In introducing the notion of the propositions developed, we want to clarify that the adaptation model implies multivariable and nonlinear configurations. However, at this initial stage in our theorizing, we have begun by drawing relationships which imply linear relationships and are largely bivariate. It is clear that much work remains to be done.

are thus applied to each of the physiological needs. Since nursing interventions related to this mode are more clearly developed, each of the chapters in Part III includes a discussion of nursing interventions. However, a clear typology of nursing interventions awaits further work. Each chapter closes with an hypothesis for practice. To carry out the process of theorizing with the psychosocial modes in Part IV each mode is viewed as a system and propositions specific to that system are developed. Finally, since nursing interventions in these modes are relatively undeveloped, the specific propositions are developed into an hypothesis which makes a given prediction about nursing practice. The book closes with Part V drawing general conclusions about the theory that has been constructed. Sharon Roberts was responsible for Part III, while Sister Callista Roy was the main author of the other parts, and Dorothy McLeod developed the regulator mechanism material.

This text is presented with the hope that it will further the discussion of theory construction in nursing, a task essential to the current stage of development of the science of nursing. It also can provide direction for the great task remaining in developing and validating that science. Ultimately, we want to demonstrate that the practice of nursing, based on the science of nursing, makes a difference in the health status of the population. The theorizing efforts presented here are preliminary, but do provide us with a sense of direction in working toward that goal.

Of the many persons contributing to this developing work, we would like particularly to thank the faculty and students working with Sister Callista Roy at Mount St. Mary's College and at the University of Portland. We are also indebted to our consultants on the various parts of the project: Dorothy McLeod, Dwight Risky, Felix Roy, Dorothy Johnson, and Margaret Hardy, and, too, faculty of the Department of Sociology at the University of California at Los Angeles, who worked with Sister Callista Roy on concepts basic to this work, especially Melvin Seeman, Ralph Turner, and Kenneth Bailey. We also appreciate the help of our capable typists, especially Ruth Garrick. Lastly, Sister Callista is particularly grateful for her interactions with other nurse theorists in the group working with the National Conference on Nursing Diagnosis. Together, much progress in nursing science is possible.

Sister Callista Roy
Sharon Roberts

Los Angeles, California

Nursing as a scientific discipline is involved in theory construction. This procedure is one step in the total process of providing a unique body of knowledge for nursing. The individual nurse can then use this knowledge in her practice of caring for persons in health and illness. This book explores and participates in the process of theory construction in nursing.

In Chapter 1, we look at theory construction in general—its uses, levels, procedures, and evaluation. A format for theorizing introduced in this chapter is used for the theory construction done in later chapters. Chapter 2 focuses on theory construction in nursing specifically. It begins by considering the kind of theory that nursing needs, then evaluates the status of theory construction in nursing. Finally, in Chapter 3, we present an example of one process of formal theory construction.

Theory Construction in Nursing

PART I

CHAPTER 1

Theory construction: uses, levels, procedures, and evaluation

Human beings have a need to comprehend the world around them. One way they comprehend is through knowledge. Knowledge comes in many ways and in many forms. There is practical knowledge based on daily experience. There is also scientific knowledge built around generations of study and research. In the process of building scientific knowledge, theories are constructed.

The simplest definition of a theory comes from the philosophy of science: A theory is a set of sentences whose purpose is to explain. These sentences, like all sentences, have semantics and syntax. The semantics are the meaning given to the elements, or words. As Hempel (1965) notes, some elements are primitive terms—those for which no definition is specified. A second set of elements includes the derived terms—those with a specifically introduced definition.

The syntax of the sentences of a theory is the relation expressed between the elements. Hardy (1974) has specified the various relationships that can be stated in theoretical statements, along with their nature and meaning (see Figure 1.1).

In a *symmetrical* relationship the concepts are related reciprocally.

Nature of relation	Meaning
Symmetrical	If A, then B; if B, then A
Asymmetrical	If A, then B, but if no A, no conclusion about B
Causal	If A, always B
Probabilistic	If A, probably B
Time order	If A, later B
Concurrent	If A, also B
Sufficient	If A, then B, regardless of anything else
Conditional	If A, then B but only if C
Necessary	If A and only if A, then B

FIGURE 1.1. Relationships between Concepts. Not all relations are mutually exclusive. Source: Hardy, Margaret E. "Theories: Components, Development, Evaluation," Copyright © 1974 American Journal of Nursing Company. Reprinted from *Nursing Research*, March-April, Vol. 23, No. 2.

For example, it may be possible to demonstrate that loss of weight leads to a change in body image and that, likewise, a change in body image can lead to loss of weight. This would be a symmetrical relationship. An *asymmetrical* relationship simply says that one factor occurs in association with another; for example, if there is loss of weight, then there will be a change in body image. In an asymmetrical relationship, however, we cannot come to the reciprocal conclusion; that is, we do not know whether a change in body image will be related to loss of weight.

A *causal* relationship shows an invariant link between two concepts. This type of relationship is extremely difficult to establish in the sciences related to human behavior. To state the relationship between loss of weight and body image causally, we would have to be able to say that if there is a loss of weight, there is always a change in body image. On the other hand, a *probabilistic* relationship states a likely occurrence of the second factor; for example, if weight loss, probably a change in body image.

Time order and *concurrent* refer to the sequencing of the occurrence of the two factors under consideration. Thus we might say that if there is weight loss, later there will also be a change in body image (time order) or, if weight loss, also a change in body image at the same time (concurrent).

Sufficient, conditional, and *necessary* describe relationships that are influenced by other factors. *Sufficient* means that the relationship exists regardless of anything else. Thus, if we know that weight loss leads to a change in body image, even if all other circumstances change, then the relationship is sufficient. A *conditional* relationship requires the existence of a third factor. For example, we might state that weight loss leads to a change in body image only if the client has concurrent psychotherapy. In a

necessary relationship the first factor must be present for the second to occur. Thus, to make the relationship necessary in our example, we would
have to say that if there is a weight loss, and only if there is a weight loss,
then there will be a change in body image.

The relations expressed in a theory are considered lawlike propositions. However, lawlike propositions in themselves are not theories. Only
when combined into interrelated systems do they constitute theory. For example, Zetterberg (1954) cites the 1045 propositions listed as research findings on human behavior. He notes that they are not theory since they are
not interrelated. Facts alone do not lead to major advances in any science.
Rather, empirical data must be organized and interrelated so that they can
be interpreted and unified. This is the function of theory.

In looking at the form that theory takes, Blalock (1969) states that
"Ideally, one might hope to achieve a completely closed deductive
theoretical system in which there would be a minimal set of propositions
taken as axioms, from which all other propositions could be deduced by
purely mathematical or logical reasoning." He admits, however, that the
model of the completely closed deductive system can only be approximated
in practice.

With this brief introduction on the nature of theory, we can turn to
the uses of theory.

Uses of Theory

We have noted that theory building contributes to knowledge. One form of
knowledge is explanation, but there are other forms as well. According to
Reynolds' (1971) summary of its goals, scientific knowledge provides:

1. A method of organizing and categorizing phenomena, a *typology*
2. *Predictions* of future events
3. *Explanations* of past events
4. A sense of *understanding* about what causes events
5. The potential for *control* of events

The elements of theory contribute to these goals of scientific
knowledge. Theory building can begin by searching for theoretical concepts
to describe social phenomena. After categories or dimensions are named,
these labels can be classified. This arrangement of labels is the typology.
The typology serves the development of scientific knowledge by outlining
the meaning (semantics) of the domain of science. Theory development then
moves from conceptual schemes or typologies to lawlike propositions that
interrelate the concepts. Predictions relate to outcomes. In a prediction we

foretell the value of one or more units making up a system or anticipate the condition or state of a system as a whole. The lawlike proposition is precisely the prediction. It states that if you change one variable in a given way, there will be a resulting change in the associated variable. Beyond prediction, scientific knowledge aims at understanding. In understanding we come to knowledge about the interaction of units. In theory building, the linkages of the propositions provide how and why connections that specify interactions. Thus as theory explains causal mechanisms it contributes to understanding. Finally, control of events is not an essential aim of scientific knowledge, but is sometimes an appropriate outcome. If a theory provides understanding of how certain variables affect one another, and if it is possible to change one of the variables, then theory can contribute to the control of events. Theory building, therefore, is closely related to the goals of scientific knowledge and is used to describe, predict, understand, and control events.

A revised definition of theory can be stated as follows: A theory is a system of interrelated propositions used to describe, predict, explain, understand, and control a part of the empirical world. Given this definition, we can enter a discussion of the levels of theory construction.

Levels of Theory Construction

If theories deal with a part of the empirical world, then levels of theory can be distinguished by the scope of the world that they are intended to describe, predict, explain, understand, or control. This scope can range from all the empirical events of an entire science or discipline to an isolated occurrence in the real world.

A theory that attempts to deal with the entire field under consideration is commonly referred to as a grand theory. Grand theories are global in nature and in the broadest outlines sweep over the whole range of phenomena under consideration. For example, some would consider the broad, general outlines of nursing practice developed by such persons as Rogers, Orem, Roy, and Johnson to be the grand theories of nursing (The Nursing Theories Conference Group, George, Chairperson 1980). These formulations specify the elements of nursing in a most general way.[1]

A theory dealing with a given event in the here and now may be called abstracted empiricism (Mills 1959). In this approach, no attempt is made to generalize beyond the phenomena under condsideration. We may, for example, develop a theory of the etiology of a given nursing diagnosis for a

---

1. According to the distinction between model and theory which is made in Chapter 2, these conceptualizations may be called more properly models of nursing practice.

given patient. We could specify the factors that contributed to a patient's refusal to maintain bedrest. As the factors are enumerated and related to one another and related to the effect, an abstract picture is formed. However, this picture is rooted in observation and experience, the bases of empiricism. We may refer to an example from sociology. A theory of the cause of a given race riot could be an example of abstracted empiricism.

Between these two extremes in levels of theory construction lies the level that Merton (1957) calls middle-range theory. This level of theory is characterized by its empirical testability and its middle level of generality. Merton notes that the concepts of such theories are specific enough to be effectively utilized in organizing the evidence bearing upon determinate ranges of phenomena and general enough to be consolidated into increasingly broader sets of generalizations. Jacox (1974) notes that theory-building efforts in nursing may more realistically be focused on this level of theory development. She suggests theories of limited aspects of nursing such as a nursing theory of pain alleviation, or one concerned with the promotion of sleep, or with teaching health measures, or with rehabilitation, or socialization of the patient into the health care system. Merton's own discussion of social structure and anomie is an example of middle-range theory from sociology.

These varying levels of theory can be constructed using specific procedural approaches, as discussed in the next section.

Procedures Used in Theory Building

Theory building takes place through the basic procedures of induction and deduction. A special form of theory derived from these procedures is the axiomatic form. Each procedure will be described briefly.

Induction

The inductive process of theory construction works from the specifics of empirical situations to generalizations about the data. This approach is perhaps best exemplified in the grounded theory of Glaser and Strauss (1967). These authors prescribe that the researcher immerse himself in the data of the research project to attempt to generate new theoretical insights. They argue for grounding theory in research itself—for generating it from data. They state their position is not logical, but phenomenological.[2]

---

2. Inductive reasoning is phenomenological in that it is based on sense data. However, this is a great oversimplification of phenomenology. For further discussion see Marvin Farber, *The Foundation of Phenomenology* (Albany: State University of New York, 1967).

The position of Glaser and Strauss is linked to the general method of comparative analysis. They encourage qualitative research in the library and field. Although they admit that it is necessary to verify as much as possible with as accurate evidence as possible while one discovers and generates one's theory, they also hold that verification should not become so paramount as to curb generation. Their point is that generation of theory through comparative analysis both subsumes and assumes verifications and accurate descriptions, but only to the extent that these are in the service of theory generation.

The steps in this inductive process are not unlike the elements of deductive theory development. For Glaser and Strauss, the elements of the theory are, first, the conceptual categories and their conceptual properties, and then the hypotheses, or generalized relations among the categories and among their properties. The difference is in the process used to derive these elements. In developing grounded theory, the researcher initially enters the field with only a general perspective and a general subject or problem area, not a *preconceived theoretical* framework. He uses "local" concepts; that is, he designates a few principle or gross features of the structure and processes in the situations that he will study. Glaser and Strauss give the example of studying a hospital and using the concepts doctors, nurses and aides, and wards and admission procedures. Conceptual categories and their conceptual properties are then indicated by the data.

Glaser and Strauss point out that a category stands by itself as a conceptual element, while a property is an aspect of a conceptual element. The example they use to illustrate this distinction is that two conceptual elements or categories of nursing care are the nurse's "professional composure" and her "perceptions of social loss" of a dying patient—that is, her view of what degree of loss the patient's death will represent to his family and occupation. One property of the category of perceptions of social loss is "loss rationales"—that is, the rationales nurses use to justify to themselves their perceptions of social loss. The authors note that both categories and properties are concepts indicated by the data (and not the data itself). By constantly comparing groups, the researcher's attention is drawn to their many similarities and differences. Considering these similarities and differences leads to the generation of abstract categories and their properties. Glaser and Strauss suggest that lower-level categories emerge rather quickly during the early phases of data collection. Higher-level conceptualizations, which they describe as overriding and integrating, and the properties that elaborate them tend to come later during the joint collection, coding, and analysis of data.

The comparison of differences and similarities among groups also leads to the generation of relations among categories, or the step of hypotheses making. For Glaser and Strauss, the step of hypotheses generation requires only that the evidence be sufficient to establish a suggestion. Such evidence is often based on relations that the field worker discovers "in vivo," that is, on relations that she literally "sees." Glaser and Strauss further state that one's hypotheses may, in the beginning, seem unrelated. However, as categories and properties emerge, develop in abstraction, and become related, their accumulating interrelations form an integrated central theoretical framework. This, then, is the core of the emerging grounded theory.

Glaser and Strauss distinguish between substantive and formal theory. Substantive theories are those that are developed for an empirical area of inquiry such as patient care or race relations. Formal theories are those developed for a conceptual area of inquiry such as stigma or deviant behavior. New grounded formal theories arise out of substantive theories. Glaser and Strauss have charted an example of the generation, from clinical data, of the elements of the two kinds of theory (see Table 1.1).

Thus Glaser and Strauss exhibit an inductive approach to theory construction in their grounded theory.

Deduction

In deductive theory construction the method proceeds from generalizations to specific deductions. The deductive method of theory construction can be examined by looking at each of the elements of theory and the procedure used at each stage in this process.

Theory consists first of a set of concepts. The purpose of a concept is to point out the phenomenon under consideration. Labels like decision making and powerlessness are intellectual pointers, highlighting what previously had been dim and obscure. Further, Hage (1972) distinguishes two kinds of theoretical concepts: (1) those that label categories or classes of phenomena, like role set and *Gemeinshaft*; and (2) those that label dimensions of phenomena, like degree of stratification and level of education. Hage calls the latter *general variables* and sees these as more significant for theory development. These concepts can be used in universal laws and they make possible subtle classifications. In discussing the advantages of general variables, he points out that these concepts take into account the complexity of reality. For example, once a society is scored on one dimension, such as population density, the researcher looks for other dimensions since he recognizes that he has only one continuum among many possible ones. The two kinds of concepts distinguished by Hage are also called descriptive and operative. Descriptive concepts or categories show what the theory is about. For example, Durkheim used terms such as individualism, suicide, and Protestantism. Operative concepts or general variables give the properties of natures. These properties may include such variables as suicide rate and in-

TABLE 1.1

Elements of Theory	Types of Theory	
Category	Substantive	Formal
Properties of category	Social loss of dying patients. Calculating social loss on basis of learned and apparent character- istics of patient.	Social value of people. Calculating social value of person on basis of learned and apparent characteristics.
Hypotheses	The higher the social loss of dying patient, (1) the better his care, (2) the more nurses develop loss rationale to explain away his death.	The higher the social value of a person the less delay he experi- ences in receiving services from experts.

Source: Adapted with permission from Barney G. Glaser and Anselm L. Strauss, *The Discovery of Grounded Theory*. New York: Aldine Publishing Company. Copyright © 1967 by Barney G. Glaser and Anselm L. Strauss.

cidence of Protestantism. Variables are concepts that can have various values and that are defined in such a way that one can tell by means of observation which value it has in a particular occurrence. The main concern and strategy of this first step of theory development is to search for the many dimensions describing a unit of analysis.

Since the first step of deductive theory construction is concept forma- tion, we may explore this topic further. Some of the significant work done in concept formation has been Lazarsfeld's (1937) approach to typology construction. We have noted that a classification of labels is a typology. The typology speaks to the meanings included in the domain of the discipline. (Later we will see that theoretical statements add syntax to the outline of the domain.)

Lazarsfeld begins his discussion by describing an attribute or property space as having as many dimensions as there are attributes according to which the individuals of the group are classified. For example, consider Barton's (1955) analysis of a qualitative property space of political position. The two trichotomous dimensions of usual party affiliation (Democratic, Republican, and Independent) and by degree of political interest (high, medium, and low) give a nine-fold property space. Barton also notes that since an IBM card provides an 80-dimensional property space and each prop- erty has 12 classes, the card provides the possibility of locating each respondent in a dichotomous attribute space of 960 dimensions. The at- tribute space is the entire area defined by the dimensions.

In regard to the property space, Lazarsfeld recommends the processes of reduction and substruction. Each of these will be defined and discussed according to their use.

Lazarsfeld says simply, "By reduction is understood any classification as a result of which different combinations fall into one class." Barton says that reduction is the combining of classes in order to obtain a smaller number of categories. This process takes place in the frame of an attribute space. The space has as many dimensions as there are attributes according to which the individuals of the group are classified. Lazarsfeld's example involves three characteristics: to have (+) or not have (−) a college degree, to belong to the white (+) or black (−) race, to be native (+) or foreign born (−). These characteristics provide eight possible combinations.[3]

Using this example, Lazarsfeld distinguishes three kinds of reduction: functional, arbitrary numerical, and pragmatic. In functional reduction there is an actual relationship between two of the attributes which reduces the number of combinations. Thus, in the example, if foreign-born persons usually do not acquire a college degree, certain combinations of variables will not occur in practice and, therefore, the system of combinations is reduced. It may be that a combination does not occur at all or it may be that it occurs so infrequently that no special class need be established.

Lazarsfeld exemplifies the arbitrary numerical reduction by using index numbers. In an analysis of housing conditions, for example, the following procedure may be followed: Several items, such as plumbing, central heating, and refrigeration are selected as indicative and each is given a certain weight. Central heating and ownership of a refrigerator, without plumbing, might be equivalent to plumbing without the other two items, and, therefore, both cases get the same index numbers. In this way the matrix is reduced to a given set of index numbers.

In pragmatic reduction certain groups of combinations are contracted to one class in view of research purposes. Lazarfeld's example of degree-race-nativity, can be so reduced. In considering the concrete problem of discrimination, for instance, perhaps no distinction will be made between the other qualifications of the blacks, and all of them will be regarded as one class. Therefore, the four combinations in which black race occurs are reduced to one.[4]

Reduction is done primarily for two purposes. The first purpose is practical and the second is theoretical. The practical reason is to keep the number of groups compared small enough so that each will have enough

---

3. As we proceed with this example, the authors recognize that Lazarsfeld's discussion could be considered to contain racist elements and is extremely simplistic according to present knowledge of race relations. Nonetheless, the concepts clearly demonstrate the process he is speaking of and thus are retained from the 1937 discussion.

4. Refer to footnote 3 in this chapter.

cases in a limited sample. In the example given earlier, pragmatic reduction can reduce the eight combinations of degree-race-nativity to four classes of an order of social advantage: the native white with college degree, the native white without college degree, the foreign-born white irrespective of education, and the black irrespective of nativity and education.[5] It is a much simpler matter to compare these four categories with some dependent variable than to use the original categories. In addition, the number of cases in each of the four cells is increased. At the same time, one can see the theoretical advantage of this reduction. One is saying more about a relationship when the attribute space has been reduced to meaningful categories. To speak in terms of groups with varying degrees of social advantage is to give some meaning to the various combinations that can occur in the total attribute space. Thus reduction is an important practical and theoretical tool in social research.

Lazarsfeld suggests the name *substruction* for the process that is the reverse of reduction. Substruction is the procedure of finding, for a given system of types, the attribute space in which it belongs and the reduction that has been implicitly used. It is not assumed that the theorist creating types had a particular procedure in mind but that, no matter how he actually found the types, he could have found them logically by such a substruction. This is evident in the case of functional reduction. When groups are combined because they occur together, they can just as well be pulled apart into their original categories. When arbitrary numerical reduction has been used, the theorist would be aware of the procedure used and could enumerate the original categories. Lazarsfeld points out that it is substruction corresponding to the pragmatic reduction which is of the greatest practical importance in empirical research. The theorist may have given impressionistic classifications of the material at hand. The procedure is to examine the categories to see what is logically implied in the categories. Whether this involves classifications of reasons for marital discord or of types of television programs, when the attribute dimensions are distinguished then the logically occurring combinations can be enumerated.

Whatever the elaborate procedure used in this initial step of concept formation, conceptual schemes, in themselves, are not deductive theories, rather the concepts, or variables, must be interrelated in theoretical statements. In this way the syntax as well as the semantics of the domain is outlined. Theoretical statements are referred to by a variety of labels depending on their place in the theory and on their empirical validation. These differing types of statements have been called propositions, postulates, axioms, theorems, hypotheses, empirical generalizations, and laws.

The term *proposition* has been used in theory development literature

---

5. Refer to footnote 3 in this chapter.

with varying meanings. Philosophers of science (for example, Braithwaite 1953) use the word proposition to describe any declarative statement that attempts to assert a truth. This truth might be as simple as the statement of a characteristic of a concept such as "social norms are generally agreed upon." More generally, however, the term proposition is used to describe those statements that identify relationships between variables (Burr 1973). For example, we shall see later that Burr uses a statement of social norms affecting behavior as a proposition. For Burr, the propositions are the basic statements of the theory from which hypotheses are derived. On the other hand, Reynolds (1971) says that in axiomatic theory, the propositions are the conclusions derived from the axioms. In this text, the term *proposition* will be used to describe the initial relationship between variables asserted by the theory.

Propositions may vary in regard to their empirical validation. They may be merely assumptions of the truth, or they may be empirically validated to the extent of being called laws. In any case, since the statements derived from the basic propositions depend for their truth upon the truth of the propositions, some assurance of the validity of the relationship asserted in the proposition is needed.

An initial statement of a relationship in a theory is also called *postulate* (Zetterberg 1954). A postulate's place in the theory is determined, but its empirical validation varies just as that of a proposition. Reynolds (1971) calls the initial statements of the theory *axioms*. Newman (1979), quoting Dubin, adds that axioms are propositions that are assumed to be true.

Theorem is the word that Zetterberg (1954) uses for the conclusion drawn from propositions, postulates, or axioms. Again, the theorem is last in the theory and depends for its truth on the truth of the initial statements which may or may not be empirically validated.

Propositions, postulates, axioms, and theorems may all contain concepts that cannot be measured directly. Their relationships to the empirical world may be remote. When we use the term *hypothesis*, however, we make a direct tie to the empirical world. An hypothesis states a relationship, as do the other kinds of theoretical statements, but it does so in measurable terms that can be compared with data collected in a concrete situation. The hypothesis is usually based on the derived statement of the theory. It is stated in empirical terms but is not yet tested.

The two remaining terms under consideration, *empirical generalizations* and *laws*, are used to describe relationships that have been empirically validated. Which of these terms is chosen is a matter of degree and circumstances. Reynolds (1971) notes that, if the same pattern of events is found in a number of empirical studies, this pattern may be called an *empirical generalization*. When an empirical generalization receives wide acceptance and scientists have great confidence in its validity, then it may be called a *law*. The physical sciences have many laws, but the less well developed social sciences have fewer such established empirical relationships. However, Reynolds (1971) quotes a law of operant behavior as follows:

An organism will regularly perform the appropriate (rewarded) behavior sooner in a learning situation if a continuous rather than an intermittent reinforcement schedule is introduced.

In deductive theory construction, then, one develops concepts by a logical process. These concepts are then related in theoretical statements generally called propositions. Finally, one deduces other statements from the original statements and often discovers relationships that have not been previously identified. For example, from one research study (Roy 1977), the following propositions can be stated:

Proposition I: Higher levels of decision making by the physically ill are related to lower levels of sensed powerlessness.

Proposition II: Lower levels of sensed powerlessness are related to greater adaptation during illness.

Proposition III: Higher levels of decision making by the physically ill are related to greater adaptation during illness.

This last statement was put into hypothesis form and later tested by Bernardini (1979) who provided some beginning empirical support for the proposed relationship.

Inductive and deductive modes of theory construction are complementary. Results of the inductive process can be used in a deductive scheme. Furthermore, in developing any theory, inductive processes can be used at one stage, (for example, identifying basic concepts), and deductive processes at another stage (for example, relating the concepts).

Theory based on these procedures can take the special form of axiomatic theory. The field of sociology has placed emphasis on axiomatic theory construction since the writings of Zetterberg in the mid-1950s. Zetterberg (1954) emphasized that theory concerned systematically organized, lawlike propositions that can be supported by evidence. He urged that theorists spell out in greater detail what kind of relation is assumed in a given proposition: reversible or irreversible, deterministic or stochastic, sequential or coextensive, sufficient or contingent, and necessary or substitutable. For the ordering of propositions, Zetterberg recommends the axiomatic form. In axiomatic formats with proposition reduction, the following process is followed: From the list of original propositions (inventories or matrices) a certain number are selected as postulates. The postulates are chosen so that all other propositions, the theorems, are capable of derivation from the postulates and no postulate is capable of derivation from other postulates. The implications of the propositions are then spelled out in the form of theorems.

In referring to the method of deduction, Zetterberg states that at this time sociology may be satisfied with the use of derivation rules implied in ordinary language. This is the propositional form:

Postulate I: The greater the A, the greater the B.
Postulate II: The greater the B, the greater the C.
Theorem A: The greater the A, the greater the C.

Zetterberg's rules for deduction have been referred to as the sign rule; that is, "the sign of the deduced relationship is the algebraic product of the signs of the postulated relationships."

In the years that followed, a limited number of axiomatic theories were provided by sociology theorists. Two notable axiomatic theories were those of Gibbs and Martin in "A Theory of Status Integration and Its Relationship to Suicide" (1958), and of Schwirian and Prehn in "An Axiomatic Theory of Urbanization" (1962).

A number of authors criticized the derivation procedures and other methods of these and other theorists. Perhaps the most influential of these critiques was that done by Costner and Leik in 1964. They sought to modify Zetterberg's position to say that only asymmetric causal relationships should be included in derivation procedures. Furthermore, they gave the following necessary conditions for using the sign rule: (1) Postulates are stated in asymmetric causal form; (2) the common variable in the two postulates is prior to one but not to both of the other two variables; and (3) a closed system is assumed.

The most important advantage to putting theoretical statements in axiomatic form is to reveal relationships that were not previously seen. However, there are also some disadvantages to using this system. First, there is difficulty, especially in the behavioral sciences, in finding relations that are either causal or of sufficiently high association to deduce with some level of confidence. And secondly, there could be lack of parsimony involved in these elaborate deductive systems.

Whatever the type of theory—grand, middle-range, or abstracted empiricism—developed by whatever procedure—induction, deduction, or axiomatic formation—theory must be subject to evaluation. Evaluative criteria for theory are considered below.

Evaluation of Theory

Theory can be evaluated by first assessing the quality of concepts used in the theory construction, and then reviewing the total system of propositions.

Evaluating concepts

The first two criteria for appropriate concepts to be used in theory construction are that they represent classes that are mutually exclusive and exhaustive (implied by Lazarsfeld 1937). By mutually exclusive is meant that an item can be classified in one and only one category. If the concepts are represented in block chart form, the classes do not overlap with one set of attributes occurring in more than one cell. By exhaustive is meant that every case can be classified within the typology. No case occurs outside of it.

A third criterion is that of parsimony (Bailey 1973). That is, the conceptual scheme should be reduced to the smallest number of concepts that express the totality of the scheme.

A fourth criterion is conceptual clarity (Burr 1973). The concept must be lucid in the sense of being free from obscurity, ambiguity, or multiple meanings. It must be communicable to others. A fifth criterion holds that one should choose variables with the greatest discriminating power. That is, a concept should clearly distinguish the category from all other related notions.

A sixth criterion refers to the level of generality: The concept used in a theory should be abstract, but it should not be so abstract that there is confusion in identifying instances of the concept (Reynolds 1971). Abstract concepts are those concepts that are completely independent of a specific time or place. If a concept is specific to a particular time or place, then it is considered concrete. For example, general community hospital is an abstract concept, but Southbay Community Hospital is a concrete concept. Theoretical concepts, then, should be abstract, but should still be able to point to specific instances of the concept.

As a last criterion, we may consider that some theorists require that a concept be operational. That is, it must be translatable into observable terms that can be measured. The reasoning in this criterion is that theories must be testable and only operational concepts can be tested.

The best candidates for concepts to be used in theory are thus concepts which produce mutually exclusive and exhaustive categories and which are parsimonious, clear, discriminating, appropriately abstract, and eventually operational.

Evaluating theoretical systems

The major criteria for evaluating theoretical systems included here are based on discussions by Hage (1972) and Gibbs (1972). These criteria include scope, including range and intensity; parsimony; precision of prediction, including testability and discrimination; accuracy of explanation; and logical consistency.

Scope generally means a measure of how many basic problems in the discipline or specialty are handled by the same theory (Hage 1972). Scope refers to assertions about large numbers of properties. A related concept is range. With greater range, there are assertions about more types of social units. Another related idea is intensity. When a theory comprises assertions about all types of temporal relations, it has maximum intensity (Gibbs 1972).

Parsimony is a property of the theoretical statements. We are interested in explaining as much as we can with as little as possible (Hage 1972). A parsimonious theory, also called a powerful one, is one that makes few assumptions. Parsimony can be judged by the rates of theorems to premises such as axioms.

Predictive power is considered the primary criterion for judging a theory and includes nearly all the other criteria (Gibbs 1972). This assertion provides the most effective basis for consensus in assessment of theories. The purpose or function of theory can be taken to be the identification or creation of order, and success in this regard can be judged by predictive power. The notion of predictive accuracy presupposes that a theory has been tested; thus, testability is a related criterion. Furthermore, to the extent that predictions are correct, the theory discriminates.

The fourth major criterion is accuracy of explanation (Hage 1972). This criterion is difficult to explain. It involves being *persuaded* that the explanation is an accurate one. The value of the theory's explanation lies in its set of premises. These, when amplified, provide a story about some chain of events. Research can be helpful in assessing this criteria when it can be so designed as to eliminate equally plausible sets of premises. One must be convinced that the given specific situation is an instance of the general law asserted by the theory and, thus, that the theory explains it.

Logical consistency is the final criterion (Gibbs 1972). The consensus on this criterion is so universal and longstanding that it tends to be accepted uncritically. A logically inconsistent theory would lead to contradictory predictions.

Based on the nature and extent of the criteria for evaluating theory, it is predictable that it will be hard to find successful versions of theory. These criteria ask a lot of any theory. It is extremely difficult to meet all criteria at once. For example, in setting up enough premises to be logically consistent in deducing a theorem, one may violate the criterion of parsimony by having too many premises. Still, these stringent criteria should not deter theory construction efforts. Much knowledge can be gained from every theory development attempt, for, to quote Bailey (1970) "surely imperfect theory is better than no theory at all."

One Format for Theorizing

In his book on *Theory Construction and the Sociology of the Family* (1973), Burr describes one format for deductive theorizing that exemplifies the notion of theory discussed in this chapter. The method involves specifying concepts, then relating them in propositions. Propositions are then arranged in an interlinking pattern. Finally, a testable hypothesis is derived from the propositions.

Burr illustrates this process by an example about one factor that probably influences premarital sexual permissiveness. He draws from the work of Christensen to state this proposition:

Proposition 1.1: The context of social norms (beliefs about what people should or should not do) influences the behavior in the group where they occur so the behavior tends to conform to the norms.

From this proposition Burr deduces that if there is a variation in the degree to which social norms in a group proscribe premarital sexual permissiveness, and if all other phenomena are invariant, then:

Proposition 1.2: The amount that social norms in a group proscribe premarital sexual permissiveness influences the amount of premarital sexual permissiveness, and this is an inverse relationship.

Burr goes on to reason that if the social norms in the United States proscribe premarital sexual permissiveness more than the norms in Scandinavia, then the amount of premarital sexual permissiveness is higher in Scandinavia than it is in the United States. A specific testable hypothesis can be based on this proposition. For example:

Hypothesis 1.1: Scores on the Reiss Premarital Sexual Permissiveness Scale are higher in Scandinavia than in the United States.

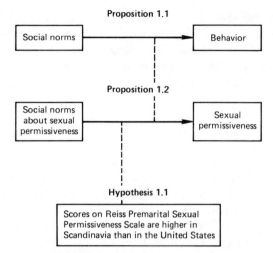

FIGURE 1.2 A Minitheory of Sexual Permissiveness. Source: Burr,
Wesley R. *Theory Construction and the Sociology of the Family.*
New York: Wiley, 1973.

The diagram in Figure 1.2 is used as a way to communicate
economically some very complex theoretical ideas.

This format is basic to the theorizing done throughout this book.
Although later propositions often are further development of earlier ones,
rather than deductions, the notion of schematically linking propositions is
frequently used.

Summary

In this chapter, we have looked at the general notion of theory construction. Theory has been defined as a system of interrelated propositions
used to describe, predict, explain, understand, and control a part of the empirical world. The specific uses of theory were explored briefly as were the
levels of theory and the procedures used in its development. Criteria were
proposed for evaluating theoretical concepts and theoretical systems. Finally,
a particular format for theorizing was introduced as a basis for the theorizing in Parts 3 and 4 of this book.

References

Bailey, Kenneth D. "Evaluating Axiomatic Theories." In *Sociological
Methodology 1970,* ed. Edgar J. Bogotta, pp. 48–71. San Francisco: Jossey-
Bass, 1970.

————. "Monothetic and Polythetic Typologies and Their Relation to Conceptualization, Measurement and Scaling," *American Sociological Review*, 38, (February 1973): 18–33.

Barton, Allen. "The Concept of Property-Space in Social Research." In *The Language of Social Research* by Paul F. Lazarsfeld and Morris Rosenberg, New York: Free Press, 1955. pp. 40–43.

Bernardini, Lois J. "Decision Making: A Factor in Adaptation of the Elderly to the Long-Term Care Facility." Master's thesis, School of Nursing, Edinboro State College, Edinboro, Pa., 1979.

Blalock, Hubert M., Jr. *Theory Construction*. Englewood Cliffs, N.J.: Prentice-Hall, Inc., 1969.

Braithwaite, Richard B. *Scientific Explanation*. Cambridge: The University Press, 1953.

Burr, Wesley, R. *Theory Construction and the Sociology of the Family*. New York: John Wiley, 1973.

Costner, Herbert L., and Robert K. Leik. "Deductions from Axiomatic Theory," *American Sociological Review*, 29, no. 6 (December 1964): 819–35.

Gibbs, Jack P. *Sociological Theory Construction*. Hinsdale, Ill.: Dryden Press, 1972.

————, and Walter T. Martin, "A Theory of Status Integration and Its Relationship to Suicide," *American Sociological Review*, 23, (April 1958): 140–47.

Glaser, Barney, and Anselm L. Strauss. *The Discovery of Grounded Theory*. Chicago: Aldine, 1967.

Hage, Jerald. *Techniques and Problems of Theory Construction in Sociology*. New York: John Wiley, 1972.

Hardy, Margaret E. "Theories: Components, Development, Evaluation," *Nursing Research*, 23, (March-April 1974): 100–107.

Hempel, Carl G. *Aspects of Scientific Explanation*. New York: Free Press, 1965.

Jacox, Ada. "Theory Construction in Nursing," *Nursing Research*, 23, (January-February 1974): 4–13.

Lazarsfeld, Paul F. "Some Remarks on the Typological Procedures in Social Research," *Zeitschrift fur Sozentforschung*, 6 (1937): 119–139.

Merton, Robert K. *Social Theory and Social Structure*. New York: Free Press, 1957.

Mills, Charles W. *The Sociological Imagination*. New York: Oxford University Press, 1959.

Newman, Margaret A. *Theory Development in Nursing*. Philadelphia: F. A. Davis Co., 1979.

The Nursing Theories Conference Group, Julia B. George, Chairperson, *Nursing Theories: The Base for Professional Nursing Practice*. Englewood Cliffs, N.J.: Prentice-Hall, Inc., 1980.

Reynolds, Paul Davidson. *A Primer of Theory Construction*. Indianapolis: Bobbs-Merrill, 1971.

Roy, Sr. Callista. "Decision-Making by the Physically Ill and Adaptation During Illness." Doctoral dissertation, University of California, Los Angeles, 1977.

Schwirian, Kent P., and John W. Prehn. "An Axiomatic Theory of Urbanization," *American Sociological Review*, 27, (December 1962): 812–25.

Zetterberg, Hans L. *On Theory and Verification in Sociology*. Totoux, N.J.: Bedminster Press, 1954.

CHAPTER 2

Theory development in nursing

There is little doubt that interest in nursing theory is one of the most significant movements in contemporary nursing. Although nursing has been interested in theory from the time of Florence Nightingale, the conferences, journal articles, and educational curricula of the later 1970s reflect a highly intensified quest for nursing theory. A searching for the theoretical basis for nursing and nursing practice and a striving for delineating nursing as a science occupies the energies of many nurses. But what kind of theory does nursing need, and where have the efforts of the last decade brought us in developing that theory?

In this chapter we shall look first at nursing science and outline the kind of theory that nursing needs. We shall then assess the progress we have made in outlining the realm of the discipline of nursing. Finally, some analysis will be made of the current development and testing of nursing practice theory.

The Science of Nursing

We shall begin by developing a clear notion of the theory that nursing needs to develop. This leads us to a consideration of nursing as a profession, a discipline, a science, and a form of health care practice.

Nursing is striving for professionalism. One of the major characteristics of a profession, is that it utilizes a well-defined and well-organized body of knowledge to provide a service vital to human and social welfare (Kelly 1975). In a recent article, Roy (1979) has noted that this criterion raises two basic difficulties for nursing as an emerging profession. First, the usefulness of nursing has not been clear historically, and, in fact, is questioned by some today. Cannot the duties of the nurse be distributed one by one to other health care workers?—the dietician, the respiratory therapist, the social worker, the physician's assistant, the chaplain? Second, it is widely disputed that nursing can claim a unique body of knowledge that clearly differentiates it from other professions. Phillips (1977) has described how nursing, in its evolutionary process, has borrowed first from medicine, then from psychology, followed by ecology and, finally, sociology. Clearly the time has come when nursing as a profession must describe its own body of knowledge. Johnson (1974) has long warned us that to describe our own body of knowledge, we must first answer the question of the nature of the service that nursing offers.

The building of the body of knowledge is the responsibility of the scientific discipline. A discipline is simply a field of inquiry. It is characterized by a unique perspective, a distinct way of viewing all phenomena. This unique view ultimately defines the limits and nature of its inquiry. For example, biology has viewed the human person as an organism while psychology has viewed the person as a behaving being. Nursing as a discipline, therefore, must describe the phenomena it will study and the kinds of questions it will ask.

When the discipline of nursing defines its body of knowledge, we shall have a science of nursing. Or, as Andreoli and Thompson (1977) put it, nursing will attain the status of a science once it has clearly identified a verifiable knowledge base that can be contested and corroborated. What do we mean by a science of nursing? First, a dictionary definition of a science is that it is a system of knowledge based on scientific principles, concerned with the observation and classification of facts and establishing verifiable theories and general laws. Nursing, then, must develop its unique system of knowledge by its own observation and classification of facts and establishment of verifiable theories and general laws about the phenomena that the discipline of nursing outlines.

We can distinguish between the developing science of nursing with its verifiable theories and general laws, and the practice based on that science. Nursing knowledge provides the basis for practice. However, scientific theory and research can only describe and predict outcomes of nursing action. To know whether or not an action is desirable and, therefore, whether it should be used in a given situation, requires a set of values about what kinds of outcomes are desirable. To know scientifically that a given action will relieve pain does not necessarily prescribe that one perform the action.

However, if one adds to the situation the view that relief of pain is "good" in this case, then one is in a position to make a judgment about the action to be taken. Tucker (1979)[1] has said that the "principle activity of science is to make well-supported value judgments." The nursing judgment method introduced by McDonald and Harms (1966) reflects this scientific value-based nature of nursing practice. According to this method, a nursing judgment is based on the probability of a given outcome and the value placed on that outcome.[2]

In developing our scientific knowledge we need both theory building and research. We have already noted that a theory is a system of interrelated propositions used to describe, explain, predict, and control a part of the empirical world. But what about theory for nursing? How shall we define it? Berthold (1968) says that theory for nursing is a conceptual structure of knowledge useful and necessary to attain the goals established by nurses.

If theory for nursing is a conceptual structure of knowledge, we must specify what types of knowledge this theory must deal with. Johnson (1968) proposes that theory for nursing deals with knowledge of order, knowledge of disorder, and knowledge of control.

To describe further these kinds of theory for nursing, we shall need to look briefly at the nature of nursing models and how models differ from but are related to theory. A conceptual model for nursing is a set of concepts that identify the essential components of nursing practice. It is a mental image of the realm of nursing, similar to a model car or plane or house. It shows all the essential parts, how they are put together, and how they work. The elements of a model are the parts that make it up. Johnson (1975) has described six elements or essential units of the nursing model:

1. *A goal of action:* The mission or ideal goal of the profession expressed as the end product desired (a state, condition, situation)
2. *A descriptive term for patiency:* That concept which best isolates who or what is acted upon to achieve the goal of action—i.e., those aspects of the person (as patient) or the organization of his functioning toward which attention is to be directed; the target of action
3. *The actor's role:* A descriptive label that indicates the nature of the actions of the nurse (as the actor) on patiency
4. *Source of difficulty:* The originating point of deviations from the desired state or condition
5. *Intervention focus:* The kind of problems found when deviations from the desired state occur; the kinds of disturbances in the patiency which are to be prevented or treated

---

1. The reader is referred to this article for further discussion of the relationship between science and values.

2. See Roy 1976 for further illustration.

Intervention Mode: The major means of preventing or treating such problems; the kinds of levers that can be used to change the course of events toward the desired end product

6. *Consequences intended:* The outcomes of action desired, stated in more abstract or broader terms than the mission, and/or including significant corollaries of the intended outcomes
Consequences unintended: Outcomes that are not intended but that might follow, and that may or may not be desirable

These elements can be restated and condensed to the following three major units which imply all the elements:

1. A description of the person who receives nursing care. (Is he an adaptive system as in Roy's model, or a developmental being as in Peplau's model?)[3]
2. A statement of the goal or purpose of nursing. (Does nursing promote adaptation or maximize growth?)
3. A delineation of nursing intervention or activities of the nurse. (Does she manipulate the environment or use the therapeutic interpersonal process?)

Each model will have a little different perspective on the person, and the goal and interventions of nursing. Although the term *model* has many scientific and unscientific meanings (see Brodbeck 1968; Williams 1979), we use it here to refer to a conceptual framework for nursing practice that has been sufficiently developed to delineate clearly the three main units listed above. How, then, does our view of a nursing model differ from the notion of nursing theory? Williams (1979) submits that the distinction lies in the range of phenomena included and the degree of specificity of the concepts and hypotheses. As models describe their concepts, they tend to be general and overriding. The vagueness of the related terms of a model makes it difficult for them to be submitted to empirical testing. Theories, on the other hand, which can arise out of models, tend to deal with more specific phenomena within the model. Their terminology is more precise and concepts are defined in a way that they can be empirically tested.

We can describe further the relationship between models and theory.[4] The nursing model describes the person and the goal. Based on the model's view of the person, we can draw upon basic science theories to give description and predictive statements about the person; for example, physiology

---

3. See Chapter 4 of this text for further elaboration of the elements of the Roy Adaptation Model as well as Riehl and Roy (1980) for discussion of Peplau and other nursing models.
4. For further discussion of the relationship between models and theory see Bush 1979.

tells us about his fluid needs and psychology tells us about the need for developing a healthy self-concept. This, then, is nursing's knowledge of theory of order. According to Johnson, it is usually "borrowed" knowledge.[5] The model also describes the goal of nursing. Based on this goal, we can develop theories of nursing practice. This is our knowledge of control. Finally, stemming from both the model's view of the person and of the goal of nursing, we get a nursing practice theory which is the knowledge of disorder, that is, of the kinds of problems or situations that nurses diagnose and treat.

We have here described the kinds of theory that nursing needs. First, nursing science needs *theories of the phenomena* that it studies. Our view of the human person will lead us to describe theoretically all the propositions relevant to the basic phenomena of our discipline. Second, nursing science needs *theories related to the service* the profession provides. Based on the nature of our service, or the goal of nursing, we shall develop a system of propositions related to what we do with patients. This theory is directly related to what happens in clinical settings. It will describe the client's problems, and predict and describe outcomes of nursing actions. This theory of nursing practice is considered unique to nursing.

From what we have said thus far, we have a beginning point for assessing the current status of nursing theory. First, we may ask the global question, How far have we come in outlining the realm of the discipline of nursing? Second, we can investigate where we are in our current efforts to develop and test basic science theory for nursing and nursing practice theory.

The Discipline of Nursing

We have noted that a discipline has a unique perspective—a distinct way of viewing all phenomena. It defines the limits and nature of its inquiry. To what extent does nursing have a common view of the human person and of the goal of nursing? Johnson (1978) notes that several conceptual models for nursing practice have been developed in recent years in an effort to define nursing. She points out that these models, however, appear to have had a greater impact on education than on research. Moreover, they differ in the goal of nursing set forth and, thus, in the phenomena and perspective delineated.

Hardy (1978) refers to this situation as the preparadigm stage of theory

---

5. We acknowledge that theories generated for a different purpose in another context may be inadequate to the needs of nursing, but also recognize that nursing can build upon the fund of knowledge from the other sciences.

development. This early stage of scientific development is characterized by divergent schools of thought which, although addressing the same range of phenomena, usually describe and interpret these phenomena in different ways. These "grand theories" or philosophies about nursing are characterized by discursive presentation and descriptive accounts or anecdotal reports to illustrate and support their claims. Hardy notes that in these formulations the theoretical terms are usually vague and ill defined, and their meaning may be close to everyday language. These early paradigms provide a perspective rather than a set of interrelated theoretical statements. We see this fact demonstrated in the writings of a number of the nurse theorists.

However, some indications would support the claim that nursing theory development is moving beyond the preparadigm stage. First, the analysis made by Donaldson and Crowley (1977) reveals the following commonalities in the ideas of nursing writers:

1. Concern with principles and laws that govern life processes, well-being, and optimum functioning of human beings, sick or well (for example, Nightingale and Rogers).
2. Concern with the pattern of human behavior in interaction with the environment in critical life situations (for example, Rogers and Johnson).
3. Concern with the processes by which positive changes in health status are effected (for example, Peplau, Kreuter, and Leininger).

These commonalities can become themes for inquiry in the discipline of nursing. They provide a beginning direction for defining the limits and nature of our inquiry. The second source of data is the comparison of the major nursing models done recently by Riehl and Roy (1980). First, one case study was analyzed according to Roy, Johnson, Orem, Peplau, and Riehl. The case was a male physician who had suffered a myocardial infarction and was not restricting his activity as ordered. The analyses were similar in that each focused on the patient's behavior. Furthermore, similar issues, namely independence, control, and role performance, were subsumed in the diagnoses arrived at using each of the nursing models. All the nursing model statements of interventions allow for the patient's expression of his feelings. Likewise, each would maintain what independent behavior is possible and would provide new ways for meeting independence needs. Four of the five models specifically use patient health teaching.

Second, in this text (Riehl and Roy 1980) the components of the major models were analyzed to outline what might become a unified model of nursing. Summarizing the authors' conclusions, this unified model views an individual, the recepent of nursing care, as a unified whole, consisting of subsystems. In interacting with the environment, this person has lines of defense and internal regulating mechanisms that function by the principles of homeodynamics. The goal of nursing is to maintain a person's system and help the individual to maximize his potential, which includes health and harmonious interaction with the environment. Nursing fulfills this goal through a problem-solving process including the use of various diagnostic and intervention means in an interactive framework.

Lastly, to support the claim that nursing is moving beyond the preparadigm stage, we have a project involving the collaborative efforts of a group of nurse theorists. The National Conference on Nursing Diagnoses has been working since 1974 to develop a diagnostic classification system for nursing. The group has been working inductively, that is, trying to proceed from the experience of nurses to general categories. There were some who were concerned about the theoretical underpinnings of the project. They felt we needed an organizing principle to tie it all together. Thus, at the Third National Conference in St. Louis in the spring of 1978, a group of nurse theorists was convened to begin the development of a conceptual scheme to organize the labels. The group met for three days to work on their task. It included such theorists as Martha Rogers, Imogene King, Sister Callista Roy, and Dorothea Orem. There were 14 theorists who, through a process of commitment, scholarship, courage, and commonality, developed the beginnings of a common conceptual scheme for nursing.

When the group reported to the Conference on the fourth day, they were challenged to make the project more clinically relevant. The group met again for two additional times to respond to this challenge. The important point about this group is that the theorists themselves worked together to evolve a common conceptual framework that will serve the needs of the significant work on nursing diagnoses. The efforts of this group are ongoing and promising.

Thus, in assessing the status of nursing theory in regard to the first step of outlining the realm of the discipline, we can say that nursing is in a preparadigm stage, but moving in the direction of a common definition of the domain of nursing.

Developing and Testing
Nursing Practice Theory

Earlier we said that, based on the unique view of the discipline of nursing, nurses need to develop nursing practice theory—that is, systems of propositions related to the diagnosis and treatment of the clients of nursing. How much progress have we made in this direction? First, Hardy (1978) says that "until there is a prevailing paradigm and exemplar paradigms to give focus to the thinking and work of nurse-scientists, knowledge in nursing will develop slowly and somewhat haphazardly.'' Adding to this pessimistic note is Johnson's (1979) observation, from an exhaustive review of research by nurses and about nursing, and her own cursory examination of the literature, that only a relatively small proportion of the investigations reported even now are concerned with the development of theory basic to nursing practice.

Johnson groups the investigations relevant to the direct care of patients into three categories: (1) those that have implications for nursing practice, but that fall essentially within the boundaries of another discipline; (2) those that attempt to describe patient behavior with some effort to couch these descriptions in terms meaningful to nursing; and (3) experimental studies on the outcomes of nursing intervention. The first and third categories are the most numerous. However, research in other disciplines, though it may serve the cause of science, fails to add directly, if at all, to the body of nursing theory. In regard to the third category, experimental studies are formulated from widely differing perspectives on what to study and what kind of questions to ask. Thus, they are not building a cumulative body of nursing knowledge. The smaller number of studies in the second category are also based on a whole range of theoretical frameworks. As Johnson remarks, there is little basis on which the diverse findings can be tied together. Johnson concludes that if the research task of nursing is to identify and explain patient problems accepted as falling within nursing's distinctive area of knowledge and to develop the theoretical (and technical) means of managing these problems, then we have barely begun.

However, there are two promising indicators that progress will be made in the near future. First is the research activity centered around some of the prevailing conceptual models of nursing. Imogene King is involved in research to validate her conceptual model. The present book is seen as outlining research hypotheses that can become the basis for a program for research. Also, we find on the East Coast and increasingly throughout the country nuclei of research activities stemming from the Rogers model. All of these activities can be ways of building up the body of knowledge unique to the discipline of nursing.

The second hopeful sign in developing nursing practice theory is what is going on in the graduate nursing programs in this country. It would seem that most Master's degree programs have introduced courses in which conceptual models for practice are explicated and students are initiated into the value of nursing models for practice and research. In some places, the student's thesis research must be drawn from one of the existing conceptual models for nursing. Furthermore, in a personal review of the curriculums of eight doctoral programs in nursing, Roy found a heavy emphasis on nursing theory. About half of the programs had the doctoral students proceed beyond theory analysis to participation in the process of formal theory construction. An example of this work is given in the next chapter. We are developing a core group of nurse scientists who can help us accelerate our slow pace of progress in theory development.

Summary

Nursing as a discipline needs a common focus. Then, based on the discipline's view of the human being and of the goal of nursing, nursing needs nursing practice theory. Theory construction in nursing may be in the preparadigm stage of development. As Jacox (1974) says, it is still a gleam in the proverbial eyes of its would-be founders. Still, the activities of nurse theorists and the directions of graduate curricula provide hope for rapid theory development in the next 25 years.

References

Andreoli, Kathleen, and Carol E. Thompson. "The Nature of Science in Nursing," *Image,* 9, no. 2 (June 1977): 32–37.

Berthold, Jeanne, "Prologue—Symposium of Theory Development in Nursing," *Nursing Research,* 17, no. 3 (May-June 1968): 196–97.

Brodbeck, May. "Models, Meaning, and Theories," In *Readings in the Philosophy of the Social Sciences,* ed. May Brodbeck. London: Macmillan—Collier Macmillion, Ltd., 1969.

Bush, Helen A. "Models for Nursing," *Advances in Nursing Science,* 1, no. 2. (January 1979): 13–21.

Donaldson, Sue K., and Dorothy Crowley. "Discipline of Nursing: Structure and Relationship to Practice." In *Communicating Nursing Research,* vol. 10, ed. Marjorie Batey, pp. 1–22. Boulder, Colorado: Western Interstate Commission on Higher Education, 1977.

Hardy, Margaret E. "Perspective on Nursing Theory," *Advances in Nursing Science,* 1, no. 1 (October 1978): 37–48.

Jacox, Ada. "Theory Construction in Nursing," *Nursing Research,* 23, (January-February 1974): 4–13.

Johnson, Dorothy. "Theory in Nursing: Borrowed and Unique," *Nursing Research,* 17, no. 3 (May-June 1968): 206–09.

———. "Development of Theory: A Requisite for Nursing as a Primary Health Profession," *Nursing Research,* 23, no. 5 (September-October 1974): 372–77.

———. "Requirements of an Effective Conceptual Model for Nursing." N. 203 class handout, University of California, Los Angeles, 1975.

———. "The State of the Art of Theory Development in Nursing." In *Theory Development: What, Why, How?,* pp. 1–10. New York: National League for Nursing, 1978.

Kelly, Lucie Young. *Dimensions of Professional Nursing,* 3rd ed. New York: Macmillan, 1975.

McDonald, F. J., and Mary Harms, "Theoretical Model for an Experimental Curriculum," *Nursing Outlook,* 14, no. 8 (August 1966): 48–51.

Phillips, John R. "Nursing Systems and Nursing Models," *Image,* 9, no. 1 (February 1977): 4–7.

Riehl, Joan P., and Sr. Callista Roy. *Conceptual Models for Nursing Practice,* 2nd ed. New York: Prentice-Hall, Inc., 1980.

Roy, Sr. Callista. *Introduction to Nursing: An Adaptation Model.* Englewood Cliffs, N.J.: Prentice-Hall, Inc., 1976.

——."Relating Nursing Theory to Nursing Education: A New Era," *Nurse Educator,* 4, no. 2 (March-April, 1979): 16–21.

Tucker, Robert W. "The Value Decisions We Know as Science," *Advances in Nursing Science,* 1, (January 1979): 1–12.

Williams, Carolyn A. "The Nature and Development of Conceptual Frameworks." In *Issues in Nursing Research,* ed. Florence Downs and Juanita W. Fleming, pp. 89–106. New York: Prentice-Hall, Inc., 1979.

CHAPTER 3

Formal
theory construction:
an example
of the process

Betty J. Hill
Carolyn S. Roberts

The discipline of nursing has arrived at that point of evolution where practice and research can be premised upon nursing theory. The purpose of nursing theory is to provide the nurse practitioner and researcher with a rationale for practice modalities and research questions. One of the measures of the utility of theory in guiding practice and research is the degree to which the theory is testable against the empirical world; that is, can testable theorems be derived from the theory?

   The focus of this chapter is the illustration of the process of deducing a testable theorem from the prescriptive nature of Roy's theory of nursing.[1] To illustrate the process, the concept of *maternal locus of control* was extrapolated from social learning theory to predict a quality of the concept *habilitation* which was derived from developmental theory at the descriptive level. Using the predicted relationship between the concepts or units *maternal locus of control* and *habilitation,* Roy's theory of nursing prescribes the manipulation of the former to affect the latter. Dubin's (1969) model of theory building serves as the framework to illustrate the process of theorem

---

1. See footnotes 1 and 2 of the Preface.

deduction, and the criteria identified by Hardy (1973) are used for evaluation.

Theoretical Frameworks

Nursing is viewed as a theoretical system of knowledge prescriptive of a process leading to interventions that, by manipulating the environment, enhance man's adaptation levels relative to the health-illness continuum (Roy 1976; Riehl and Roy 1974). Significant others are viewed as part of man's environment at each of the three levels of stimuli. For most children, their mother is the caretaker and, as such, acts as a focal stimulus in the child's environment. Roy's theory of nursing, then, allows for the prescription of nursing interventions directed towards the mother to effect the goal of improved adaptation level of the child on the health-illness continuum.

Among children at risk of failing to achieve an optimum level of adaptation are those with birth defects and in need of habilitation, a concept that shares commonalities with the concepts of parenting patterns and rehabilitation. The connotation is that the child requires of his caretaker interventions in addition to parenting. The literature indicates that, across children with the same adaptation problem, caretakers vary widely in their ability to habilitate the child.

Social learning theory predicts that one of the salient variables in the habilitation of handicapped children is the perceived locus of control of the child's mother, where she is the caretaker (Lefcourt 1976). Locus of control is the generalized belief that outcomes are or are not contingent upon one's own behavior. Internal locus of control refers to the individual's belief that the outcomes of events are a consequence of one's behavior and hence, under one's control. Conversely, a belief in external locus of control is the perception that one's own behavior is unrelated to the outcome of the event. The theory predicts that mothers of handicapped children are at risk for perceived external locus of control and that the greater their perceived external locus of control, the less able they are to habilitate their children. That is, maternal locus of control may account for some of the variability in the ability of mothers to habilitate their children.

Dubin's Model of Theory Development

Dubin (1969) states that the notion of a concept is familiar to almost everyone involved in theory and science, but the word *concept* has many meanings. Therefore, Dubin translates the word *concept* to the more neutral term *unit*. The word *unit* refers to the aspects of "things" of the world about which a scientist tries to make sense. More specifically, scientists build theories about the *properties* of things rather than about the things themselves. Theories are focused on selected characteristics (properties) of objects rather than upon the objects themselves because humans are simply not able to comprehend things whole. Therefore, Dubin's term *unit* refers to the properties of things. Theory building involves linking the relevant units of a scientific discipline together in various ways to form models of the empirical world. The two major units used in this chapter are *child habilitation* and *maternal locus of control*.

Characteristics of the units

Units of a theory may be classified as either attributes or variables. Dubin defines an attribute as a property of a thing that is always present, while a variable is defined as a property of a thing that is present in degree. Child habilitation and maternal locus of control are both variable units in the theorem under consideration, as both of these properties may be present in various degrees. Dubin clearly states that while variable units are considered to have greater precision than attribute units, both types of units have a place in theory building.

A second distinction related to the units of a theory is made between a real and a nominal unit. This distinction is based on the probability of finding an empirical indicator for the unit. Because empirical indicators are available for both child habilitation and maternal locus of control, these concepts can be termed real units. Dubin further classifies units as being either primitive or sophisticated. Units of a theory are seen as primitive if they are undefined starting points, and sophisticated if they are defined. Both of the units, child habilitation and maternal locus of control, can be defined and are therefore viewed as sophisticated units.

All sophisticated units of a theory are classified by Dubin into five types: enumerative (E), associative (A), relational (R), statistical (S), and summative (S), using the misspelling of the word ears as a mnemonic device. A unit may belong to more than one of these classes. Both child habilitation and locus of control can be considered of the enumerative unit type, which is defined as a property characteristic of a thing in all its conditions. The two concepts under discussion are variable enumerative units because child habilitation and maternal locus of control are always present in some degree in a "thing" in all its conditions. For example, whether habilitation is successful or not, a level of habilitation is a property present in a child. Similarly, with the unit maternal locus of control, whether locus of control is internal or external, it is present in some degree if the mother is present. It follows, then, that neither of the units are associative units, which are defined by Dubin as having a real zero or absent value.

A relational unit is a property characteristic of a thing that is derived from at least two other properties. Child habilitation is a relational unit by virtue of the interaction between the concept of child and the concept of habilitation. Similarly, the interaction between the concepts *maternal* and *locus of control* makes this a relational unit also, having a property that distinguishes it from all other units and that is contingent upon the interaction.

According to Dubin, a statistical unit not only refers to a property of a thing but also summarizes the distribution of that property in a thing. Both child habilitation and maternal locus of control may be considered statistical units of the type that locates things by its relative position in a distribution. In fact, it is the relative position or degree of maternal internal control that is to be manipulated by the nursing intervention to effect (improve) the relative position of the second unit or child habilitation.

Summative units are the most complex of all. There is no limit to the number of properties being related because summative units stand for an entire complex thing. Such global units are of limited value in theories and theory-building models, according to Dubin. Neither child habilitation nor maternal locus of control are summative units. Thus the units under discussion have characteristics of enumerative, relational, and statistical units, illustrating the ways in which units may be classified.

Laws of interaction

Linkages among units of a model are labeled by Dubin as laws of interaction. The statement or phrase of the sentence that expresses the connection or relationship between two or more units is the law of interaction. A law of interaction is never itself measured, but can be tested only if values can be empirically assigned to the units used in the law. Dubin identifies three general categories of laws of interaction which encompass all forms of expressing a relationship: (1) categoric interactions, which state that values of a unit are associated with values of another unit; (2) sequential interactions in which a time dimension is used to order a relationship among units; and (3) determinant interactions in which determinate values of one unit are associated with determinate values of another unit.

The type of law in the theorem under development is a categoric law of interaction. The value of maternal locus of control is associated with the value of child habilitation.

Boundary criteria

Because the units and laws of interaction must fit within the boundaries, the boundaries of a theoretical model must be stated before propositional statements are derived. Boundary criteria or limiting values may be derived from the characteristics of the units in the theory, or from the characteristics of the laws by which the units interact.

The theorem developed in this chapter is concerned with maternal locus of control as this affects the habilitation of a child, specifically one with birth defects. Locus of control is defined as the belief that outcomes are or are not contingent upon one's behavior. Habilitation is defined as level of adaptation related to genetic and environmental factors impinging on a child, relevant to a particular type of birth defect. Dubin indicates that there is an inverse relationship between the number of boundary-determining criteria given in a model and the size of the domain covered by the model. Depending on the specificity of the definitions of the units in a theory, the domain of the deduced theorem is constricted or expanded. The theorem in this chapter is seen as having a tightly defined domain when one considers the extensive domain of the nursing theory model and the developmental and social learning theories from which the theorem was deduced.

The number of boundary-determining criteria of a model has an influence on the homogeneity of the model's domain. The more boundary-determining criteria, the greater the homogeneity of the domain, and vice versa. Generalization of a specific model is dependent upon the size of the domain it represents. That is, a model with a tightly defined domain has a greater specificity of generalizability. On the other hand, models with domains that are defined too broadly have a wider generalizability, but these are more tenuous.

Deduction of a Theorem

Theorems may be deduced from theory once the units and their characteristics and boundaries have been identified, rendering them amenable to laws of interaction. The term *laws of interaction* in Dubin's model is similar to the concept of axioms, which are defined as propositions assumed to be true (Blalock 1969). Propositions and testable theorems, such as the one in this chapter, are developed by deductive reasoning from the laws of interaction or axioms. Roy's nursing theory provides laws of interaction among the major units as well as between the concepts of adaptation and nursing, thus providing the basis for the deductive process of theorem development. Table 3.1 illustrates the major relevant theory derivations.

As can be seen from the relevant theory derivations outlined in Table 3.1, a large number of units and laws of interaction may be deduced. Of the range of possibilities, only those which may be deduced in a direct sequence from the theories to arrive at the theorem were selected.

Theorem deduction

Man is an adaptive being with an adaptation level.

The greater the adaptation level, the greater the independence in activities of daily living.

The greater the independence in activities of daily living, the greater the habilitation level.

A greater habilitation level is related to internal locus of control of the habilitating agent.

The habilitating agent for handicapped children is the mother.

The more external the maternal locus of control, the lower the habilitation level and, hence, the adaptation level of the child.

The lower the adaptation level of the child, the greater the need for nursing interventions directed towards the child's environment.

The child's environment includes maternal locus of control.

Therefore:

The more nursing interventions shift maternal locus of control from externality to internality, the greater the habilitation level of the child.

Units to be measured:

Changes in maternal locus of control (independent variable)

Changes in child habilitation (dependent variable)

Measurement is contingent upon:

1. Specific hypotheses
2. Empirical indicators of the independent and dependent variables
3. Measureable nursing manipulation of the independent variable

TABLE **3.1** Relevant Theory Derivations

Roy's Premises	Developmental Unit—Child Habilitation	Social Learning Unit—Maternal Locus of Control
Man is an adaptive being.	Habilitation is an adaptation problem.	Generalized expectancy of control is directional towards internality or externality.
If man is an adaptive being, he has an adaptation level. The adaptation level is a function of the interaction between adaptation mechanisms and the environment.	The greater the adaptation level, the greater the habilitation level. The habilitation level is a function of the interaction between adaptation mechanisms and the environment.	
	The greater the deficits in habilitation, the greater the impairment of adaptation level. The greater the impairment of adaptation level, the greater the impairment in activities of daily living. The greater the impairment of adaptation level, the greater the significance of the environment.	A significant stimulus in a child's environment is the mother.
		The greater the maternal internal locus of control, the greater the parenting patterns fostering independence of a child. The greater the maternal external locus of control, the less the parenting patterns fostering independence of a child.

TABLE **3.1** con't.

Roy's Premises	Developmental Unit—Child Habilitation	Social Learning Unit—Maternal Locus of Control
Nursing intervention is directed towards manipulation of the environment.	The less the habilitation level of the child, the greater the need for nursing intervention.	The less the parenting patterns fostering independence of a child, the less the habilitation level of the child.

The theorem is seen as testing that portion of Roy's theory that addresses the focus of nursing interventions (namely, stimuli in the environment), to effect a positive change in adaptation level. At the same time it is seen as testing a variable predicted by social learning theory to be relevant to the adaptation level of specified patients. It is possible to derive a number of hypotheses from the theorem, contingent upon the aspect of interest and empirical indicators selected. For example, the researcher or practitioner may be interested in children with a specific birth defect, or specific birth order, or both. Similarly, aspects of the maternal locus of control unit may be more tightly circumscribed according to the researcher's interest. Other laws of interaction within the nursing theory may be of interest. For example, the researcher may be interested in the relationship between locus of control and adaptive modes or, perhaps, a level-two assessment of maternal locus of control as this relates to child adaptation.

Finally, the theorem is seen as illustrating the prescriptive nature of Roy's nursing theory. That is, the theorem uses the prescriptive nature of Roy's theory to manipulate a relationship predicted by social learning theory. Thus, the primacy of prescriptive theory over predictive theory is supported, and the theorem contributes to nursing as a theoretical system of knowledge.

Evaluation of the Proposed Theorem

Because theorems are deduced from theory, they should be amenable to the same kinds of evaluative scrutiny as theories. The emphasis in evaluation is on a theory's relative utility to nursing practice because the raison d'être of nursing research is ultimately the practice of nursing. Criteria articulated by Hardy (1973) for evaluating theory have been used to evaluate the theorem proposed.

Are the assumptions reasonable? The assumptions underlying the theorem are those upon which Roy's theory of nursing is premised and evaluated as reasonable elsewhere. In addition, the assumption of a generalized expectancy of control as part of man's interaction with his environment has been reasonably demonstrated, as have the assumptions underlying the unit *habilitation.*

Is the theorem explicit and the reasoning logical? Dubin's theory-building model renders the deduction of the theorem explicit and logical through the process of identifying the characteristics of the units, the laws of interactions, and the boundaries of the theorem.

Does the literature review lead coherently to the question of interest? The unit *habilitation* is described in the developmental theory literature, and its relationship to the unit *maternal locus of control* is predicted by social learning theory. Roy's theory of nursing prescribes the application of the prediction to man's adaptation level on the health-illness continuum. The relationships between the units, and between their laws of interaction and Roy's theory were logically derived from the relevant literature.

What new ideas and understandings are generated by the theorem? As Phillips (1977) notes, concepts from other disciplines need to be viewed through the context of nursing's unique perspective to be of value to the discipline of nursing. The theorem takes the units "borrowed" from other disciplines, links them, and proposes to verify their fruitfulness to nursing in testing the prescriptive nature of Roy's theory. The theorem is seen as generative of new understandings consistent with the predictive component of social learning theory and the prescription of Roy's theory of nursing.

Is the theorem parsimonious? Of the range of possible propositions that could be generated from the major units selected, only those that contribute to a direct sequence from theory to theorem were included. The propositions identified were derived from a series of laws of interaction generated by the units, which in turn were generated by the review of the relevant literature.

Can empirically testable hypotheses be derived from the theorem? The units of the theorem can be defined in empirical terms for measurement. The theorem, as noted, is generative of a range of hypotheses that may be of interest to the researcher or practitioner.

Summary

The process of deducing a testable theorem from a theory of nursing was illustrated, using Dubin's theory-building model as the framework. The development and characteristics of the units of the theorem, and their laws of interaction and boundaries were explored. The deduction of the theorem from prescriptive and predictive theory was illustrated, and its relationship to hypotheses discussed. Finally, the theorem was evaluated against criteria suggested by Hardy (1973).

The refinement of the theoretical basis for nursing practice is contingent upon consistent, rigorously developed theorems that are deduced from and that test nursing theory.

References

Blalock, Hubert M. *Theory Construction.* Englewood Cliffs, N.J.: Prentice-Hall Inc., 1969.

Dubin, R. *Theory Building.* New York: Free Press, 1969.

Hardy, Margaret E. "The Nature of Theories." In *Theoretical Foundations for Nursing,* ed. M. E. Hardy, pp. 10–25. New York: M.S.S. Information Corporation, 1973.

Lefcourt, H. M. *Locus of Control: Current Trends in Theory and Research.* New York: John Wiley, 1976.

Phillips, John R. "Nursing Systems and Nursing Models," *Image,* 9, no. 1 (February 1977): 4–7.

Riehl, Joan P., and Sr. Callista Roy. *Conceptual Models for Nursing Practice.* New York: Prentice-Hall, Inc., 1974.

Roy, Sr. Callista. *Introduction to Nursing: An Adaptation Model.* Englewood Cliffs, N.J.: Prentice-Hall, Inc., 1976.

The first part of this book looked at theory construction in general and at theory development in nursing. An example of an exercise in theory construction was given. The following sections of the book provide some ongoing theorizing, according to the method described, using the Roy Adaptation Model of Nursing. Part 2, is thus a transitional section. It focuses on the model for nursing that is utilized and upon the theory about the person as an adaptive system that is developed based on the elements of the model.

We have defined theory as a system of interrelated propositions used to describe, explain, predict, and control a part of the empirical world. By a model we mean a schematic representation of reality showing the parts of the reality and their relation to one another. Models of nursing have three basic parts: (1) a view of the person who receives nursing care, (2) a view of the goal of nursing, and (3) a view of nursing interventions. Nursing models specify which theories are to be developed or borrowed for nursing. Models then provide the broad outline and theory provides the working insides.

Chapter 4 outlines the essential elements of the Roy Adaptation Model and Chapter 5 draws upon the major concepts of the model to describe a theory of the person as an adaptive system.

Adaptation Model and Theory

PART II

CHAPTER **4**

The Roy
Adaptation Model
of nursing

Theories for nursing will be based on the conceptual models for nursing practice. The model's view of the human person will be the basis for a theory or theories of the functioning of the human person. The model's view of the goal of nursing will be the major determining factor in deriving nursing practice theory. This book is about theory development and purports to do some formal theorizing based on the Roy Adaptation Model for nursing practice. This chapter will describe the Roy model by reviewing its essential elements: the person, the goal, and nursing intervention.[1]

The Client

The client of nursing may be a person, a family, a group, a community, or society. The abstract concept or model that the adaptation model uses to think about the client was developed on the individual level, that is, in rela-

1. The reader is reminded that according to the distinction between theory and model made in Chapter 2, the Roy framework is a model, not a theory, and thus should not be subjected to the procedures for the development and evaluation of theory. See footnote 1 of the Preface.

tion to the human person. However, this notion is applicable to the other levels that involve groups of persons, an application that will be discussed briefly later.

The Roy Adaptation Model of Nursing identifies the recipient of nursing care as an adaptive sytem. A system is described in its simplest form as a mechanism involving input, internal and feedback processes, and output. Inputs for the person as an open system come both externally from the environment[2] and from the self. These inputs have been generally termed stimuli. Certain stimuli pool to make up what Helson (1964) calls the person's adaptation level. We shall discuss this more in a moment. For now let us say that it represents a variable standard against which the feedback can be compared. It is like the setting of the thermostat except that with the living person the setting does not stay at a fixed point. We constantly have new levels of ability to cope. The adaptation level, then, is a constantly changing point which represents the person's own standard of the range of stimuli that he will tolerate with ordinary adaptive responses.

Let us next consider the output side. The output of the system is adaptive and ineffective responses. Adaptive responses are those that promote the integrity of the person in terms of the goals of survival, growth, reproduction, and self-mastery. Ineffective responses are those that do not contribute to these goals. These responses act as feedback which is further input for the person as a system. Just as the thermostat knows from the temperature whether to increase or decrease heat production, the person knows whether to increase or decrease efforts to cope with the stimulus.

The person has two major internal processor subsystems, the regulator and cognator. These are explored in greater depth in Chapter 5. To further describe the client of nursing, let us look at the four adaptive modes that are outlined below: physiological needs, self-concept, role function, and interdependence. The regulator and cognator are seen as mechanisms for adapting or coping. It is proposed that these coping mechanisms act in relation to the four modes. These modes provide the particular form or manifestation of cognator and regulator activity. They are the effectors of adaptation.

Physiological needs involve the body's basic needs and ways of dealing with adaptation in regard to fluid and electrolytes; exercise and rest; elimination; nutrition; circulation and oxygen; and regulation, which includes the senses, temperature, and endocrine regulation.

Self-concept is the composite of beliefs and feelings that one holds about oneself at a given time. It is formed from perceptions, particularly of

---

2. By environment we mean simply what the dictionary says, that is, all the conditions, circumstances, and influences surrounding, and affecting the development of an organism or group of organisms. Further clarification of environment as distinct from internal stimuli awaits additional theoretical work on the model.

other's reactions, and directs one's behavior. Its components include: (1) the physical self, which involves sensation and body image; and (2) the personal self, which is made up of self-consistency, self-ideal or expectancy, and the moral, ethical self. (Driever 1976).

Role function is the performance of duties based on given positions in society. The way one performs a role is dependent on one's interaction with the other in the given situation. The major roles that one plays can be analyzed by imagining a tree formation. The trunk of the tree is one's primary role, that is, one's developmental level—for example, generative adult female. Secondary roles branch off from this—for example, wife, mother, and teacher. Finally, tertiary roles branch off from secondary roles—for example, the mother role might involve the role of P.T.A. president for a given period of time (Malaznik 1976). Each of these roles is seen as occurring in a dyadic relationship, that is, with a reciprocal role.

The interdependence mode involves one's relations with significant others and support systems. In this mode one maintains psychic integrity by meeting needs for nurturance and affection (Poush and Van Landingham 1977).

Let us summarize to this point. We have said that Roy's abstract concept of the client of nursing is the person as an adaptive system with cognator and regulator acting to maintain adaptation in regard to the four adaptive modes. When we think of the family, community, or society as the client, we can also conceptualize these groups as adaptive systems. With some additional theorizing, these systems can be described in terms of their own inputs, coping mechanisms, and outputs. Whatever level the nurse is dealing with, her client is viewed, according to this model, as an adaptive system.

The Goal

The goal of nursing refers to the outcome of nursing action—that is, what the nurse is trying to accomplish. The goal of nursing action, according to this model, can be stated most simply as to promote patient adaptation in regard to the four modes. To understand this goal and to prepare for our discussion on intervention, we shall spend a little time describing the notion of adaptation utilized by the model.

The adaptation concept utilized by this model follows the work of Helson (1964). Helson says that adaptive responses are a function of: (1) the stimulus coming in—for example, how hot it is, or how painful it is— and (2) the adaptation level. Adaptation level is made up of the pooled effect of three classes of stimuli: (a) the focal stimuli or the stimuli immediately confronting the individual, that is, the same stimulus as in number 1, the heat or the pain; (b) the background or contextual stimuli, that is, all other stimuli present—for example, the humidity that intensifies the effect of the heat, or the noisy environment that intensifies the pain—and finally (c) the residual stimuli which include factors that may be relevant in the current situation but whose effect cannot be validated—for example, the person's general attitude toward hot weather, or the person's previous experience with pain.

The adaptation level sets up a zone that indicates the extent of stimuli that will elicit a positive response. Stimuli that hit outside of this zone bring about a negative response. We all have a threshold of pain that we can endure. Eventually, when that level is reached, we respond negatively. We try to get away from the pain, or we cry or moan. Some of these responses may be effective in maintaining our integrity but some may be ineffective. According to Helson, adaptation is a process of responding positively to environmental changes.[3] This positive response decreases the response necessary to cope with the stimuli and increases sensitivity to other stimuli. Thus we know that we have made an adaptive response to pain if our response has dealt with the situation so adequately that we can turn our attention to other things.

The person encounters adaptation problems in changing environments, especially in situations of health and illness. These problems are the concern of the nurse and her goal will be to solve the problem and bring about adaptation. The projected outcome is, therefore, an adapted state in the patient which frees him to respond to other stimuli. This freeing of energy makes it possible for the goal of nursing to contribute to the overall goal of the health team, higher-level wellness. When energy is freed from inadequate coping attempts, then it can promote healing and wellness. Thus the goal of the model, promoting adaptation, leads to the intended consequence of the model, that is, higher-level wellness.

This goal provides the conceptual basis for deciding whether or not a person needs nursing. When unusual stresses or weakened coping mechanisms make the person's usual attempts to cope ineffective, then the person needs a nurse. This person may be a child whose body fluids are depleted by diarrhea or an elderly person who sees limited options for meeting his affectional needs. In either case the nurse aims at changing the stimuli to help the person's coping mechanisms to bring about adaptation.

---

3. This notion of adaptation does not negate the fact that humans do not merely respond to stimuli in the environment, but can take the initiative to change the environment. This fact needs further exploration in relation to the model.

Nursing Intervention

The last critical component with which we shall deal is nursing intervention. When we think of nursing as a process, what is it that the nurse actually does? The model's view of nursing intervention comes directly from its view of the client and of the goal of nursing. If the client is an adaptive system, and if the goal of adaptation is reached when the focal stimuli is within the patient's adaptation level, then nursing intervention involves manipulating the focal, contextual, and residual stimuli so that the patient can cope with the stimuli.[4]

Nursing intervention is carried out in the context of the nursing process. We can understand the step of nursing intervention better if we look at the whole nursing process.

The theoretical view of the client provides the guidelines for the assessment phase of the nursing process. Since the client of this model is viewed as having four modes of adaptation, assessment involves collecting data relevant to each adaptive mode. For example, in regard to the physiological mode and specifically its component of exercise, the nurse makes observations concerning posture, mobility, and body alignment. For another physiological component, the need for rest, she collects date on the client's behaviors related to sleep and comfort. Likewise the psychosocial modes direct her collection of data. For example, in assessing the physical self, she notes references to body image and the client's mannerisms concerning his body parts. Or considering self-esteem, she listens for the client's statements that refer to his perceptions of worth. Assessment concepts thus include, first, significant behaviors in each of the adaptive modes.

According to this model, there is a second level of assessment. As we have seen, adaptation is a function of the gradient between the focal stimulus and the pooled effect of the focal, contextual, and residual stimuli. Thus, after the nurse assesses behaviors, she looks for the cause of these behaviors in terms of provoking stimuli, or the input to the system. Common classes of stimuli include: environmental changes, developmental level, and cultural patterns.

As the American Nurses' Association (ANA) Standards of Practice indicate, from the assessment data the nurse determines the nursing diagnosis. To understand the nature of a nursing diagnosis based on the Roy Adaptation Model, let us explain briefly what goes wrong in the system in a situation of ineffective behavior (previously defined as behavior that does not

---

4. Work on the clarification of nursing action modes according to the adaptation model is currently being done by Joyce Van Landingham formerly of Mount St. Mary's College, Los Angeles, Calif.

contribute to the goals of survival, growth, reproduction, and self-actualization). Changes in the internal or external environment can trigger off need deficits or excesses. Within the appropriate adaptive mode, coping activation is stimulated. When the coping mechanism is ineffective in meeting the demand, ineffective behavior results. The nature of the diagnostic categories are thus the deficits or excesses of basic needs leading to ineffective behavior. Roy (1973) outlines a beginning typology of adaptation problems. We are continuing to work on the diagnostic labels that are appropriate to this conceptual framework for nursing. In the meantime, a diagnosis may be expressed as the behavior with its predominate stimulus. For example, in regard to exercise and rest, a problem may be stated as lack of restful sleep related to change in environment and routine.

If the behavior of the client has been clearly specified, then writing the goal section of the nursing process is a simple matter. The nurse simply states that she wishes to maintain the adaptive behavior or to change the ineffective behavior. For example, the goal may read: Patient will sleep accustomed number of hours and wake up feeling rested.

Now we come to the specific intervention part of the nursing process. We have said that to promote adaptation, the nurse manipulates the stimuli so that they fall within the patient's zone of positive coping. She may increase, decrease, or modify internal and external stimuli. For a patient with a sleeping problem, for example, she may have assessed certain factors that were falling outside the patient's coping range, or were causing the range to be narrowed. Thus she does such things as decrease light and noise, increase opportunity for bedtime rituals, and modify bed by placing an accustomed bedboard under the mattress. Intervention is based specifically on the nursing assessment. We hope that, with additional work on the model, we can organize categories of nursing interventions.

In speaking of nursing intervention it is appropriate to mention the role of the patient in the nursing process. We must be entirely clear that manipulating stimuli is very different from manipulating persons. According to this nursing model, the person is to be respected as an active participant in his care. It is the information that the patient shares with the nurse that forms the assessment. The goal arrived at is one of mutual agreement between nurse and patient. Interventions are the options that the nurse provides for the patient. At times the nurse may have to act to safeguard the physiological integrity of the patient. This would be true in the case of infants, and unconscious or suicidal patients. Still, she is constantly aware of the active responsibility of the patient to participate in his own care when he is able to do so.

Based on this model, some nursing interventions will be traditional techniques such as comfort measures or health teaching. However, our theoretical work may allow us to discover entirely new activities that are the unique responsibility of the nurse when she is viewed as the promoter of patient adaptation.

Summary

In this chapter we presented the basic elements of the Roy Adaptation Model of Nursing. The person was viewed as an adaptive system having regulator and cognator coping mechanisms that act through the four adaptive modes to promote patient adaptation. The nurse enters the system by using the nursing process to manipulate stimuli to promote adaptation.

References and Additional Readings

Brower, H. T. F., and B. J. Baker. "The Roy Adaptation Model: Using the Adaptation Model in a Practitioner Curriculum," *Nursing Outlook,* 24 (1976): 686–89.

Driever, M. J. "Theory of Self Concept," In *Introduction to Nursing: An Adaptation Model,* ed. Sr. Callista Roy. Englewood Cliffs, N.J.: Prentice-Hall, Inc., 1976.

Galligan, A. C. "Using Roy's Concept of Adaptation to Care for Young Children," *American Journal of Maternal Child Nursing,* 4 (1979): 24–28.

Helson, Harry. *Adaptation Level Theory.* New York: Harper & Row, 1964.

Malaznik, Nancy. "Theory of Role Function." In *Introduction to Nursing: An Adaptation Model,* ed. Sr. Callista Roy. Englewood Cliffs, N.J.: Prentice-Hall, Inc., 1976.

Porth, C. M. "Physiological Coping: A Model for Teaching Pathophysiology," *Nursing Outlook,* 25 (1977): 781–84.

Poush, Mary, and Joyce Van Landingham, "Interdependence Mode Module," Class handout, Mount St. Mary's College, Los Angeles, 1977.

Riehl, Joan P., and Sr. Callista Roy. *Conceptual Models for Nursing Practice,* 2nd ed. New York: Prentice-Hall, Inc., 1980.

Roy, Sr. Callista. "Adaptation: A Conceptual Framework for Nursing," *Nursing Outlook,* 18 (1970): 42–45.

––––––. "Adaptation: A Basis for Nursing Practice," *Nursing Outlook,* 19 (1971): 254–57.

––––––."Adaptation: Implications for Curriculum Change," *Nursing Outlook,* 21 (1973): 163–68.

––––––. *Introduction to Nursing: An Adaptation Model.* Englewood Cliffs, N.J.: Prentice-Hall, Inc., 1976.

––––––. "The Roy Adaptation Model: Comment,"*Nursing Outlook,* 24 (1976): 690–91.

––––––. "Relating Nursing Theory to Education: A New Era." *Nurse Educator,* 4, no. 2 (1979): 16–21.

Wagner, P. "The Roy Adaptation Model: Testing the Adaptation Model in Practice." *Nursing Outlook,* 24 (1976): 682–85.

CHAPTER 5

Theory
of the person as
an adaptive system

Sister Callista Roy
Dorothy McLeod

The Roy Adaptation Model of Nursing describes the recipient of nursing care as an adaptive system. The model thus directs one to articulate a theory of the adaptive system. Theories underlying a model's view of the recipient of nursing care generally come from the basic sciences. Investigation of adaptive systems is evident in the literature of a number of fields including genetics, biology, physiology, physics, psychology, anthropology, and sociology. All of these approaches can be helpful in conceptualizing the adaptive system. Yet each approach views the person or the group from the perspective of that discipline. The nursing model directs that the nurse view the patient holistically. We need a theory of the holistic person as an adaptive system.[1] Since the basic sciences do not provide nurses with a single working theory, the nurse using the adaptation model must create one for herself. This chapter is a beginning effort to do this—to create a theory of the holistic person as an adaptive system.

The first section of the chapter will explore the notion of an adaptive system by describing systems and examining the meaning of adaptation.

---

1. Though we have noted that the recipient of nursing care may be an individual person or a group, such as a family or community, for the sake of simplicity this initial theorizing will be confined to the individual level.

Then a depiction of the person as an adaptive system will be offered. The person's two subsystems, the regulator and the cognator, will be treated according to the approach to theory construction introduced earlier. The emerging theory of the person as an adaptive system will be related in a general way to the adaptive modes proposed by the Roy Adaptation Model of Nursing. Finally, the two subsystems will be interrelated.

Meaning of the Terms *System* and *Adaptation*

To view the person as an adaptive system one must have a clear notion of the meaning of the terms *system* and *adaptation*. This section describes each term briefly and focuses on the meaning given the terms within the theoretical system being developed.

System

In its broadest meaning, a system is a set of units with relationships among them. Rapoport (1968) adds to this general definition the statement that a system is a whole that functions as a whole by virtue of the interdependence of its parts. A system may be as simple as a mechanical heating device or it may be as complex as the process model of sociocultural operations in society. It will be helpful first to describe a simple mechanical system.

Systems can be analyzed in terms of input, output, and feedback processes. A simple mechanical control system is made up of an output device, a control device, involving a detector of input, and a feedback loop. Figure 5.1 shows these parts in diagrammatic form.

In an electrical heating system, the output device may be a high-resistance wire heated by the passage of an electric current supplied by a central voltage source. This device has a switch that can be opened or closed to turn the current on or off. The control device is the mechanism that operates the switch according to the environmental temperature. This device may be made up of a sensing and regulating thermometer and an electromagnet that will throw the switch. The input is, first, the location of

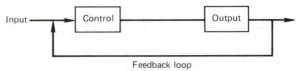

Feedback loop

Figure **5.1.** Simple Mechanical Control System.

the preset point on the thermometer indicating the desired temperature. Second, the feedback (that is, something from the output) allows the control device to compare the heat produced by the output device with the amount of heat needed to reach the desired temperature. Input is often referred to as information.

Just as feedback leads to correction of error in mechanical systems, so too feedback is important in the regulation of living systems. It is, in fact, negative feedback that maintains steady states. The term *negative feedback* can be misleading, however, in that it seems to imply a negative quantity. To understand the notion of negative feedback let us use the image of the mechanical heating system. Negative feedback means that the control system subtracts the input in the form of the standard from the feedback and the sign of the difference is opposite to the sign of the regulated change in output. Thus if the thermostat is set at 70° (input standard) and the heat being produced warms the room to 75° (feedback), 70° is subtracted from 75° and a +5° obtained. The sign of this difference is the opposite of the sign of the regulated change in output and a change of −5° in output is directed.

The diagram can thus be read: The output device produces its output; something from the output is fed back to the control device; under the joint influence of the fed-back material and the input in the form of a standard, the control device instructs the output device as to further action.

If we add to this simple mechanical control system the notion that the input setting is not fixed but, rather, is variable, we have what is called a *servo system.* An example of this type of system is the automatic gunsight that responds to a moving target. This servo system improves its performance by getting more information from scanning the moving target. Reiner (1968) notes that, in adaptive control devices, the standard of operation is variable as it is in a servo system. Furthermore, he treats the living organism as an adaptive control system.

Living systems are comprised of matter and energy organized by information. Matter simply means anything that has mass and occupies space. Energy is the ability to do work. According to the laws of physics, matter and energy can be converted to one another. Information is the name for the content of what is exchanged with the outer world. The processing of information is termed *communication.* Information-processing capabilities have been referred to as adaptiveness (Buckley 1967).

In moving from mechanical systems to living systems we make a transition from closed systems to open systems, from mechanism to dynamism. Closed systems tend to increase in entropy. Entropy is defined as the disorder, disorganization, lack of patterning, or randomness of organization of a system. It is that quality of energy within a system that is not capable of work. An increase of entropy is the running down of the system.

It is a decrease in information. Miller (1965) uses the example of figures carved in ice. Since there is no principle of the conservation of information, as there are principles of the conservation of matter and energy, the figures melt into a puddle. Closed systems respond to environmental demands with a loss in organization or a change in the direction of dissolution of the system.

Open systems, on the other hand, engage in interchange with the environment and this interchange is an essential factor underlying the system's viability, its reproductive ability or continuity, and its ability to change. The response of open systems to environmental demands is elaboration or change of their structure to a higher or more complex level. This increasing complexity is termed *negentropy*. Negentropy is also a measure of the order of the system and may be referred to as energy that is available to do work. Miller (1965) notes that living systems maintain a steady state of negentropy even though entropic changes occur in them. Basically, living systems take in inputs of matter and energy higher in complexity—that is, lower in entropy—than their outputs. In the living system's dynamic interchange with the environment, four decisions are possible, according to Miller: (1) alter self, (2) alter the environment, (3) withdraw from the environment, and (4) alter the desirable state.

Living systems also have the basic characteristic of being composed of subsystems. A subsystem is the totality of all the structures in a system that carry out a particular process. Thus, the circulatory subsystem in the person can be identified by the process it carries out, namely, circulation. In living systems the subsystems are integrated together to form actively self-regulating, developing, reproducing unitary systems with purposes and goals. Subsystems are generally arranged in a hierarchy.

Systems in general, and living systems in particular, are assumed to have a tendency toward balance. When balance is thought of as reaching a fixed point, the system is considered in equilibrium—for example, body temperature at 37 °C. When the balanced relationship of the parts is not dependent upon a fixed point or level, the system is maintaining a steady state—for example, healthy rhythms of exercise and rest. A dynamic equilibrium exists when the equilibrium shifts to a new position of balance after disturbance—for example, greater coping ability following the resolution of a crisis.

Living systems are characteristically subject to stress.[2] Miller (1965) notes that input or output of either matter-energy or information which, by some lack or excess, forces the variables beyond the range of stability, constitutes a stress and produces a strain within the system. Adjustment pro-

---

2. A thorough discussion of the concept of stress is beyond the scope of this chapter; however, the reader is encouraged to consult the references cited since a fuller understanding of stress is relevant to the theory of the adaptive person.

cesses are those processes of the subsystems that maintain steady states in systems. These processes keep variables within their ranges of stability despite stresses.

The living system is, in summary, a whole made up of parts or subsystems that function as a unity for some purpose. The input of the system involves variable standards and negative feedback which act to maintain the system in dynamic equilibrium. As an open system, the living system is negentropic and subject to internal and external stress.

Adaptation

White (1974) says that "adaptation is something that is done by living systems in interaction with their environment." It can be described as a process that occurs in groups such as in the anthropological approach of Cohen (1968). Also on the group level, adaptation can mean an end state as seen in the Davis and Moore's (1945) sociological functional analysis. When adaptation is viewed on the individual level, again some theorists view it as a process, such as the ego psychology of Hartman and Rapoport (Klein 1968). Other theorists view it as an end state, for example, the adaptation level theory of Helson (1964). These different conceptualizations have in common the notion of adaptation as a response to the environment which results in survival. This goal of survival is common to all systems. In dealing with living systems, the goals of growth and reproduction are added. When the living system is a human person, most theorists would postulate an additional goal which is described in such terms as self-determination (Angyal 1941) and mastery (Howard and Scott 1965). We shall therefore broaden our description of adaptation to include the person's response to the environment which promotes the general goals of the person including survival, growth, reproduction, and mastery.

We have noted that the person's adaptive response to the environment can be viewed as either a process or an end product. Of the many theoretical formulations of human adaptation, the nursing model under consideration directs attention to the work of Helson (1964) who views adaptation as an end product. Helson's adaptation level theory took the concept of adaptation from biology and sensory physiology, then developed it in psychophysics, and finally applied it to the social psychology of the person.

In explaining his concept of adaptation, Helson speaks of the *state* of adaptation. He says that this state corresponds to a given level of activity and that, conversely, the level of activity is a reflection of the state of adaptation. Helson points out two aspects of adaptation: (1) the decrement in response of some receptors following durative or repeated stimulation, and (2) the heightened response on the part of other receptors. Adaptation to the color red makes the subject more sensitive to blue-green and adaptation to warm makes one sensitive to cold. The end state of adaptation, therefore, involves heightened as well as lowered performance. Helson further stresses that this end state is one of dynamic equilibrium as opposed to static equilibrium.

Helson's work points to adaptation as a dynamic state of equilibrium involving both heightened and lowered responses brought about by autonomic and cognitive processes triggered by internal and external stimuli. This approach to adaptation appears to narrow the description given earlier, namely, that adaptation involved the person's response to the environment which promotes the general goals of the person. However, if we look at the process of adaptation, then relate it to systems theory, we shall see how Helson's view of adaptation fits into and clarifies the larger description given.

The process of adaptation will be presented by synthesizing some of the literature related to stress adaptation. The transaction between the environmental demand for adaptation and the person's response has been given the general term *stress*. Lazarus (1966) emphasizes that stress should be defined in terms of transactions between individuals and their situations rather than as either one in isolation. Mechanic's (1970) contribution to the concept of stress adaptation emphasizes consideration of both a personal and societal perspective at the same time.

In Dohrenwend's (1961) paradigm of the stress response, stressors and mediating factors interact and lead to stress, which triggers off an adaptation syndrome resulting in adaptive or maladaptive responses. Although his work considers the social psychological nature of stress, Dohrenwend's framework parallels Selye's (1978) presentation of his research on physiological stress adaptation. In his model of psychological stress, Lazarus (1966) postulates coping processes (identified as primary and secondary appraisal) between the antecedents and consequences of stress.

Based on these notions, and borrowing some terminology from Helson, the view of stress adaptation depicted in Figure 5.2 can be synthesized.

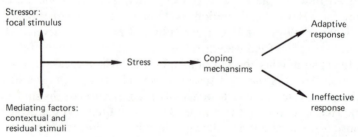

FIGURE 5.2 Stress Adaptation.

The process of adaptation can be described as stressors, or focal stimuli, being mediated by contextual and residual factors (which include both a personal and a societal perspective) to partially produce the interaction called stress. The other half of the stress interaction is the coping mechanisms that are triggered off to produce adaptive or ineffective responses. To further clarify the proposed nature of the process of adaptation, the meaning given to each term used in the diagram will be explored.

The focal stimulus is generally identified as the degree of change that precipitates adaptive behavior. It is the stimulus most immediately confronting the person, the one to which he must make an adaptive response. This demand for an adaptive response can also be referred to as a stressor. Stressors can range from relatively mild fluctuations such as the weather to severe bombardments such as repeated artillery shellings during wartime. They can be physical, physiological, psychosocial, or a combination of these; spouse beating, for example, has elements of each of these kinds of stressors. Stressors may be located in the external environment as with all of the examples noted here, or they may be internal to the person—for example, the meaning the person gives to a painful memory. They may be negative occurrences, or they may be more positive occurrences such as a job promotion. (See, for example, the life change patterns research of Rahe 1968.) The process of stress adaptation is thus initiated by a stressor, or focal stimulus, which is a change that requires an adaptive response.

Mediating factors are those that contribute to the effect of the stressor. Helson (1964) classifies mediating factors as contextual and residual. Contextual stimuli are all other stimuli present in the situation of the stressor—for example, the degree of humidity during the temperature change. Again, these stimuli can vary in intensity; they include psychological and social factors as well as physical and physiological ones; they may be internal or external and positive or negative.

Residual stimuli are of the same nature as contextual stimuli; that is, they are contributory to the focal stimuli. Furthermore, residual stimuli have the same variety of characteristics that we have noted for focal and contextual stimuli. Residual stimuli differ, however, in that they are presumed to effect the current situation, although this effect cannot be validated or measured. Often such factors as beliefs, attitudes, experience, or traits are considered residual stimuli.

In considering the focal, contextual, and residual stimuli, we should note a particular outcome of the interaction of these factors that has been identified by Helson (1964). The pooled effect of these three classes of stimuli (focal, contextual, and residual) determines what Helson calls the adaptation level. Adaptation level is a condition of the person relative to adaptation. We shall return to this notion of adaptation level when we relate the process of adaptation to systems theory.

We have already indicated the meaning given to the term *stress*. Stress is the general term given to the transaction between the environmental demand for adaptation and the person's response. Much of the literature on stress focuses on either the input side of the stressors or on the output side of the stress responses. The view of stress being emphasized here is that stress is interactive of both demand and response.

The next term used in our diagram of the process of adaptation is *coping mechanisms*. Coping is a construct closely linked in the literature with the notion of adaptation. This is particularly so in the psychology literature (see, for example, Coelho 1974). Though coping has a variety of meanings, it has been defined most broadly as any attempt to master a new situation that can be potentially threatening, frustrating, challenging, or gratifying (Murphy 1962). Other authors would reserve the term coping for efforts in relatively difficult conditions. (See, for example, Lazarus, Averill, and Opton 1974, White 1974.) However, since adaptation is seen as a process involved in all of the person's interactions with the environment, and since coping mechanisms are seen as operating to produce adaptive responses, the broad definition of coping will be utilized. Coping will refer to routine, accustomed patterns of behavior to deal with daily situations as well as to the production of new ways of behaving when drastic changes defy the familiar responses.

Both Lazarus, Averill, and Opton (1974) and White (1974) clearly point out the need for a theoretically based system of classification for coping responses. This system, according to Lazarus and his colleagues, is at present more of a need and a wish than a reality. It must be evolved, linked to more general theories of the human person, and then tied to observable antecedents and consequences.

One way of approaching the classification of coping responses is to explore the coping mechanisms that produce these responses. The definition of coping has already been given. The meaning of *mechanism* that is used here is the arrangement of parts to produce an effect. Based on some general notions introduced by Helson (1964), Roy (1970) has postulated two major coping mechanisms, the regulator and the cognator. This conceptualization is an attempt to unify the work done on physiological adaptation and psychosocial adaptation into a holistic view of human coping. The regulator and cognator mechanisms, and the effects they produce, are developed theoretically later in this chapter. The remaining chapters of the book then link these mechanisms to the functioning of the person in health and illness.[3]

---

3. This approach may be considered one attempt among many to classify coping responses, to link them to a theory of the human person, and to tie them to observable antecedents or consequences. But whether or not it makes any appreciable contribution to basic science theory of the human person, it fulfills the present purpose of providing an important link in the development of the theory for nursing that is in progress.

The last terms in the schematic outline of stress adaptation are adaptive and ineffective responses. We have already broadly described adaptation as involving the person's response to the environment which promotes the person's general goals including survival, growth, reproduction, and mastery. Thus, as Roy (1976) has elsewhere defined it, an adaptive response is behavior that maintains the integrity of the individual. Conversely, ineffective response is behavior that does not lead to these goals or that disrupts the integrity of the individual.

White's (1974) discussion of strategies of adaptation provides two insights particularly useful in this exploration of adaptive and ineffective responses. First, White notes an unwitting tendency to think of adaptive behavior in a dichotomy of good and bad. Adaptation, for him, does not mean either a total triumph over the environment or a total surrender to it, but rather a striving toward acceptable compromise. The maintenance of integrity is always a relative notion. A daredevil cyclist may risk his survival goal to promote his self-mastery goal. Furthermore, White notes in militaristic terms that adaptation often calls for delay, strategic retreat, regrouping of forces, abandoning of untenable positions, seeking fresh intelligence, or developing new weapons. An example would be the adaptive purpose served by the period of denial following a loss. Conversely, on the physiological level we see many responses that are initially adaptive—for example, fever—that do not serve the organism in the long run.

From this discussion we can draw two basic principles to be used in judging adaptive and ineffective responses. Judgments of such behavior will be relative within some valued hierarchy of goals. Adaptation for the individual depends on what is important to him. Secondly, judgments will be made on the basis of the long-term effects of the behavior. The immediate effect of most actions is adaptive, but if these actions are continued over time they may be ineffective.

The second discussion from White that is useful at this point is his listing of variables in adaptive behavior. Behaviors are more likely to be more adaptive when the person can: (1) keep securing adequate information about the environment; (2) maintain satisfactory internal conditions for both action and for processing information; and (3) maintain his autonomy or freedom of movement and freedom to use his repertoire in a flexible manner. These variables will be reflected in the propositions related to adaptive behavior that are given later.[4]

Adaptation is viewed here, then, as a process of coping with stressors (as illustrated in Figure 5.2) as well as the end state produced by this process.

---

4. Though the propositions were written before reading the article by White (1974) their relationship to his ideas was seen to be clarifying.

The Adaptive System of the Person

By relating the explanations given of the two terms *system* and *adaptation,* we can create a depiction of the person as an adaptive system. Beginning with the diagram of a simple mechanical system (see Figure 5.1), we noted that systems have input, a control device, an output device, and a feedback loop. Living systems are characterized by being open systems, exchanging energy and matter with the environment. Their input also involves variable standards and negative feedback which act to maintain the system in dynamic equilibrium including ever higher levels of organization. The control device of living systems is made up of subsystems which each have a function, but which work as a unity for the common purpose of the system.

Adaptation was presented as both a process and an end state. The process of adaptation, outlined in Figure 5.2, was described as stressors, mediated by contextual stimuli, leading to activity of the coping mechanisms which produce adaptive and ineffective responses. The resulting end state may be described broadly in terms of conditions that promote the goals of the person including survival, growth, reproduction, and mastery. It is more specifically a dynamic state of equilibrium involving both heightened and lowered responses.

Simplifying the major components of the explanations of the terms systems and adaptation, the diagram in Figure 5.3 represents in broadest outline the current understanding of the person as an adaptive system.

A theory of the person as an adaptive system will thus involve a description of the functioning of this system by way of descriptions of the working of the subsystems, together with propositions predicting effects of the relationships between the variables in the total system. Before presenting this theoretical work, some general observations will be made about the input and output sides of this system.

Inputs for the person as an open system come both externally from the

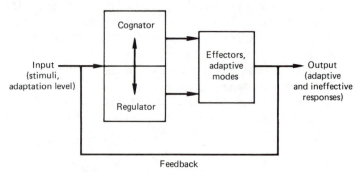

FIGURE **5.3** The Person as an Adaptive System.

environment and internally from the self. These inputs have been generally termed stimuli, some of which are labeled stressors since they provoke adaptive mechanisms. However, it should be noted that the portrayal here is philosophically far removed from a notion of the person as a constant victim of bombardment by hostile elements from within and without. Rather the modern person faces a great many changing circumstances (stimuli or stressors), most of which are challenges to further growth and self-mastery. The richness and variety of these inputs lead the person on to new accomplishments. Thus the mountain climber does not shrink from the higher, more rugged mountain. Rather he approaches it with zest and excitement.

Another observation about the input of the human adaptive system relates to a characteristic presented earlier, that this type of system involves a variable standard. The mechanical closed system had a preset standard—for example, the thermostat set at 70 °F. But with living open systems, the standard is not fixed. Further, it was noted that Helson (1964) speaks of a certain condition of the person relative to adaptation which he terms *adaptation level*. It is here proposed that adaptation level represents the system input that provides the variable standard against which the feedback is compared to direct the further output of the system.

The adaptation level is determined by the pooled effect of the three classes of stimuli: focal, contextual, and residual. It is a constantly changing point that represents the person's own standard of the range of stimuli that he will tolerate with ordinary adaptive responses.

This brings us to a consideration of the output of the human system, which we hope will unify our broad and specific descriptions of the end state of adaptation. There are two ways that the person can make adaptive responses. First, the gradient between the focal stimuli and the adaptation level may be such that usual responses are adequate to cope with the situation. This response is adaptive in both senses of the term. On the narrower level (Helson's definition), if the stimulus is easily handled, there will be a lowering of responses to this stimulus and a heightening of responses to other stimuli with the result of a continuing dynamic state of equilibrium. In other words, energy is not needlessly expended in efforts to cope. Since there is no threat to the individual, the integrity of the person in terms of the goals of survival, growth, reproduction, and mastery is maintained (broader definition).

When there is a steeper gradient between the focal stimulus and the adaptation level, an adaptive response is still possible for the person. Initial efforts to cope with the stimulus are fed back into the system and compared with the adaptation level and its gradient to the focal stimulus. If the effort is not sufficient to cope with the stimulus, the coping mechanisms will be further activated to produce greater responses—for example, novel solutions to the problem. If these efforts are successful, these responses will eventually be lowered, since they are no longer needed, and other responses will be heightened. Again, with this adaptive response, the person has contributed to his goals of survival, growth, reproduction, and mastery. It should be noted that the new adaptive state has effected the adaptation level so that the dynamic equilibrium of the person is at an ever higher level. Greater ranges of stimuli can be dealt with successfully by the person as an adaptive system.

Regulator Subsystem

The regulator subsystem is described by the inputs, major parts, processes, effectors, and feedback loops. From the description propositions can be derived that indicate the role of the regulator subsystem in the adaptation of the living human system.

Inputs are stimuli from the external environment and from changes in the internal state of dynamic equilibrium. The inputs are chemical in nature or have been transduced into neural information. Inputs such as light, touch, pain, odor, and position in space are all transduced into electrical, neural inputs. The inputs may be in the positive or negative direction and include information from the body responses via the feedback mechanisms.

The major parts of the subsystem are the neural, endocrine, and perception-psychomotor portions. The perception-psychomotor part is basically neural in nature as is shown by stimulation and lesion experiments. The details of the process are not known by neurophysiologists. The perception-psychomotor part overlaps with the cognator subsystem and, therefore, serves to connect the two subsystems.

The processes have been simplified to include only the major and necessary steps and are shown in Figure 5.4. External and internal neural stimuli must be transduced into electrical impulses and travel through intact pathways to the central nervous system and to the effectors setting up automatic reflex responses. The effectors are neurally controlled muscles or glandular structures. These reflexes may be conscious or unconscious in nature. Other neural impulses will stimulate endocrine glands to produce their hormones. Circulating chemicals also stimulate the endocrine glands to produce hormones. The target organs or tissues must be responsive to the circulating hormones in order to produce a body response.

These neural inputs which generally come into conscious awareness are acted upon by the "perception process." The perception that results is altered by cultural and social factors and must remain in short-term memory long enough for a psychomotor choice of response to be made. The

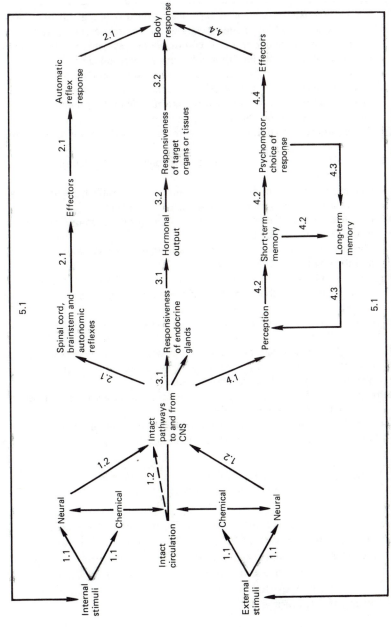

Figure **5.4** Regulator Subsystem. Numbers refer to propositions in Table 5.1.

TABLE **5.1** Propositions — Regulator Subsystem

1.1	Internal and external stimuli are basically chemical or neural; chemical stimuli may be transduced into neural inputs to the central nervous system.
1.2	Neural pathways to and from the central nervous system must be intact and functional if neural stimuli are to influence body response.[1]
2.1	Spinal cord, brainstem, and autonomic reflexes act through effectors to produce automatic, unconscious effects on the body responses.
3.1	The circulation must be intact for chemical stimuli to influence endocrine glands to produce the appropriate hormone.
3.2	Target organs or tissues must be able to respond to hormone levels to effect body responses.
4.1	Neural inputs are transformed into conscious perceptions in the brain (process unknown).
4.2	Increase in short-term or long-term memory will positively influence the effective choice of psychomotor response to neural input.
4.3	Effective choice of response, retained in long-term memory, will facilitate future effective choice of response.
4.4	The psychomotor response chosen will determine the effectors activated and the ultimate body response.
1.1 through 2.1, 3.2, 4.4	The magnitude of the internal and external stimuli will positively influence the magnitude of the physiological response of an intact system.
3.1 through 2.1, 4.4	Intact neural pathways will positively influence neural output to effectors.
1.1 through 3.2	Chemical and neural inputs will influence normally responsive endocrine glands to hormonally influence target organs in a positive manner to maintain a state of dynamic equilibrium.
1.1 through 5.1	The body's response to external and internal stimuli will alter those external and internal stimuli.
1.1 through 5.1	The magnitude of the external and internal stimuli may be so great that the adaptive systems cannot return the body to a state of dynamic equilibrium.

1. This is generally the case though there are exceptions; for example, persons with spinal cord injury have a separation of cognitive and reflex activity.

choice of response or the short-term memory may enter long-term memory and feedback in a positive feedback loop to alter perception. The psychomotor response acts through the effectors to influence the body response. Each of these relationships is depicted in the propositions listed in Table 5.1.[5] These propositions are based on the relationships established in the literature of physiology.

5. As noted in the Preface with the notion of propositions developed, we want to clarify that the adaptation model implies multivariable and nonlinear configurations. At this initial stage in our theorizing, however, we have begun by drawing relationships which imply linear relationships and are largely bivariate. We recognize the extensive work that needs to be done.

Cognator Subsystem

The cognator subsystem can be described in terms of its input, parts, processes, and effectors. Propositions related to the functioning of the cognator subsystem in the adaptation of the total system can then be presented, based on this description.

The inputs to the cognator subsystem are the same as those described for the system as a whole. The inputs are internal and external stimuli that vary in intensity, include psychological and social factors as well as physical and physiological ones, and are positive or negative. The internal stimuli include the output of the regulator mechanism.

The parts of the cognator mechanism that have been proposed are the psychosocial pathways and apparatus for: (1) perceptual/information processing, (2) learning, (3) judgment, and (4) emotion. Though the exact nature of these pathways and apparatus may not be conclusively known, there is some general agreement that they exist.

Four distinct kinds of processes have been identified relative to these parts of the cognator. In regard to the perceptual/information processing, the processes of selective attention, coding, and memory have been identified. The learning apparatus seems to give rise to processes such as imitation, reinforcement, and insight. The part of the cognator called judgment involves the processes of problem solving and decision making. Lastly, the emotional apparatus gives rise to defenses to seek relief and affective appraisal and attachment.

Effectors for the cognator subsystem involve the bodily musculoskeletal system and all the psychomotor parts that act together to produce internal and external verbalizations. White (1974) highlights the significance of motor activity in the organism's adaptive repertoire. It makes possible the basic responses of orientation, approach, avoidance, flight, or hiding. For the human person, the ability to represent reality and manipulate it for oneself and others in the form of spoken or unspoken words is even more significant. The effectors that produce the cognator adaptive and ineffective responses thus lie in these two major areas.[6]

This view of the cognator subsystem is summarized in Figure 5.5. Internal and external stimuli trigger off the four kinds of cognator processes. These processes depend on the corresponding intact pathways and apparatus. The various processes produce a psychomotor choice of response which is carried out through the effectors. The resulting response may be

---

6. In-depth discussion of the cognator apparatus, its processes, and effectors is beyond the scope of this chapter. However, the author's view of how they work in the human person will be further clarified as the cognator subsystem's functioning in the adaptive modes is explored in later chapters.

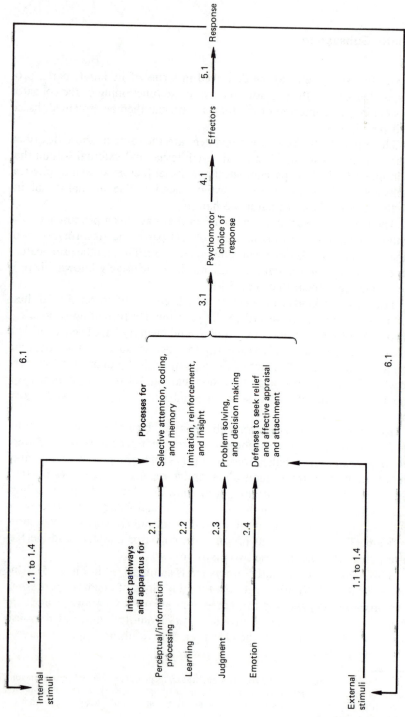

FIGURE 5.5 Cognator Subsystem. Numbers refer to propositions in Table 5.2.

adaptive or maladaptive for the cognator subsystem and for the person as a whole system.

Based on logical or empirical relationships within the cognator subsystem, we may propose a series of theoretical propositions. These are grouped into two sets of relationships and four single relationships.

The first set of relationships link the amount and clarity of input to the adequacy of each of the cognator processes. These propositions are indicated as 1.1 to 1.4 on Figure 5.5 and can be read from Table 5.2. They can be seen as illustrative of White's (1974) first variable in adaptive behavior. He refers to the need to keep securing adequate information from the environment. It should be noted further that the propositions specify an optimum amount and clarity of input. The highest amount of input and the greatest clarity are not always optimum. The plethora of memos that come across administrators' desks often illustrates that more information is not always better. In a related matter, Mechanic (1974) speaks of a misconception in stress literature; that is, the notion that successful adaptation requires an accurate perception of reality. He suggests, for example, that

TABLE 5.2 Propositions—The Cognator Subsystem

1.1	The optimum amount and clarity of input of internal and external stimuli positively influences the adequacy of selective attention, coding, and memory.
1.2	The optimum amount and clarity of input of internal and external stimuli positively influences the adequacy of imitation, reinforeement, and insight.
1.3	The optimum amount and clarity of input of internal and external stimuli positively influences the adequacy of problem solving and decision making.
1.4	The optimum amount and clarity of input of internal and external stimuli positively influences the adequacy of defenses to seek relief, and affective appraisal and attachment.
2.1	Intact pathways and perceptual/information-processing apparatus positively influences the adequacy of selective attention, coding, and memory.
2.2	Intact pathways and learning apparatus positively influences imitation, reinforcement, and insight.
2.3	Intact pathways and judgment apparatus positively influences problem solving and decision making.
2.4	Intact pathways and emotional apparatus positively influences defenses to seek relief, and affective appraisal and attachment.
3.1	The higher the level of adequacy of all the cognator processes, the more effective the psychomotor choice of response.
4.1	The psychomotor response chosen will be activated through intact effectors.
5.1	Effector activity produces the response that is at an adaptive level determined by the total functioning of the cognator subsystem.
6.1	The level of adaptive responses to internal and external stimuli will alter those internal and external stimuli.

there is perhaps no thought so stifling as to see ourselves in proper perspective.

In the second set of relationships, each of the intact pathways and apparatus is postulated to have a positive influence on the adequacy of the related cognator process. These propositions are labeled as 2.1, 2.2, 2.3, and 2.4 in both Figure 5.4 and Table 5.1. Again these seem to be specific applications of one of White's (1974) variables. He notes the need for the organism to maintain satisfactory internal conditions both for action and for processing information.

The next single proposition, labeled 3.1, specifies that the higher the level of adequacy of all the cognator processes, the more effective the psychomotor choice of response. This proposition seems to speak to White's third variable of adaptive behavior, that the organism maintain its autonomy or freedom of movement and use its repertoire in a flexible fashion. This effective choice of response, or flexibility in behavior, is often equated with adaptability.

From proposition 4.1, we note that the psychomotor response chosen will be activated through intact effectors. This speaks to another specific internal condition that must be maintained satisfactorily.

The proposition specified by 5.1 is the last link in the chain and serves to summarize the cognator activity. It specifies that the effector activity produces the response that is at an adaptive level determined by the total functioning of the cognator subsystem.

However, as with any system, the output of the adaptive system is fed back into the system by its effect on the input. Thus we have the final proposition, 6.1, which states that the level of adaptive responses to internal and external stimuli will alter those internal and external stimuli. The propositions stated here seem to be reasonable assumptions based on the current level of knowledge in the behavioral sciences.

Relationship of Theory to the Adaptive Modes

We have been developing a theory of the person as an adaptive system to be used with the Roy Adaptation Model of Nursing. As discussed in Chapter 4, Roy (1970) has proposed that the person has four adaptive modes, that is, ways or methods of adapting or coping. According to the theory outlined, the regulator and cognator must be seen as the ways or methods of adapting or coping. It is proposed, however, that these coping mechanisms act in relation to the four modes of adaptation: physiological needs, self-concept, role function, and interdependence. These modes[7] will provide the par-

---

7. Fortunately, the term *mode* also connotes the revised meaning as well as the earlier meaning given to the term.

ticular form or manifestation of cognator and regulator activity. They are, therefore, more the effectors of adaptation than the means of adaptation. In the following chapters we shall apply the theory developed to the manifestations of patients' functioning within the adaptive modes. First, however, a few observations will be made on the relation of the two subsystems to the four adaptive modes.

The regulator subsystem is related predominately to the mode of physiological needs. Since very little is known physiologically about the process of perception formation, memory, and choice of psychomotor responses, the other modes of self-concept, role function, and interdependence must relate to the meaning of a given perception for the individual human system. The meaning of the perception will, therefore, influence the body response.

The cognator subsystem is seen as related to each of the adaptive modes in at least three major ways. First of all, a review of the literature on the facets of each mode reveals specific relevant inputs for the cognator subsystem. For example, cultural habits will be an important mediating factor in considering the nutritional mode. Likewise role cues will be significant input with the role-function mode. Secondly, the adaptive mode under consideration will specify the relevant pathways and apparatus. For example, in the self-concept mode perceptual/information-processing apparatus seem to be highly significant. Lastly, within each mode it will be possible to view specific cognator processes. An example of a cognator process that is active in relation to a physiological need is the process of imitation, reinforcement, and insight involved in toilet training. Similarly, threats to self-concept can be profitably viewed in terms of the cognator process of defenses to seek relief.

The Relationship
Between Cognator and Regulator

We have noted that the regulator and cognator are linked together in the process of perception. Inputs to the regulator are transformed into perceptions. Perception is a process of the cognator. The responses following perception are feedback into both the cognator and the regulator. We have noted that subsystems are generally arranged in hierarchies. The hierarchical arrangement of the regulator and cognator in relation to each other can be the subject of further theoretical exploration.

Within each of the following chapters, theoretical propositions for each of the adaptive modes will be developed on the basis of how the functioning of the regulator and cognator subsystems are manifested within each mode in the promotion of the adaptive goals of the total person system—that is, survival, growth, reproduction, and mastery.

Summary

In this chapter, we have explored the beginning development of a theory of the person as an adaptive system. After an introductory section that explored the meaning of the terms *system* and *adaptation*, the person was conceptualized as having two subsystems for adapting, the cognator and regulator. Each of these subsystems was explored by describing its inputs, major parts, processes, effectors, and feedback loops. Propositions related to the two subsystems were derived from the descriptions of the cognator and regulator. The relationships between these two subsystems, and among the subsystems and adaptive modes were discussed briefly. This beginning theory of the person as an adaptive system becomes the basis for the additional theorizing in the next two parts of this book.

References

Angyal, A. *Foundations for a Science of Personality.* New York: Commonwealth Fund, 1941.

Buckley, W. *Sociology and Modern Systems Theory.* Englewood Cliffs, N.J.: Prentice-Hall, Inc., 1967.

Coelho, G. V.; David A. Hamburg; and John E. Adams, eds. *Coping and Adaptation.* New York: Basic Books, 1974.

Cohen, Y. A. *Man in Adaptation: The Biosocial Background,* vol. 1. Chicago: Aldine, 1968.

Davis, K., and W. E. Moore, "Some Principles of Stratification," *American Sociological Review,* 10, no. 2 (April 1945): 242–49.

Dohrenwend, Bruce P. "The Social Psychological Nature of Stress: A Framework for Causal Inquiry," *Journal of Abnormal and Social Psychology,* 62, no. 2 (1961): 294–302.

Helson, Harry. *Adaptation Level Theory.* New York: Harper & Row, 1964.

Howard, A., and R. Scott. "A Proposed Framework for Analysis of Stress in the Human Organism," *Behavioral Science,* 10 (1965): 141.

Klein, Georgé. "Psychoanalysis: Ego Psychology." In *International Encyclopedia of the Social Sciences,* ed. David L. Sills, pp. 19–23. New York: Macmillan/Free Press, 1968.

Lazarus, R. S. *Psychological Stress and the Coping Process.* New York: McGraw-Hill, 1966.

———; J. R. Averill; and E. M. Opton, Jr. "The Psychology of Coping: Issues of Research and Assessment." In *Coping and Adaptation,* ed. G. V. Coelho, D. A. Hamburg, and J. E. Adams, pp. 249–315. New York: Basic Books, 1974.

Mechanic, D. "Social Structure and Personal Adaptation: Some Neglected Dimensions." In *Coping and Adaptation,* ed. G. V. Coelho, D. A. Hamburg, and J. E. Adams, pp. 37–44. New York: Basic Books, 1974.

———. "Some Problems in Developing a Social Psychology of Adaptation to

Stress." In *Social and Psychological Factors in Stress,* ed. J. McGrath, pp. 104–23. New York: Holt, Rinehart and Winston, 1970.

Miller, James G. "Living Systems: Basic Concepts," *Behavioral Science,* 10 (July 1965): 193–237.

Murphy, L. B. *The Widening World of Childhood: Paths Toward Mastery.* New York: Basic Books, 1962.

Rahe, R. H., and R. J. Arthur. "Life Change Patterns Surrounding Illness Experience," *Journal of Psychosomatic Research,* 11 (1968): 341.

Rapoport, Anatol. "Foreword." In *Modern Systems Research for the Behavioral Scientist,* ed. Walter Buckley. Chicago: Aldine, 1968.

Reiner, John. *The Organism as an Adaptive Control System.* Englewood Cliffs, N.J.: Prentice-Hall, Inc., 1968.

Roy, Sr. Callista. "Adaptation: A Conceptual Framework for Nursing," *Nursing Outlook,* 18, no. 3 (March 1970): 42–45.

————. *Introduction to Nursing: An Adaptation Model,* Englewood Cliffs, N.J.: Prentice-Hall, Inc., 1976.

Selye, H. *The Stress of Life.* New York: McGraw-Hill, 1978.

White, Robert W. "Strategies of Adaptation: An Attempt at Systematic Description." In *Coping and Adaptation,* ed. G. V. Coelho, D. A. Hamburg, and J. E. Adams, pp. 47–68. New York: Basic Books, 1974.

The theory of the adaptive person, developed in Chapter 5, proposes that the person utilizes cognator and regulator coping mechanisms to adapt to the changing environment. Cognator and regulator activity is effected through the four adaptive modes proposed by the Roy Adaptation Model of Nursing. In the next two parts of this book we look at the theory of the adaptive modes, applying it first to physiological needs, then to psychosocial needs.

In Part 3 the propositions from the regulator subsystem are applied to each of the physiological needs. The physiological basis for the proposed relationships is explored. Each of the physiological needs—exercise and rest, nutrition, elimination, fluid and electrolytes, oxygen and circulation, and regulation—is discussed. However, since the focus of nursing is not biological systems (this is the focus of medicine), it is important to discuss each need in relation to the regulator activity rather than to explore the body system. Therefore, each chapter is organized around five sets of propositions as they pertain to the adaptive regulatory responses and the ineffective regulatory responses. To relate this theorizing to nursing practice, the ineffective responses are examined according to the nursing process of assessment of regulatory behaviors, focal stimuli, and intervention by manipulating stimuli. Lastly, examples of hypothesis testing are presented at the end of each chapter. It is through testing of hypotheses that theories unique to the regulatory subsystem are further developed.

Theory of Adaptive Modes: Physiological Needs

PART

CHAPTER **6**

Exercise
and rest

Exercise and rest are vital to the well-being of the individual. The individual strives to achieve a balance between the two. There are times when the balanced ratio may be altered due to stressors that increase exercise and decrease rest. Exercise or the ability to be mobile in one's environment is a primary characteristic through which an individual defines and experiences himself. Furthermore the degree of exercise or mobility tolerated becomes a measure of the individual's health and physical fitness. Because mobility is a significant aspect of one's daily life, ineffective alterations that lead to its restriction become a nursing care problem. Likewise sleep is also necessary because it enables physiological and psychological systems to essentially regenerate themselves. When external and internal stimuli exceed the body's ability to adapt, the response may be immobility and sleep deprivation.

The physiological mode of exercise and rest will be examined according to five sets of theoretical relationships. The first four sets of relationships focus on adaptive regulatory responses of internal and external stimuli. The last set of relationships focuses on ineffective responses. The ineffective response will be examined according to regulatory behaviors, focal stimuli, manipulation of contextual stimuli, and a brief discussion of residual stimuli.

First Set of Relationships

The first set of relationships is as follows: The magnitude of the internal and external stimuli will positively influence the magnitude of the physiological response of an intact system. This is predicated on the propositions indicated as 1.1 to 2.1, 3.2, and 4.4 in Table 5.1

The control of movement requires input from external and internal stimuli originating from the following: sensors, feedback circuits, and muscles to bring about the movement. External sensory stimuli are transported to the central nervous system. The stimuli inform the CNS as to the intact muscular system's progress in achieving the desired motor outcome. The transmission pathways for the sensors vary from the simple spinal stretch reflexes that maintain posture to the complex decision-making pathways of visual feedback. Ordinarily input from the visual sensory modality is necessary for safe movement. One must see the environment and objects within it so that mobility is safely possible. Likewise one receives auditory stimuli that causes the body to turn in the direction of the stimuli. Without external sensory stimuli, the individual's mobility would be greatly reduced.

Internal stimuli from three sensors are operational in the movement of the extremity. The first internal sensor is in the muscle itself. This sensor responds to the changing length of the muscle. It is a receptor that is arranged in parallel with muscle fibers. When a muscle fiber is lengthened through stretch mechanisms, the receptor responds. The adaptive response causes impulses to travel to the central nervous system and back to those muscle fibers lying parallel to the receptor. As a result, the muscle fibers contract and the muscle shortens. It should be pointed out that the receptor itself is suspended between two muscle fibers. The muscle fibers serve the purpose of regulating the tension on the receptor. For example, a small degree of tension in the main muscle must be greatly stretched before the receptor will respond.

The second internal sensor is in the tendon and is sensitive to tension. The third sensor, in the joint, gives the individual an awareness of a limb's position. The latter two sensors or receptors in the extremity respond to tension and provide postural input. As Milhorn (1966) points out

> The postural control system's purpose is to maintain the orientation of a limb in opposition to gravity, mechanical disturbances, and fatigue. It accomplishes its purpose by monitoring muscle position using this information to alter the instructions to the actuators of the limb. It depends on the central nervous system for basic orientation and fixed instructions which are modified by its actions. This control system is oriented by biasing the output of the position transducers (muscle spindles) via the gamma efferent pathways, depending on the peculiarities of the position-maintaining task.

These sensors provide all the input necessary to make it possible for an extremity to be guided quickly and appropriately.

Internal and external stimuli are communicated through a diverse and complex feedback system. The feedback involves signals from the brain to cause rapid movement of the desired body part. The feedback signals work together so that both large skeletal muscle fibers and muscle spindle fibers contract in unison. The skeletal reflex operates as a feedback mechanism to control the length of a muscle. Likewise the tendon reflex can also operate as servofeedback mechanism to control muscle tension.

> That is, if the tension on the muscle becomes too great, inhibition from the tendon organ decreases this tension back to a lower value. On the other hand, if the tension becomes too little, impulses from the tendon organ cease; and this loss of inhibition allows the anterior motorneurons to become active again, thus increasing muscle tension back toward a higher level. [Guyton 1971]

Signals originating from the brain are communicated to the cord center which in turn sets the gain of the tendon feedback system. The process is accomplished by changing the degree of facilitation of the neurons themselves in the feedback loop.

Lastly external and internal stimuli affect muscles to bring about the desired movement. The muscle cell is a highly organized structure. Therefore, any alteration in the functional state of one cellular system may influence others. Stimulation of the cell's exterior is conducted towards its interior. It is here that the contractable filaments undergo abrupt changes from a stationary state to a new, dynamic state. A small change in input of energy leads to the release of a large amount of energy. According to Winegrad (1965)

> The magnitude of the response of a cell may be relatively independent of the size of the change in the control mechanism, as long as that change exceeds a certain threshold. The control is an on-off switch. Once the contractile machinery is triggered into action, however, the actual energy output of the cell is determined by an external factor, the load on the muscle.

Movement through muscular control involves muscles, sensory organs which monitor system performance, neural inputs which process the sensory signals into positive commands directed to appropriate muscles, and nerve fibers which serve as the communication linkages with the nervous system.

As mentioned earlier, rest and sleep are the mechanisms through which the body restores and repairs itself. Sleep exists when the individual has a reduced capacity to interact with external environmental stimuli.

Studies on the effects of external stimuli during NREM (Non-Rapid Eye Movement) phases have failed to show that sounds, lights, and tactile stimulation applied during such sleep leads to production of REM sleep. According to Foulkes (1966)

> It is doubtful that occasional external stimuli would play as large a role in sleep-onset dreaming as would occasional organismic stimuli, for the sleep-onset period is one during which the sleeper seems to try to "tune out" external stimulation and in which the boundaries of awareness begin to shrink from the external world to the body itself. Except, then, for cases where external stimulation is sufficiently intensive to impinge upon this shrinking awareness but not sufficiently intense to awaken one, it is doubtful that external stimulation leads to interspective sensory imagery at sleep onset.

During sleep the afferent neural fibers from the receptor of the sensory modes have been structurally altered so that their messages are no longer transported to the brain. It should be pointed out that structured changes have not taken place, yet the sensory system responds as if changes have occurred. The altered function is due to reduced and monotonous stimuli. In a sleep state, internal rhythm and restricted sensory input need to periodically alter the threshold of the reticular activating system to incoming stimuli. The response is a partial functional shutdown of the wakefulness system. Meaningful verbal and auditory stimuli may keep the individual awake.

During the beginning stage of sleep, individuals indicate an increased awareness of their body position, body sensation, muscular fatigue, and pain. According to Foulkes (1966), "The self seems to be exhanging its interest in the external world for concern with its own bodily processes, a shrinkage of the scope of one's interest that undoubtedly facilitate the induction of sleep."

The magnitude of internal and external stimuli are influenced by the factors cited and in turn influence the physiological response of movement or muscular action and rest. Alterations in internal and external stimuli are received through receptors and communicated by means of the neural pathways. This process involves the second set of relationships.

Second Set of Relationships

In the second set of relationships, the intact neural pathways will positively influence neural output to effectors. This is predicated on the labeled 3.1 to 2.1, and 4.4 in Table 5.1. Motor function and resulting mobility is dependent upon the intact function of the central nervous system, muscles, and bones. The sensors provide information that is passed directly into the motor system. The overall response is gross movement. More refined and discrete movements require intact neural pathways from the cerebellum and stimulation from the motor nerves. The cerebellum involves a complex circuitry which ties it to the motor cortex, to other parts of the brain, to muscles that alter receptor action, and to various types of receptors. The cerebellum's significant role lies in maintaining coordination. The input into the cerebellum provides information from the motor cortex, muscles, tendons, and joints. Output from the same system influences the motor cortex, muscles, and receptors (Langley 1965).

Muscular contraction occurs in response to stimulation of a motor nerve. Three stages are involved in muscular contraction: "transmission of the nerve impulses across the myoneural junction with activation of the motor end-plate, propagation of the impulses along the muscle itself, and, finally, the actual physical phenomena of muscular contraction with its attendant biochemical change" (Sodeman 1968). The basic unit of muscle contraction is the motor unit. The motor unit consists of a group of muscle fibers all connected by a terminal branch of a single motor axon.

Two other structures that facilitate the influence of intact neural pathway's over neural output to effectors are the tendon organ and the muscle spindle. First, the tendon organ detects muscle tensions. The tendon organ responds with overexcitation to the onset of increased muscle tension. In a relatively short period of time, the tension is reduced to a lower level of steady-state firing. The tendon organ is significant because it provides instantaneous data to the central nervous system concerning the degree of tension in each small segment of the involved muscle. Signals from the tendon organ are controlled through alpha nerve fibers. The fibers transmit signals into local areas of the cord and the spinocerebellar tract from which they are transmitted on into the cerebellum (Guyton 1971).

The second factor is the muscle spindle. The spindle's overall purpose is to detect muscle length. It should be pointed out that

> All reflexes require a receptor, an effector, and a medium for transmission of signals from the receptor to the effector. The stretch reflex, also called the myotatic reflex, employs the fewest number of neurons of any cord reflex: a single sensory neuron and a single motorneuron. This reflex is initiated by stretch of the primary receptor of the muscle spindle, and it causes the stretched muscle to contract. [Guyton 1971]

As with exercise and mobility, rest also involves intact neural pathways that seek to positively influence neural output to effectors. Researchers have discovered a system that extends from the brain's base to the cerebral cortex that provides a neuroanatomical basis for the passive theory of sleep. According to Foulkes (1966)

The ascending reticular activating system (ARAS) arises in the brain stem reticular formation and diffusely projects to the cerebral cortex. When incoming sensory impulses are supported by impulses passing through the ARAS, one is awake and aware of the environmental events causing the sensory impulses. When the ARAS does not support incoming sensory stimulation, a person is not aware of environmental events causing such impulses and is asleep.

When the individual sleeps, the autonomic nervous system responds with a decreased arterial blood pressure, decreased heart rate, decreased respiratory rate, slightly increased gastrointestinal function, and generalized muscle relaxation. These regulatory behaviors are usually typical of NREM sleep. When REM sleep begins there is a transitory increase in arterial blood pressure, pulse, and respiration. These increased rates usually do not reach the waking levels.

The intact neural system and its receptors influence neural output to effectors. If the neural system and its neural pathways did not positively influence neural output to effectors, muscle contraction and sleep pattern would reach a state of disequilibrium.

Third Set of Relationships

The second set of relationships and related propositions are a significant link to the third set of relationships. In the third set of relationships, chemical and neural inputs are postulated to influence normally responsive endocrine glands to hormonally influence target organs in a positive manner to maintain a state of dynamic equilibrium. This is predicated on the propositions labeled 1.1 to 3.2 in Table 5.1. This set of propositions seems to specify the interrelationship between the chemical and neural regulatory systems. Each system attempts to respond to alterations in the other to maintain a state of equilibrium.

Chemical input influences muscular contraction. The energy production of muscle cells is dependent upon the degree of activity of its specialized function, namely, contraction. On the other hand, the cell's rate of oxidative metabolism is determined by the secretion of the thyroid gland. Winegrad (1965) points out that

All cellular activity is controlled by the rates of various chemical reactions occuring within these compartments, which include the nucleus, the mitochondria, the endoplasmic reticulvm, and the sarcoplasm. Function within each compartment is not independent, since the membraneous boundaries are permeable and movement of permanent cellular substances across them occurs continuously.

The phase boundaries of the compartment within the cells act as diffusion barriers that limit the movement of substances between the compartment. The membrane's permeability and electrical potential gradient determine what materials are exchanged.

Acetylcholine is a chemical agent that facilitates muscular contraction. As acetylcholine combines with the reactor site, the muscle membrane's physical properties become altered. The response is an increase in the permeability to ions, a decrease in membrane potential, and electrical excitation which is impulse formation. The producing source of energy for muscle contraction is ATP (adenosine triphosphate) which has a high-energy phosphate bond. The breakdown of this bond by the enzyme ATP present in the myosin fibrils represents the energy releasing event closest to the contraction itself.

Additional chemical input takes the form of electrolytes such as calcium, potassium, and magnesium. The electrolytes are related to the ATP system. Some people believe that the muscle weakness resulting from hyperkalemia and hypokalemia is actually due to disturbances of cofactor enzyme activity at ATP levels. Guyton (1971) has outlined the chemical and physical events that take place during contraction. The events consist of the following:

1. The actin filaments at their reactive sites are negatively charged.
2. The cross-bridges of the myosin filaments attach ATP which is negatively charged. This takes place because of absent calcium ions.
3. The calcium ions combine with the negative charges of actin and myosin filaments which then bind them together.
4. Calcium ions cause the myosin filament to develop an ATPase capability. The myosin has the capability of splitting ATP and liberating energy from the myosin molecule.
5. Besides actin another protein called tropomyosin, while not understood, is essential for normal function.
6. Other proteins present in the myofibrils have the ability to inhibit or suppress the ATPase activity of myosin. They also have the ability to modify the binding characteristics of myosin and actin.

Therefore the basic biochemical alterations at the muscle cell level are also accompanied by impulses from the central nervous system. The impulses initiate coordinated skeletal muscle activity. The muscle cell departs from the stationary state either by chemical changes, such as changes in the composition of the fluid bathing the cell, or by neural activity.

Neural input originates from the central nervous system. The nervous system in conjunction with chemical factors coordinates the specialized function of a cell with the overall function of the individual. This is accomplished through neural transmission or humoral substances that alter the cell membrane or its interior. Stimulation of the motor nerve causes acetylcholine to be released at the myoneural junction. The overall response is diffusion of acetylcholine between the nerve and muscle which then results in changed permeability of the postjunctional muscle membrane.

Muscular activity is initiated by the nervous system. This is accomplished by releasing acetycholine which increases membrane permeability thereby leading to a reduction in the postsynaptic membrane potential. "The change in the permeability of the postjunctional membrane that occurs following nervous stimulation produces a rapid depolarization of that membrane and a net movement across it of ions in accordance with their new electrochemical gradients" (Winegrad 1965).

In terms of neural input there are primary and secondary receptors. Primary receptors are large and very sensitive. They transmit vast numbers of impulses following very slight stretch. The original excitation is transmitted to the central nervous system and depicts the rate of change of the receptor length. Next, the steady-state signals transmit information depicting the actual length of the receptor.

Secondary receptors are not quite as instantaneous in their responses. Instead they require several milliseconds to reach a full response. As responses take place, the degree of excitation is determined almost entirely by the length of the receptor itself. Consequently the receptor transmits to the central nervous system a signal depicting only the length of the receptor itself (Guyton 1971).

Chemical and neural input influences the target organ (the muscular system) which ultimately contracts in a positive manner to maintain a state of dynamic equilibrium. Likewise chemical and neural input is also necessary in rest and sleep. However, the distinction and application of the inputs is not as specific as the ones discussed in muscular contraction. There has been interest in chemicals that produce either an increase in the need for sleep or an increase in sleep itself. When a chemical agent such as a drug decreases sleep it is due to disturbance in sleep rather than a decreased sleep requirement. Drugs like the amphetamines are "thought to act by stimulating the release and preventing the reuptake of the catecholamines in the brain [and] have classically been used in combating sleep deprivation and in increasing wakefulness or alertness. There is considerable evidence, then, that dopamine and norepinephrine are involved in the maintenance of wakefulness." (Hartmann 1973).

Neural input in rest and sleep involves the reticular activating system of cortical arousal. As incoming stimuli are reduced and fatigue becomes the dominating force, the cortical system becomes less aroused making sleep possible.

Both chemical input in the form of electrolytes, acetylcholine, or drugs, and neural input from motor nerves or the reticular activating system influence the muscular system and sleep state. When the chemical and neural inputs are unable to positively influence the endocrine glands and subsequently the hormone's influence upon target organs, then the system becomes disorganized. When this response occurs, the individual becomes aware of his own ineffective behavior.

Fourth Set of Relationships

A fourth set of relationships provides the transition between adaptive and ineffective behavior. This set of relationships involves the body's response to external and internal stimuli and states that such stimuli will alter those external and internal stimuli. This is predicated on the propositions labeled 1.1 to 5.1 in Table 5.1.

The nature of the information-transmitting mechanism will influence the magnitude and speed with which other cellular systems react. When transmission occurs by diffusion coupled with local concentration alteration of a substance, the response time may be very slow. The control mechanism also influences the amount of cell involved in a given response. "Local potential changes or localized current flow can restrict the regions of the cell which respond to the initial change, whereas a change in membrane permeability will affect the concentration of substances in most or in all of the cell (Winegrad 1965).

Internal stimulation of the muscle via the large anterior motor neurons causes instantaneous and quick contraction of the muscle. This occurs without any limit to the degree of shortening that will take place. Other stimuli from the gamma system cause the muscle to contract to a predetermined length. Of significance is the fact that the stimuli cause the muscle to continue its contraction until it has shortened to equal the degree of contraction of the spindle (Guyton 1971).

The tone of the skeletal muscle is caused by stimuli that constitute a slow rate of discharge of the alpha nerve fibers to each repetitive muscle. Increases in the basal rate of nerve discharge result in increases in the intensity of the muscle tone. Likewise the tone is decreased when the rate of discharge is also decreased. Stimuli from the anterior motorneuron can be continuous. Guyton (1971) believes that

> One factor that causes the anterior motorneuron to emit continuous discharge is its facilitation by afferent impulses from the muscle spindle. When the rate of discharge of the spindle impulses increases, the tone of the muscle also increases. When the rate of discharge decreases, the tone of the muscle also decreases.

Besides alpha nerve fibers, the gamma efferent system is also involved in muscular contraction. The bulboreticular facilitatory region of the brain stem is responsible for excitation of the gamma system. Furthermore, impulses are also transmitted from the cerebellum, basal ganglion, and cerebral cortex into the bulboreticular facilitatory area.

> The bulboreticular facilitatory area is particularly concerned with postural contraction, which emphasizes the possible or probable important role of the gamma efferent mechanism in the control of muscular contraction for positioning the different parts of the body. [Guyton 1971]

Likewise the alpha motorneurons from the spinal cord innervate small groups of muscles that work together and against each other to provide fine control of position, velocity, and force in a person's limb.

External and internal stimuli work together to influence muscle coordination. There are times when a disturbance in transmission of stimuli at the myoneural junction does occur. Such a disturbance can result from any of four factors: (1) acetylcholine may be produced in insufficient amounts at the termination of the motor nerve; (2) acetylcholine may be destroyed before reaching the reactor site of the motor end plate; (3) a substance may compete with acetylcholine from receptor sites; and (4) acetylcholine having completed its purpose may persist for an abnormal period of time on the end plate (Sodeman and Sodeman 1968).

Manipulation of steady-state external environmental variables produces disturbed sleep resulting in decreased total sleep. External environmental stimuli can result from sounds, lights, people, or temperature changes. Internal stimuli can result from illness or a diseased body part. The greater the illness or disease process resulting in noxious stimuli the greater will be the influence upon other internal stimuli. According to Hartmann (1973),

> In terms of stimulation, for instance, what we are looking for is not a stimulus somewhere which will quickly induce or interrupt sleep, but a situation in which a period of stimulation, for instance, will produce a clear increase or alteration in subsequent sleep or one of the sleep states in a repeatable manner.

The composition of sleep, sleep patterns, and rapidity of awakening are related to age. It seems that the overall length of time an individual spends sleeping decreases with maturity. On the other hand the ability of the individual to attain normal working function in awakening is negatively related to age. The younger individual takes longer to achieve his functional abilities in awakening from sleep.

The individual who experiences a deficit or excess of exercise or rest behaves in such a way as to restore balance. Consequently, action upon internal and external stimuli causes exercise or rest to be regulated at a level above or below that which contributed to negative feedback. The entire process is considered to be adaptive.

The fourth set of relationships signifies a linkage between adaptive and ineffective regulatory responses. There are times when the fourth set of relationships fails to successfully alter internal stimuli and external stimuli in an adaptive way. Instead the intact system or systems responds in an ineffective manner.

Fifth Set of Relationships

In the fifth set of relationships, the magnitude of the external and internal stimuli may be so great that the adaptive systems cannot return the body to a state of dynamic equilibrium. This set includes propositions 1.1 to 5.1 in Table 5.1.

When mobility and need for rest deviate excessively from the body's ability to restore equilibrium, regulatory mechanisms cannot be depended upon to resist further imbalances. External and internal stimuli may be so great that the body cannot return to equilibrium; instead it experiences disequilibrium. If the regulatory mechanism fails, the result is disorganization and possibly death.

The ineffective responses to be discussed consist of problems associated with immobility and sleep deprivation. Each ineffective response within these two categories will be discussed according to regulatory behaviors, focal stimuli, manipulation of contextual stimuli, and a brief discussion of the residual stimuli.

Immobility

Immobility involves various levels of inactivity whereby movement is restricted or decreased. The degree of immobility present is determined by physical inactivity due to reduced body movement; physical restriction caused by supportive or treatment procedures, motor paralysis, or other restrictive illnesses; prolonged maintenance of a particular body part; and sensory deprivation of kinesthetic stimuli. Immobility can cause ineffective responses in biological and psychological systems. As the degree and duration of immobility are prolonged, the greater the probability of pathological changes. Several of the ineffective responses can be reversed. However there are times when the ineffective responses are irreversible and lead to cellular death.

Regulatory Behaviors.   Because immobility affects all systems of the body, the regulatory behavior can be categorized according to the system involved and the subproblems associated with each (see Table 6.1).

The above subproblems could possibly be prevented if a body part or system could be mobilized or used. If necessary the affected body part or system can remain immobilized. The overall goal is to maintain adaptive function of body parts through activity so that ineffective pathological responses can be controlled.

Focal Stimuli.   Landau and O'Leary (1970) point out that disturbances of muscle activity consist of the following: primary muscle disorders, general body condition affecting muscles, disorders affecting the neuromuscular junction, peripheral nerve disorders, central nervous system disorders, and general body conditions affect peripheral nerves and/or central nervous system.

It should be noted that there are both negative and positive results of a central nervous system lesion. On the negative side, a motor cortex lesion leads to the loss of skilled movement. The positive response is organization of the remaining neural tissue that results in simpler, less variable adaptive movement and less hyperactive reflexes. The nervous system becomes the

TABLE 6.1 Regulatory Behaviors in Immobility

System	Subproblems
Cardiovascular	Orthostatic hypotension
	Increased workload
	Dependent edema
	Thrombosis and embolus formation
Pulmonary	Hypostatic pneumonia
	Oxygen–carbon dioxide imbalance
Gastrointestinal	Constipation
	Indigestion
Neuromusculoskeletal	Sensory and perceptual restriction
	Osteoporosis
	Contractures
Renal	Renal and urinary tract stones
	Urinary retention
Metabolic	Negative nitrogen balance
Psychological	Perceptual distortion

primary organ of adaptation. This implies that its flexibility and variability of response are functions of the number of connections.

There are levels of neural integration. Three such levels have been recognized. The lowest level involves protective and ambulatory movements which are controlled by the anterior horn cell coupled with the local segmental reflex connection. The middle level of adaptive response results in organized behavior and is the responsibility of the brain stem and motor cortical connection. The highest level of behavior is obviously the result of a complete nervous system.

There are many movement disorders leading to varying levels of immobility. Because the focal stimuli resulting in altered mobility are numerous and involved, they will only be listed rather than discussed. The focal stimuli are grouped according to impaired movement, distortions of movement and posture, and spontaneous movement (Landau and O'Leary 1970).

1. Impaired movement
   (a) Muscular dystrophy
   (b) Polymyosites
   (c) Metabolic myopathies
   (d) Periodic paralysis
   (e) Myasthenia
   (f) Peripheral neuropathy
   (g) Anterior horn cell disease
   (h) Upper motor neuron syndrome
2. Distortions of movement and posture
   (a) Spasticity
   (b) Parkinsonian rigidity
   (c) Myotonia
   (d) Ataxia
   (e) Dystonia
   (f) Athetosis
3. Spontaneous movement
   (a) Fibrillation
   (b) Fasciculation
   (c) Spasm
   (d) Tremor
   (e) Chorea
   (f) Ballism
   (g) Oculogyration
   (h) Palatal myoclonus
   (i) Clonic convulsive movement

Mobility or movement can be influenced by many variables. The magnitude of the variable in terms of their internal and external stimuli may exceed the body's ability to adapt, thereby contributing to the many ineffective responses associated with prolonged immobilization.

Sleep deprivation

Sleep deprivation is the lack of adequate sleep as related to normal requirements by an individual. The need for sleep may increase during illness or disease; however, external and internal stimuli may contribute to sleep deprivation.

Regulatory Behaviors.   The significance of sleep for the normal function of individuals is apparent when one looks at the altered psychological responses that occur in sleep-deprived states. The phenomena sleep deprivation involves changes in the individual's thinking, mood, motor activity, affect, and perception. The following are regulatory behaviors associated with sleep deprivation:

1. Fatigue
2. Difficulty in concentration
3. Disorientation and misperception
4. Paranoia
5. Irritability
6. Hallucinations
   (a) Visual
   (b) Auditory
7. Confusion
8. Delirium
9. Time and place disorientation

The regulatory behaviors have been assessed more frequently during the early morning hours and less frequently in the afternoon or early evening. The length of time necessary to induce a sleep-deprived state varies according to the individual and his or her unique biological crisis.

Focal Stimuli.   Hospitalized individuals are usually unable to maintain their normal presleep habits and sleep patterns. Factors that contribute to an altered sleep state consist of the following:

1. Exercise near bedtime
2. Pain

3. Disease or illness
4. Anxiety
5. Drugs
   (a) Barbiturates
   (b) Amphetamines
6. Depression
7. Stress

As the individual is deprived of sleep, he is unable to destructure the neurophysiological data storage stimuli that have accumulated throughout the course of the day. Most of this information is irrevelant to a person's long-range goals and takes up needed space. Sleep, therefore, functions to destructuralize the data. The destructuralizing aspect of sleep's function is adaptive because it clears out the brain's storage system. The storage area will thus be empty during the next active waking part of the cycle for new data storage.

An additional purpose of sleep is the reinforcement of the individual's character for adaptive purposes. A sleep-deprived individual's normal function of character reinforcement is also deprived. The overall result affects both physiological and psychological regulatory behaviors. Focal stimuli vary according to what is considered normal sleep for the individual and his response to hospitalization and illness.

Manipulating the stimuli

Given that the magnitude of the external and internal stimuli are so great that the adaptive system cannot return the body to a state of dynamic equilibrium, the nurse intervenes by manipulating stimuli in an attempt to maintain or restore adequate movement and rest. In order to manipulate stimuli, the nurse assesses various influencing factors that contribute to the ineffective responses. The influencing factors consist of focal, contextual, and residual stimuli. Focal stimuli were previously discussed in terms of pathophysiological maladaptive responses. Contextual and residual stimuli will be discussed in relationship to nursing interventions.

Contextual stimuli

In dealing with problems of mobility, the nurse alters ineffective regulatory responses from external and internal stimuli through manipulation of the following contextual stimuli: positioning, conditioning exercises, joint mobility exercises, and environmental organization.

Through appropriate body position, the nurse can prevent deforming and debilitating contractures, orthostatic hypotension, hypostatic pneumonia, circulatory status resulting in thrombosis formation, dependent edema, constipation, and sensory deprivation. The goal of proper positioning is to prevent prolonged pressure in one body part resulting in damage to superficial nerves, stasis, and eventual tissue breakdown. Furthermore, frequent changes in body position stimulate postural mechanisms such as the muscle tone that maintains muscular contraction of the legs and the orthostatic neuromuscular reflexes that control the vessels. The nurse assists those individuals who are unable to change their own position or are unable to sense pressure points necessitating the need to move. When patients are able to move independently, they should be encouraged to sit in a chair or ambulate several times during the day.

The second contextual stimuli to be manipulated is conditioning exercise designed to maintain muscle strength. The nurse can utilize such techniques as isometric and isotonic contraction. In isometric contraction the length of the muscle is not altered; in isotonic contraction the length of the muscle is shortened. There are sitting and resistive exercises. Sitting exercises, an isometric technique, involves contracting muscles such as abdominal, gluteal, or quadriceps as hard as possible, then relaxing them. Resistive exercises consist of contracting muscles by pulling against a stationary object. Exercise that applies muscular pressure against an immovable object such as a footboard facilitates peripheral muscular tone and venous return to the heart.

Care is taken to assess the appropriateness of isometric exercises in individuals with a compromised cardiovascular system. If the individual has experienced prolonged immobility resulting in an increased cardiac workload as manifested by increased heart rate, cardiac output, and stroke volume, isometric exercises are contraindicated. Such exercises can temporarily elevate blood pressure, increase cardiac workload, and reduce coronary artery perfusion. The overall ineffective response can be myocardial ischemia.

Joint mobility is the third contextual stimuli to be manipulated. Joint mobility involves movement of each joint through its full range of motion. The goal is to maintain muscle and joint flexibility through active and passive range-of-motion exercises. Whether active or passive exercises are selected is determined by the patient. With active exercises, the patient is an independent participant and determines the extent of his own mobility. In chronic conditions such as arthritis, the range of movement may be small or extensive. Patients who are immobilized due to paralysis or weakness depend upon the nurse to passively range their joints. In either instance, contractures and loss of muscle tone is minimized.

Lastly the nurse can manipulate environmental stimuli by either increasing or decreasing meaningful stimuli. Depending upon where the patient is hospitalized, external environmental stimuli may be excessive. Care must therefore be taken to reduce sensory overload. Likewise patients can experience stimuli deprivation due to immobilizing illnesses or diseases. Meaningful and personal sources of stimuli can be placed where they can be seen and touched by the patient.

The nurse attempts to enhance mobility of body parts several times during the day so that ineffective regulatory behaviors need not occur. Likewise the nurse also manipulates stimuli to provide rest and prevent sleep deprivation.

In dealing with problems of rest, the nurse alters ineffective regulatory responses from external and internal stimuli through manipulation of the following contextual stimuli: minimizing of stimulus input and maintaining sleep rhythm.

In order for the nurse to minimize situations of stimulus input leading to sleep deprivation, she must be aware of the situations in which excess input occurs. The stimuli creating sleep deprivation are found in the patient's external environment. As discussed earlier, patients require sleep to destructuralize stored data collected from the day's activity. By minimizing the degree or quality of stimulus input, the nurse may also minimize the actual amount of sleep needed by the patient. Stored data comes from both verbal and nonverbal input.

Verbal input comes from the patient's doctor or nurse. Doctors may eagerly enter a patient's room and actively discuss specific technical problems amongst themselves. Unfortunately their discussion may have no meaning to the individual and may serve to frighten him. Nurses can act in a leadership role to encourage the patient to ask questions or seek clarification; if the patient is not ready, then the nurse can share this data when the patient achieves the appropriate readiness level. The nurse will need to assess the amount of verbal input actually needed in order to prevent verbal overload. The patient needs time to integrate events and data into his character structure. If the amount of meaningless verbal input is minimized, it is quite possible that the quality of sleep can be enhanced. Meaningful verbal input consists of information the patient is able to comprehend and use. All other data become useless and take valuable storage space in the individual's already troubled mind.

Nonverbal input involves three types of stimuli emanating from the patient's environment: lights; noises from nurses, doctors, other patients, and mechanical devices; and touch. Some areas of the hospital maintain light surveillance of their patients. Continual lighting of the patient's environment contributes to his inability to differentiate between day or night, and may have unwanted effects on his biological systems.

Noise comes from both human and mechanical sources. Doctors and nurses contribute their noise through constant chattering in the distance.

Patients themselves provide noise through moaning, groaning, and snoring. Noise from mechanical or supportive devices can also create sleep deprivation. Supportive devices that hum, buzz, click, or beep along as they perform their functions can reassure the patient that technology is monitoring his biological being, and make him feel secure. On the other hand, even though the equipment's physical pressure can be reassuring, often it has little meaning to the individual thereby contributing to a deprived state. The stimuli created by various alarms, lights flashing, or clicks may further annoy the patient who is trying to sleep.

The last source of nonverbal stimulus is touch. Touch appropriately used can be meaningful but, when used inappropriately, it can lead to excess stimulus input. Many of the treatments and procedures done to patients involve touch. The nurse touches her patient when she takes the blood pressure and temperature or pulse, changes dressings, bathes him, and makes the bed. There are times when the patient's illness demands intensive touch surveillance. Touch is an excellent support measure when appropriately utilized.

The nurse's goal is to minimize extraneous stimulus input. She can attempt to reduce stimuli from unnecessary lights, noise from people or machines, and inappropriate touch. While minimizing the stimulus input, she may attempt to help the patient maintain a relatively normal sleep pattern in situations that require more sleep.

The schedule of each individual's night sleep rhythm is somewhat consistent. It was mentioned earlier that one's sleep pattern changes with age. When a patient is hospitalized, normal sleep pattern is altered by anxieties aroused from illness, pain associated with illness, and situational changes disrupting sleep. When possible, the nurse's goal can be to formulate individualized planning for adequate sleep periods.

The nurse can create a sleep-oriented environment. She can gradually prepare her patient for sleep by learning his presleep ritual. If the patient normally begins his preparation by taking a shower, the nurse can provide him with water so he can at least wash his face and hands. If this is biologically impossible, the nurse can assume the responsibility. He may then brush his teeth and get into his sleep clothes, helped by the nurse as necessary. The final presleep activity the nurse should undertake is to minimize extraneous noises and dim artificial lights. All the preparatory stages get the patient into a sleeping mood, which must be continued throughout the night in order to facilitate a constant sleep state.

Depending upon the severity of the illness, the patient may need more than normal sleep to integrate various changes into a new personality structure. The nurse listens to her patient's fears and concerns in an attempt to alleviate factors that could interfere with sleep. Sleep is necessary if the patient is to destructuralize the stored data compiled from various environmental stimulus input. Too much stimulus input and too little time to destructuralize may only serve to confuse the patient. Sleep also reinforces a threatened or changed character structure. It may be the process of dreaming that allows forbidden thoughts to enter the patient's consciousness. The patient retreats into the world of sleep to recharge his depleted battery and become ready for the next day's events. The nurse should intervene to minimize meaningless stimulus input and to maintain a relatively normal sleep rhythm.

Residual stimuli

Residual stimuli may include a history of mobility and sleep disturbances; previous hospitalization for mobility problems; sleep history; use of hypnotics to induce sleep; and presleep habits.

Example of Hypothesis for Practice

We have focused on the process of theorizing with the exercise-rest physiological mode. Based on our theorizing with the exercise mode, we can postulate any number of hypotheses that can be tested. In addition, these hypotheses can be used as a guide for practice. Two examples will be given: the exercise hypothesis and the rest hypothesis.

The exercise hypothesis may be stated as follows: If the nurse helps the patient maintain muscle tone through proper exercising, the patient will experience fewer problems associated with immobility. The reason for this hypothesis is drawn from the propositions stated earlier as shown below.

General Statement: The magnitude of the internal and external stimuli will postively influence the magnitude of the physiological response of an intact system.

Specific Statement: The amount of mobility in the form of exercising positively influences the level of muscle integrity.

The nurse's use of exercise to maintain muscle tone depends upon the patient's ability to exercise. This implies that the nurse will assess the patient's psychobiological readiness for varying levels of mobility.

The rest hypothesis can be stated as follows: If the nurse provides the patient with uninterrupted sleep where REM can be achieved, the patient will not experience sleep deprivation. The rest hypothesis is based upon earlier propositions and can be shown as follows:

General Statement: The magnitude of the internal and external stimuli will positively influence the magnitude of the physiological response of an intact system.

Specific Statement: The quality of uninterrupted REM sleep positively influences the patient's avoidance of REM sleep deprivation and dream deprivation.

The nurse can determine the prehospital sleep pattern of the patient in an attempt to develop a sleep care plan. The nurse organizes nursing care to provide periods of uninterrupted sleep.

Summary

Exercise and rest have been examined according to four sets of theories that focus on adaptive regulatory responses. These responses take into consideration external and internal stimuli. The body attempts to adapt to chemical and neural inputs as they apply to fluid and electrolytes.

However, ineffective responses occur when the magnitude of external and internal stimuli are greater than the body's ability to maintain a state of dynamic equilibrium. The overall results lead to mobilization problems and sleep deprivation.

When the external and internal stimuli exceed the system's ability to adapt, the nurse assesses focal stimuli and regulatory behaviors, and then manipulates contextual and residual stimuli as they apply to exercise and rest. Based on the propositions discussed, examples of hypothesis generation were given for the exercise-rest physiological mode.

References and Additional Readings

Albert, Ira. "Penetrating the Mysteries of Sleep and Sleep Disorders," *RN* (August 1974): 36–39.

Burdick, J. A. "Heart-Rate Variability in Sleep and Wakefulness," *Cardiology,* 55 (1970): 79–83.

Donohoe, Katherine. "An Overview of Neuromuscular Disease," *Nursing Clinics of North America,* 14, no. 1 (March 1979): 95–106.

Ellestad, M. "Standards for Adult Exercise Testing," *Circulation,* 59 (February 1979): 421–30.

Foulkes, David. *Psychology of Sleep.* New York: Scribner's, 1966.

Gaardner, Kenneth. "A Conceptual Model of Sleep," *Archives of General Psychiatry,* 14, (March 1966): 253–60.

Grant, Donna Allen. "For Goodness Sake Let Your Patients Sleep," *Nursing,* (February 1974): 53–57.

Guyton, Arthur. *Textbook of Medical Physiology.* Philadelphia: Saunders, 1971.

Hartmann, Ernest. *The Function of Sleep.* New Haven, Conn.: Yale University Press, 1973.

Landau, William, and James L. O'Leary. "Disturbances of Movement," In *Signs and Symptoms,* ed. Cyril MacBryde and Robert Blacklow. Philadelphia: Lippincott, 1970.

Langley, L. L. *Homeostasis.* New York: Reinhold Publishing Corporation, 1965.

Milhorn, Howard. *The Application of Control Theory to Physiological Systems.* Philadelphia: Saunders, 1966.

Pratt, M. "Physical Exercise: A Special Need in Long-Time Care," *Journal Gerontological Nursing,* (September-October 1978): 38–42.

Roberts, Sharon. "Sleep Deprivation." In *Behavioral Concepts and the Critically Ill Patient.* Englewood Cliffs, N.J.: Prentice-Hall, Inc., 1976.

Sivarajan, Erika, and Jean Halpenny. "Exercise Testing." *American Journal of Nursing,* 79, no. 12 (December 1979): 2162–70.

Smith, Richard. "Sleep and Cardiac Arrhythmias," *Archives of Internal Medicine,* 130 (November 1972): 751–53.

Sodeman, William, and William Sodeman, Jr. *Pathologic Physiology: Mechanisms of Disease.* Philadelphia: Saunders, 1968.

Walker, Betty. "The Postsurgery Heart Patient: Amount of Uninterrupted Time for Sleep and Rest During the First, Second, and Third Postoperative Days in a Teaching Hospital," *Nursing Research,* 21, no. 2 (March-April 1972): 164–69.

Winegrad, Saul. "Energy Exchange in Striated Muscle Cells." In *Physiological Controls and Regulations,* ed. William Yamamoto and John Brobeck. Philadelphia: Saunders, 1965.

Zelechowski, Gina. "Helping Your Patient Sleep: Planning Instead of Pills," *Nursing,* (May 1977): 63–65.

———. "Sleep and the Critically Ill Patient," *Critical Care Update,* 6, no. 2 (February 1979): 5–13.

CHAPTER 7

Nutrition

Food is important to the survival of all human beings. The continuous supply of oxygen, fluid, and nutrients is vital to the maintenance of cellular function. Nutrients are stored in the body so that they can be continuously utilized by the cell. There are times when the body is called upon to sacrifice some of its nutritional substances for energy. This process adapts energy output to energy intake. Alteration in either can lead to weight loss or weight gain. Cellular nutrients involve the same homeostatic process as do other biological systems. Nutrition implies the appropriate intake of food together with a physiological system designed to recieve the food, act upon it, and transfer nutrients from the external and internal environment. The gastrointestinal system is responsible for this endeavor.

The gastrointestinal system involves a series of autoregulatory processes in the intestinal tract which seek to move food along at an appropriate pace. The food is propelled slowly enough to allow both digestion and absorption as well as to provide the body with its necessary stimuli.

The physiological mode of nutrition will be examined according to the five sets of theoretical relationships. Discussion will center upon the gastrointestinal system as it adaptively functions to digest, absorb, and deliver nutrients to the body's cells. Therefore the first four sets of relationships focus on adaptive regulatory responses of internal and external stimuli. When the adaptive processes fail, ineffective responses occur leading to malnutritional states. The last set of relationships focuses on maladaptive responses. The ineffective response will be examined in terms of regulatory behaviors, focal stimuli, manipulation of contextual stimuli, and a brief discussion of residual stimuli.

First Set of Relationships

The first set of relationships is as follows: The magnitude of the internal and external stimuli will positively influence the magnitude of the physiological response of an intact organ. This is predicated on the propositions indicated as 1.1 to 2.1, 3.2, and 4.4 in Table 5.1.

Cellular nutrition requires input from external and internal stimuli. External stimuli involve the individual's sensory modalities, environmental temperature, and desire or motivation. The sensory modalities involved are visual, olfactory, gustatory, and tactile. Dietary intake is influenced by the visual appearance of food, its aroma, and its taste. If any one of these is unpleasant, the remaining two modalities respond with like displeasure. If food is to be touched, as with finger foods, its texture should pleasantly stimulate the tactile sensors.

Environmental temperature can influence the individual's intake of food. A warm environment tends to decrease the desire for foods. Therefore the individual responds by increasing fluid intake or limiting the intake of food. An increased fluid intake distends the stomach, thereby giving the individual a feeling of fullness that leads to decreased food intake. Likewise a cold environment stimulates the hypothalamus and the individual responds by increasing his dietary intake of foods.

The individual's desire and motivation for food will influence his intake. Food can be appealing to all the senses; however, other emotional factors may influence whether or not the individual is motivated to eat. A depressed individual loses interest in food. Likewise some medications or disease processes can cause anorexia, the absence of desire for food.

Internal stimuli involve hunger and blood sugar level. The gastrointestinal tract is protected from internal stimuli in a variety of ways. The entire tract is protected by a mucous membrane that functions as a mechanical barrier to the transfer of substances from the external to internal environment. The internal environment is also protected from both microorganisms and toxic substances by the liver. Bacteria in the blood that circulates through the liver are destroyed by the reticuloendothelial cells.

Furthermore the lymph nodes and phagocytes also protect the gastrointestinal tract from injurious substances (Beland 1975).

Hunger is an important internal stimulus. Hunger contraction provides the sensation of hunger and the desire for food. Even when the nerves that innervate the stomach muscle are severed, thereby eliminating contraction, the individual still experiences hunger. The hypothalamus receives and initiates stimuli indicating hunger. It responds to the stimuli by controlling the intake of food. The hypothalamus is the center for integration of autonomous control. It is responsible for the sensation of hunger. It also communicates to the individual when sufficient food intake has been achieved. The hypothalamus consists of groups of nuclei that become aggregates of nerve cell bodies. The bodies consist of lateral and medial nuclei.

> Experiments indicate that when energy output exceeds energy intake, the lateral nuclei send messages which by evoking hunger contractions and the sensation of hunger stimulate the animal to eat. As food is taken in, the medial nuclei become progressivly more active, messages are sent to the lateral nuclei which are inhibitory and thus shut off the drive for food; the hunger is satiated and eating is terminated. [Langley 1965]

The satiety center is comprised of cells from the medial nuclei. These cells are glucoreceptors. The glucoreceptors are sensitive to the level of glucose in the blood. When the blood glucose level increases, the cells send messages to the lateral nuclei or feeding center causing the individual to increase his intake of food. The glucoreceptors are referred to as glucostats.

> When the blood sugar is low, as it is several hours after eating, or a shorter period if one is very active, the glucostats in the medial nuclei of the hypothalamus are quiescent. They send no messages to the lateral nuclei, the feeding center. The feeding center, in a way not yet understood, appears to be continuously active unless inhibited. Thus, in the absence of inhibition from the glucostats, the feeding center sends out a barrage of messages. Some of these messages cause hunger contractions of the stomach. [Langley 1965]

Therefore when one eats, the blood glucose level increases and the glucostats fire more rapidly in an attempt to inhibit the feeding center. When the individual feels satiated, he stops eating.

The magnitude of external and internal stimuli are influenced by the factors cited and in turn influence the physiological response gastrointestinal activity. Alterations in internal and external stimuli are received through receptors and communicated by means of the neural pathways. This process involves the second set of relationships.

Second Set of Relationships

In the second set of relationships, the intact neural pathways will positively influence neural output to effectors. This is predicated on the propositions labeled 3.1 to 2.1, and 4.4 in Table 5.1. The intact neural pathways involve the autonomic nervous system and intramural plexus.

The gastrointestinal tract receives its nerve supply from components of the autonomic nervous system. The autonomic system controls neural input from the parasympathetic and sympathetic nervous system. The parasympathetic system, which causes increased tone and mobility of the gastrointestinal tract, is divided into cranial and sacral divisions (McGuigan 1970). The cranial component to the intestinal tract is transmitted primarily through the vagus nerve. "The postganglionic neurons of the parasympathetic system are part of the myenteric plexus. . . . This in turn excites the gut wall and facilitates most of the intrinsic nervous reflexes of the gastrointestinal tract" (Guyton 1971). Stimulation of the myenteric plexus positively influences the intact gastrointestinal tract causing four principal effects: increased tone of contraction; increased intensity of the rhythmic contraction; increased rate of rhythmic contraction; and increased velocity of conduction of excitatory waves along the gut wall (Guyton 1971).

The sympathetic nervous system neural input to the gastrointestinal tract originates from the spinal cord between T-8 and L-3. Sympathetic innervation of the gastrointestinal tract is primarily inhibitory in its action. Stimulation of this component causes responses opposite to those of the parasympathetic system. The sympathetic system does have two excitatory effects, namely, excitation of the ileocecal sphincter and of the internal anal sphincter.

The intramural plexus is responsible for local neurogenic reflexes in the intestinal tract. The reflexes function to increase excitability of localized secretion of digestive juices through stimulation of the submucosal glands. The plexus is also involved in the coordination of motor movements of the gastrointestinal tract (Guyton 1971). According to Brooks and Davis (1965),

> A tentative model of an intramural control system might include a receptor responsive to changes in gastric content or tension in the gastric wall and linked via the myenteric plexus to the secreting cells. Neurohumors could be released both at the receptor and at the parietal cell. The role of the pyloric antrum requires that provisions be made for the release of gastrin by the action of stimuli on the mucosa of the antrum as well as in response to reflexes originating in the body of the stomach.

Acetylcholine, a neurohumor released by the parasympathetic system, will stimulate gastric secretion and histamine. Drugs that interfere with the muscarinic action of acetylcholine decrease the acid secretion in response to many stimuli.

In summary, the brain is the ultimate regulator of eating. It acts in conjunction with the alimentary canal, the peripheral nervous system, and the bloodstream. All of these factors contribute to the regulation of food intake.

The intact neural system and its receptors influence neural output to effectors. If the neural system and its neural pathways did not postively influence neural output to effectors, the gastrointestinal system would reach an ineffective state of disequilibrium.

Third Set of Relationships

The second set of relationships and related propositions are a significant link to the third set of relationships. In the third set of relationships, chemical and neural inputs are postulated to influence normally responsive endocrine glands to hormonally influence target organs in a positive manner to maintain a state of dynamic equilibrium. This is predicated on the propositions labeled 1.1 to 3.2 in Table 5.1. This set of propositions seems to specify the interrelationships between the chemical and neural regulatory systems. Each system attempts to respond to alterations in the other to maintain a state of equilibrium.

Chemical input involves such factors as drugs, hormones, and metabolic sensory pathways that influence the absorption of vital nutrients. Chemical stimulation of the hypothalamus can produce eating behavior when the lateral region is stimulated by a chemical agent such as an andrenergic drug. On the other hand, the chemical effect of a cholinergic drug is to stimulate drinking.

Chemical input from hormones is important in the breakdown, transfer, and absorption of nutrients. Chemically the gastrointestinal hormones are either proteins or polypeptides.

> In the stomach and intestine several different gastrointestinal hormones help to regulate the volume and character of the secretions. These hormones are liberated from the gastrointestinal mucosa in response to the presence of foods in the lumen of the gut. They then are absorbed into the blood and are carried to the respective glands which they stimulate. [Guyton 1971]

The breakdown of food is accomplished by action of gastric secretion. When food enters the stomach or duodenum there is an increase in the output of gastric and pancreatic juice. Furthermore, hormonal stimulation or input to the gallbladder will facilitate its emptying bile into the duodenum.

Gastric secretion is thus regulated by two factors, neural and hormonal. The hormonal regulation of gastric secretion is the responsibility of the hormone *gastrin*. Gastrin is absorbed into and transported by the blood to the gastric glands where it stimulates the parietal cells. Likewise histamine, which is a derivative of amino acid, also stimulates gastric secretion although it does not have the potency of gastrin.

Gastric secretion is under the control of a feedback mechanism. As the acidity of gastric juice increases, the gastrin mechanism for stimulating gastric secretion is blocked. Guyton (1971) identified two factors that make the feedback possible. First, greatly enhanced acidity depresses or blocks the extraction of gastrin itself from the antral mucosa. Second, the acid extracts an inhibitory hormone from the gastric mucosa to cause an inhibitory reflex that inhibits gastric acid secretion. The feedback mechanism serves to protect the stomach against an increase in acid secretion. Glandular secretion is also dependent upon sufficient water and electrolytes.

Metabolic and sensory pathways are the third component of chemical input. The nutrients eaten are broken down into glucose, amino acids, fatty acids, and various other metabolites. Receptors in the brain are specific for any one of these chemicals. The chemoreceptors respond when any one of the chemical levels is low by causing the individuals to search for food. The metabolic pathway is slow because food must be broken down into its components and absorbed before metabolites enter the circulation (Mitchell 1973). Sensory pathways can stimulate the cessation or continuance of eating. According to Mitchell (1973),

> There appears to be an immediate feedback system regarding hunger and satiety via stretch receptors and chemoreceptors in the stomach, liver, and intestines. Distention of the stomach creates the sensation of satiety of fullness, thus providing an immediate feedback regarding the quantity of food ingested. In addition, specific nutrients seem to stimulate receptors in the stomach, and intestine, which relay this immediate information about quantity of food to the central nervous system.

The sensory modalities involving taste, smell, viscosity, and texture of food initiate sensory signals in the nose and mouth. These signals can influence whether or not the individual eats. At this time neural input becomes important. Perceptual nerves communicate the input from the sensory signals to the brain. The information is analyzed by the cortex. The cortex makes its decision based upon previous experience with food. Input from the sensory modes through the pathways can influence regulatory circuits either to continue or to stop eating. If the individual remains hungry, input of food continues. However if all the above mechanisms are intact and functioning, and sufficient nutrients have been consumed the individual ceases eating.

Neural input can be the result of local stimuli. It should be pointed out that mechanical presence of food in gastrointestinal tract causes glands of the region involved and adjacent regions to secrete digestive juices. The local effect is partly due to direct stimulation of food with the surface of the glandular cells. According to Guyton (1971) there are three methods of local stimulation:

1. Tactile stimulation in chemical irritant of the mucosa can elicit reflexes that pass through the intramural nervous system of the intestinal wall in the surface in the deeper glands of the mucosa.
2. Distention of the gut can also elicit nervous reflexes that stimulated secretion.
3. Either tactile stimuli or distention and the motility in turn can then increase the rate of secretion.

Chemical and neural input are responsible for gastric secretion. Stimulation of the parasympathetic nerves to the gastrointestinal tract will increase glandular secretion. Vagus nerves are also involved in the process. Nervous signals that contribute to gastric secretion originate in the dorsal motor nuclei of the vagi. They then pass by means of the vagus nerve to the myenteric plexus, previously discussed, of the stomach and gastric glands. Lastly, neural input indicates to the brain whether or not the stomach is distended, thereby increasing or decreasing food intake.

Chemical input in the form of drugs, hormone and metabolic-sensory pathways, and neural input from local stimuli and the autonomic nervous system influence the gastrointestinal system's ability to digest, transfer, and absorb nutrients. When the chemical and neural inputs are unable to positively influence the endocrine glands and, subsequently, the hormones' influence upon target organs, then the system becomes disorganized. When this response occurs, the individual experiences ineffective responses.

Fourth Set of Relationships

The fourth set of relationships provides the transition between adaptive and maladaptive behavior. This set of relationships involves the body's response to external and internal stimuli and states that such stimuli will alter those external and internal stimuli. This is predicated on the propositions labeled 1.1 to 5.1 in Table 5.1.

The body's response to internal and external stimuli involves absorption of nutrients in the small and large intestine. Absorption involves active transport and diffusion. Active transport gives energy to the substance as it is being transported for the purpose of either concentrating it on the other side of the membrane or moving it against an electrical potential. Diffusion is the transport of substances through the membrane due to its movement along an electrochemical gradient.

Absorption in the small intestine involves two components, namely, absorption of nutrients and absorption of water and electrolytes. Absorbed nutrients consist of three elements: carbohydrates, protein, and fats (Guyton 1971). Carbohydrates are absorbed as monosaccharides through the process of diffusion. The magnitude of monosaccharides transported is dependent upon two mechanisms: (1) the chemical nature of the monosaccharides that are actively transported as opposed to those that are poorly transported, and (2) blockage of glucose transport and the takeover of glucose transport by the sodium transport system.

Proteins are absorbed in the form of amino acids. The absorption of amino acids through the intestinal mucosa occurs more quickly than protein digestion in the intestine. Thus, the normal rate of absorption is dependent upon the rate at which the amino acids are released from the protein during digestion. There are three components involved in the transport of amino acids: the basic amino acid, prolene, and hydroxyproline. As with the transport of monosaccharides, amino acid transport ceases when sodium transport is blocked. The energy for amino acid transport is therefore dependent upon the transport of sodium through the membrane.

Fats are absorbed through the intestinal membrane in the form of fatty acids and monoglycerides. Some diglycerides and triglycerides are also involved. The fatty acid molecule is lipid soluble and becomes dissolved through the epithelial cell membrane into its interior. There the fatty acid molecule comes in contact with the endoplasmic reticulum and is used to resynthesize triglycerides. The triglycerides are then discharged through the intracellular channel into the submucosal fluids.

The second component involving the small intestine is absorption of electrolytes and water (Guyton 1971). The rate of absorption of electrolytes is greater in the upper part of the small intestine. Sodium, potassium, chloride, nitrate, and bicarbonate are easily absorbed through the intestinal membrane. On the other hand, calcium, magnesium, and sulfate are poorly absorbed. Sodium is actively transported out of the epithelial cells through their sides. Calcium ions are actively absorbed from the duodenum and jejunum. They are controlled in relation to the need of the body for calcium. The parathyroid gland is also responsible for controlling calcium absorption.

Water is absorbed by osmosis. The magnitude of solution, hypertonic or hypotonic, placed in the intestine can influence absorption of water. When electrolytes and nutrients are absorbed, the intestinal fluids become hypotonic. This then causes water to be absorbed by osmosis.

Absorption in the large intestine occurs in the proximal portion of the colon and involves absorption of sodium, chloride, and water. The large intestine is capable of absorbing sodium. When sodium is removed from the lumen of the intestine, chloride and other negative ions move into the interstitial fluids. As a result, little sodium chloride is lost via the intestinal tract. Furthermore the absorbing colon contains colon bacilli that are capable of digesting cellulose, thus enabling cellulose to provide some of the calories of nutrition needed by the individual. There are other substances such as vitamins K, B_{12}, thiamin, and riboflavin that are formed by bacterial activity.

Internal and external stimuli affecting absorption in the small and large intestine will alter those external and internal stimuli. A reduced sodium intake is a stimulus that may greatly influence the transport of glucose and protein in a negative direction.

The fourth set of relationships has a interadaptive quality signifying a linkage between adaptive and ineffective regulatory responses. There are times when the fourth set of relationships fails to successfully alter internal stimuli and external stimuli in an adaptive way. Instead the intact system responds in a ineffective manner.

Fifth Set of Relationships

In the fifth set of relationships, the magnitude of the external and internal stimuli may be so great that the adaptive systems cannot return the body to a state of dynamic equilibrium. This is predicated on the labeled 1.1 through 5.1 in Table 5.1.

When gastrointestinal activity deviates excessively from the body's ability to restore equilibrium, regulatory mechanisms cannot be depended upon to resist further imbalances. External and internal stimuli may be so great that the body can not return to equilibrium. If regulatory mechanisms fail, the result is disorganization and possibly death.

Because anorexia, nausea, and vomiting are not considered normal events, they will be viewed as ineffective responses. Each ineffective response will be defined and discussed separately. Furthermore anorexia, nausea, and vomiting will only be discussed in terms of regulatory behaviors and focal stimuli causing them. The nurse may need to assess their uniqueness and subsequent treatments as they pertain to patients experiencing flu, diabetes, or other related disorders. Focal stimuli leading to each will be grouped together rather than discussed individually. Manipulation of contextual and residual stimuli will also be collectively discussed.

Anorexia, nausea, and vomiting

Anorexia is the lack or loss of appetite for food. Lack of interest in specific food may reflect individual and personal preferences. Anorexia is associated with a general disinterest in food.

Nausea is an unpleasant sensation associated with the revulsion toward any ingestion of food. Anorexia is followed by nausea which may then be followed by vomiting. According to Guyton (1971),

> Nausea is the conscious recognition of subconscious excitation in an area of the medulla closely associated with part of the vomiting center, and it can be caused by irritative impulses coming from the gastrointestinal tract, impulses originating in the brain associated with motion sickness, or impulses from the cortex to initiate vomiting.

Stimuli that cause anorexia can also cause the individual to be nauseated.

Nausea is associated with decreased motor activity of the stomach and pallor of the gastric mucosa. This may be caused by vascular changes within the gastric mucosa. Distention in the distal esophagus, stomach, or duodenum can cause nausea. With distention of the duodenum or lower small intestine, the intestine responds by contracting forcefully while the stomach relaxes thus allowing the intestinal contents to reflex into the stomach.

Vomiting is the sudden expulsion of the stomach's contents. It therefore becomes the means by which the upper gastrointestinal tract relieves itself when the gut is irritated or overdistended. Distention or irritation of the stomach or duodenum is the strongest stimuli leading to vomiting. Impulses are transmitted by vagal and sympathetic afferents to the vomiting center of the medulla. The motor impulses that cause vomiting are communicated through the fifth, seventh, ninth, tenth, and twelth cranial nerves to the upper gastrointestinal tract through the spinal nerves to the diaphragm and abdominal muscles. The overall vomiting act results, therefore, from a squeezing action of the muscles of the stomach and abdomen associated with opening of the esophagal sphincter. The result is that gastric contents are expelled.

Vomiting can also arise from inpulses in the brain outside the vomiting center. Stimulation of the chemoreceptor trigger zone can cause vomiting. The stimuli can originate from drugs such as morphine or digitalis. Rapidly changing motion of the body can also contribute to vomiting. The motion stimulates the receptors of the labyrinth. The impulses are then transmitted to the chemoreceptor trigger zone and finally to the vomiting center.

Regulatory Behaviors.   Nausea is accompanied by specific regulatory behavior. The following behaviors are attributed to nausea:

1. Profuse watery salivation
2. Drenching sweating
3. Tachycardia
4. Sensation of unpleasantness located in the epigastrium or abdomen

The nauseated individual experiences distressing sensations in the throat. Abdominal sensations need to be separated from visceral abdominal pain of mild degree which is also poorly localized in the abdomen.

The act of vomiting is also preceded by specific regulatory behaviors. The following behaviors are precursors to vomiting:

1. Watery salivation
2. Sweating
3. Vasoconstriction with pallor
4. Tachycardia or bradycardia
5. Tremor
6. Weakness
7. Dizziness
8. Retching

The patient's blood pressure may fall before the act of vomiting. The change in blood pressure is due in part to reduced cardiac output associated with abrupt changes in intrathoracic pressure. Several of the regulatory behaviors are common to both nausea and vomiting. This is because nausea usually precedes the act of vomiting.

Focal Stimuli.   Anorexia, nausea, and vomiting can be the ineffective responses associated with a variety of psychophysiological and organic disorders. Psychic stimuli such as violent scenes or odors can cause vomiting. Furthermore stimulation of certain areas in the hypothalamus can also result in nausea, anorexia, and vomiting. The following focal stimuli are contributing factors leading to anorexia, nausea, and vomiting (McGuigan 1970):

1. Psychic and neurological factors
   (a) Anorexia nervosa
   (b) Severe anemia
   (c) Vascular occlusion
   (d) Decreased cardiac output

    (e) Increased intracranial pressure
    (f) Vascular shock
2. Drugs and toxic agents
3. Intra-abdominal disorders
    (a) Mechanical obstruction of the gastrointestinal tract
    (b) Intra-abdominal inflammatory disorders
    (c) Pregnancy
4. Other factors
    (a) Febrile illness
    (b) Uremia
    (c) Diabetic ketoacidosis
    (d) Endocrine disorder
    (e) Cardiac disease
    (f) Malnutrition
    (g) Motion sickness
    (h) Ménière's disease

The focal stimuli causing ineffective response of anorexia, nausea, and vomiting are varied. If the ineffective response continues for a prolonged period of time, malnutrition and severe weight loss may occur.

Manipulating the stimuli

Given that the magnitude of the external and internal stimuli are so great that the adaptive systems cannot return the body to a state of dynamic equilibrium, the nurse intervenes by manipulating stimuli in an attempt to maintain or restore nutritional balance through an adapting gastrointestinal system. In order to manipulate stimuli, the nurse assesses various influencing factors that contribute to the maladaptive responses. The influencing factors consist of focal, contextual, and residual stimuli. Focal stimuli were previously discussed in terms of pathophysiological ineffective responses. Contextual and residual stimuli will be discussed in relationship to nursing interventions.

Contextual stimuli

The nurse alters maladaptive regulatory responses from external and internal stimuli through manipulation of the following contextual stimuli: fluid, activity, nutrition, communication, aeration, and pain.

Fluid.   The nurse can take care to assure that fluid intake is balanced with fluid loss when the ability of the gastrointestinal system as a regulatory system is impaired. The nurse therefore accurately assesses fluid loss so that correct replacement can be achieved.

INTERSTITIAL EDEMA. Depending upon the focal stimuli causing anorexia, nausea, and vomiting, edema may result from a change in the colloid osmotic pressure and hydration. Changes in colloid osmotic pressure caused by hypoproteinemia lead to a shift of fluid into the interstitial tissue. Fluid is therefore drawn out of the large and small intestine, thus reducing the amount of nutrients absorbed by these systems. The nurse can assess edematous points and intervene to protect the patient until his adaptive regulatory processes can restore his fluid balance and lessen edema.

INTAKE. Intake involves physiological intake of oral or parenteral fluids and environmental intake. Because the patient is losing fluid through frequent emesis, oral intake may be limited until the vomiting episode ceases. When possible, chilled fluids such as Seven-up or ginger ale may be provided. The fluids correct dehydration and provide glucose for energy. The dehydrated patient experiences a deficit in intracellular and extracellular water volume. Therefore the nurse seeks to increase fluid intake. Such restoration returns body fluids, electrolytes, and acid-base balance to normal.

Parenteral fluids may be necessary when antiemetic drugs are unable to immediately control vomiting. The fluid administered should approximate the normal interstitial fluids. If the individual's anorexia or nausea continues to make food intake impossible, hyperalimental fluids may be needed. Hyperalimentation provides nutrients in amounts large enough to sustain life. Electrolytes, as well, can be supplied to the patient through parenteral intake.

The patient's environment should be assessed for the presence of noxious stimuli that could contribute to anorexia, nausea, or vomiting. Strong odors from dressings, emesis, food, or other patients should be eliminated from the environment.

OUTPUT. Output consists of sensible fluid loss in urine, stool, and emesis; diagnostic procedures including blood pressure, pulse, respirations, temperature, specific gravity, daily weight, and central venous pressure; and appropriate laboratory tests.

Fluid loss is replaced with equal amounts of fluid in an attempt to maintain a state of balanced hydration. Because the patient is losing fluid in each emesis, urinary output may be greatly reduced. Therefore the nurse realizes that a urinary output of 500 cc for 16 hours is to be expected.

The sensible loss through emesis is most significant for the patient with nausea and vomiting behavior. The amount, color, and consistency of the vomitus should be assessed by the nurse. Prolonged vomiting can rupture capillaries along the wall of the stomach and esophagus. Therefore blood-tinged vomitus needs to be reported to the patient's physician. Likewise the contents should be assessed for the presence or absence of digested food particles. If the patient vomits over a period of time, the contents will be primarily bile and mucus. Specific measurement of the loss should be taken so that accurate parenteral fluid intake can be adminstered.

Blood pressure variations can occur during and after the patient's vomiting episode. While he is vomiting, the patient's blood pressure may fall because of reduced cardiac output associated with changes in the intrathoracic presssure. In addition, blood pressure variations can be helpful in assessing the patient's hydration status. Dehydration due to excessive fluid loss can decrease arterial pressure. A significant decrease in arterial pressure can compromise the intact renal system thereby decreasing glomerular filtration rate. Furthermore variations in blood pressure may lead to fainting as the patient begins ambulating. Therefore the nurse may assess the patient's blood pressure prior to ambulation.

The patient's pulse rate usually increases prior to the act of vomiting. After the emesis, the pulse rate may again rise. Such fluctuations may compromise an already compromised cardiac system and could reduce cardiac output. This can contribute to further reduction in the patient's arterial pressure. Changes in pulse and arterial pressure can create angina in the cardiac patient.

Respiration also changes during vomiting. It has been reported that respiration ceases during the act of vomiting. Prior to the act of vomiting, the patient experiences a sudden increase in his respiratory rate coupled with some irregularity of breathing. It is at this time the nurse intervenes to prevent aspiration of vomitus. To accomplish this goal the nurse simply turns her patient on his side.

Temperature alteration can occur because of dehydration. Dehydration can increase temperature which can then increase metabolic activity and cause further fluid loss. Therefore the nurse is alert to the significance of a febrile state for the patient with fluid loss due to vomiting. Because temperature elevation may also be due to intra-abdominal tumor or hepatic disturbances, the nurse assesses other causes of her patient's febrile state if his hydration status is normal.

Specific gravity and body weight also provide information regarding the fluid and nutritional status of the patient. A dehydrated patient's urine is concentrated with a higher than normal specific gravity. The anorexic and nauseated patient will lose weight. The patient's caloric intake may be supplemented with hyperalimentation solution. The health team uses daily weight to assess whether or not the patient is maintaining his body weight or experiencing additional loss.

Central venous pressure provides information regarding the patient's fluid status. A decreased venous pressure reflects hypovolemia or dehydration.

Laboratory tests of significance to the patient experiencing a gastrointestinal disturbance include measurements of serum electrolytes such as potassium, sodium, calcium, chloride and magnesium; BUN (blood urea nitrogen), creatinine, and uric acid; hemoglobin and hematocrit; amylase; and liver profile.

Activity.   The nurse in assessing her patient's activity assesses four components: physical activity, cardiopulmonary activity, metabolic activity, and mental activity.

The patient with fluid deficit, electrolyte imbalance, or extreme nutritional depletion may need to have his physical activity restricted. Electrolyte imbalance can contribute to neuromuscular changes. Likewise, nutritional depletion causes weakness and the inability to tolerate physical mobility. Physical mobility may be impossible for the patient experiencing acute abdominal pain.

Because movement predisposes to nausea and vomiting, necessary changes in body position should be made slowly to prevent stimulating the chemoreceptor trigger system to initiate vomiting.

Electrolyte disturbances due to fluid and electrolyte loss from excessive vomiting can cause cardiac arrhythmias. Depending upon the severity of electrolyte disturbance, the patient may need to be connected to a cardioscope. The pulmonary system may also become involved with gastrointestinal disturbances.

Hyperventilation can occur prior to the vomiting act. Continued hyperventilation leads to respiratory alkalosis and secondary electrolyte disturbances. Pulmonary activity can also be compromised if the patient aspirates any vomitus. Aspiration of vomitus can possibly lead to pneumonia.

Metabolic changes associated with gastrointestinal disturbances involve both metabolic acidosis and alkalosis. Metabolic acidosis results from malnutrition in which the rate of mobilization of fat is increased. On the other hand metabolic alkalosis can be the result of specific endocrine disorders that cause anorexia, nausea, and vomiting.

Nausea is an uncomfortable feeling. Likewise the act of vomiting is both unpleasant and exhausting. Severe electrolyte changes resulting from loss in emesis can cause irritability and confusion. Vomiting due to cerebral vascular changes or increased intracranial pressure may also contribute to behavioral alterations. Therefore any behavioral changes should be diagnosed, evaluated, and altered.

Nutrition.   The patient's diet normally contains five categories of necessary nutrients (Malaznik 1976):

1. Calories
2. Proteins
3. Fat-soluble vitamins
   (a) Vitamin A
   (b) Vitamin D
   (c) Vitamin E
4. Water-soluble vitamins
   (a) Vitamin C
   (b) Folacin
   (c) Niacin
   (d) Riboflavin
   (e) Thiamine
   (f) Vitamin B_6
   (g) Vitamin B_{12}
5. Minerals
   (a) Calcium
   (b) Iodine
   (c) Iron
   (d) Magnesium

It was mentioned earlier that the patient may need intravenous hyperalimentation in order to receive sufficient nutrients. The desired goal is to achieve or maintain tissue synthesis, positive nitrogen balance, and anabolism. Hyperalimentation is indicated in patients with intrinsic inflammatory bowel disease. The general composition of hyperalimental solution is 20 percent glucose, 5 percent protein hydrolysate and 5 percent vitamins and minerals.

Spiritual nutrition is also a significant aspect of patient care. Depending upon the focal stimuli resulting in ineffective responses, the patient might be well supported by a minister of his choice. For the patient experiencing an irreversible illness, supportive care from a compassionate health team is vital.

Communication.   The patient needs to know his fears are accepted and considered normal for his particular maladaptive problem. Prolonged episodes of vomiting necessitate direct intervention through use of antimetic drugs and emotional support. While the specific focal stimuli causing the vomiting are diagnosed, the patient may fantasize his own diagnosis. Weight loss associated with anorexia can create body image disturbances especially if the loss is severe.

Aeration.   Psychological and environmental aeration have already been discussed. Pulmonary aeration is assessed according to the lungs' ability to compensate for either metabolic alkalosis or acidosis. The lungs compensate in acid-base disturbances by either increasing or decreasing the rate of ventilation. Acidosis can be the result of ketoacidosis associated with diarrhea and/or starvation. Metabolic acidosis is a problem with patients who have Addison's disease, hepatic disease, or loss of hydrochloric acid. The patient's pulmonary system should be protected so that is continues to maintain its adaptive functions.

Pain.   The focal stimuli causing anorexia, nausea, and vomiting can be painful. Cerebral vascular changes leading to headaches, intra-abdominal tumors, cardiac disease, endocrine disorders, or obstruction of the gastrointestinal tract can be accompanied by physiological pain. When realistic and appropriate, drugs can be given to alleviate the pain associated with nausea and vomiting.

Residual Stimuli

Residual stimuli may include a history of gastrointestinal disturbances, extreme weight loss or weight gain, previous hospitalization for gastrointestinal disorders, previous surgical correction, drugs utilized to alter nausea or vomiting, pain, and use of diets.

Example of Hypothesis for Practice

We have focused on the process of theorizing with the gastrointestinal aspect of the physiological mode. Based on our theorizing with the nutrition mode, we can postulate any number of hypotheses that can be tested. The theorizing encompasses the four sets of relationships and their related propositions. In addition the hypotheses can be used as a guide for practice. An example of a possible hypothesis will be discussed.

The hypothesis may be stated as follows: If the nurse assesses the patient's dietary needs in relationship to his dietary preference, the patient will achieve an optimal level of nutritional intake. The reasons for this hypothesis are drawn from the propositions stated earlier as shown below.

General Statement: The magnitude of the internal and external stimuli (food) will positively influence the magnitude of the physiological response of an intact system (gastrointestinal).

Specific Statement: The diet that is based on both biological needs and patient preference will positively influence the amount of dietary intake.

With the help of a nutritionist the nurse can facilitate a diet which combines the patient's preference and biological necessity for elimination or inclusion of certain foods. The nurse therefore assesses specific biological problems and their dietary implications. In addition the nurse attempts, when possible, to incorporate the patient's preference. The magnitude of the patient's illness, however, may sometimes necessitate the total elimination of favorite foods.

Other hypotheses can be generated around the nutritional mode. One example of such a hypothesis is the following: If the nurse establishes an environment conducive for dietary intake, the patient will be less likely to experience anorexia or nausea. This hypothesis is also based upon the same earlier propositions.

General Statement: The magnitude of the internal and external stimuli will positively influence the magnitude of the physiological response of an intact system.
Specific Statement: An environment conducive for eating will positively influence the level of anorexia or nausea.

The nurse can generate hypotheses as to which environment would be the most conducive for individual patients or groups of patients. When possible, the patient can be permitted to eat in a location other than his bed or room.

Summary

The gastrointestinal system, a component of the physiological mode of nutrition, was examined according to four sets of relationships which focus on adaptive regulatory responses. These responses take into consideration external and internal stimuli. It is theorized that the body attempts to adapt to chemical and neural inputs as they apply to the gastrointestinal system. However ineffective responses occur when the magnitude of external and internal stimuli are greater than the body's ability to maintain a state of dynamic equilibrium. The overall results leads to disequilibrium and disease.

When the external and internal stimuli exceed the system's ability to adapt, the nurse assesses focal stimuli and regulatory behaviors manipulates contextual stimuli, and assesses residual stimuli. While doing so, the nurse uses the various propositions and theorizing to generate any number of hypotheses that contribute to the body of scientific nursing knowledge regarding the nutrition mode.

References and Additional Readings

Beland, Irene. *Clinical Nursing: Pathophysiology and Psychosocial Approaches.* New York: Macmillan, 1975.

Brooks, Frank, and Richard Davis. "Nervous Control of Gastric Secretion." In *Physiological Controls and Regulations,* ed. William Yamamoto and John Brobeck. Philadelphia: Saunders, 1965.

Buergel, Nancy. "Monitoring Nutritional Status in the Clinical Setting," *Nursing Clinics of North America,* 14, no. 2 (June 1979): 215–28.

Guyton, Arthur. *Textbook of Medical Physiology.* Philadelphia: Saunders, 1971.

Ivey, Marianne. "The Status of Parenteral Nutrition," *Nursing Clinics of North America,* 14, no. 2 (June 1979): 285–304.

Keithley, Joyce. "Proper Nutritional Assessment Can Prevent Hospital Malnutrition," *Nursing,* 9, no. 2 (February 1979): 68–72.

Langley, L. L. *Homeostasis.* New York: Reinhold, 1965.

Luke, Barbara. "Nutrition in Renal Disease: The Adult on Dialysis," *American Journal of Nursing,* 79, no. 12 (December 1979): 2155–57.

Malaznik, Nancy. "Nutrition." In *Introduction to Nursing: An Adaptation Model,* ed. Sr. Callista Roy, pp. 60–61. Englewood Cliffs, N.J.: Prentice-Hall, Inc., 1976.

McGuigan, James. "Anorexia, Nausea, and Vomiting." In *Signs and Symptoms,* ed. Cyril MacBryde and Robert Blacklow, p. 369. Philadelphia: Lippincott, 1970.

Mitchell, Pamela Holsclaw. *Concepts Basic to Nursing.* New York: McGraw-Hill, 1973.

Owen, Anita. Counseling Patients about Diet and Nutrition Supplements, *Nursing Clinics of North America,* 14, no. 2 (June 1979): 247–68.

CHAPTER **8**

Elimination

Elimination is a normal process by which the individual removes waste products derived from intake of food and subsequent metabolism. The physiological mechanism for elimination consists of urine, feces, and fluid loss through the skin, and lungs. Failure to eliminate waste products can have an effect upon other body systems. The body attempts to maintain a balance by eliminating that which it can no longer utilize while reabsorbing essential electrolytes and fluids. This is accomplished through homeostatic regulation of the gastrointestinal, urinary, and integumentary systems. While each system functions somewhat independently, they nevertheless have a combined regulatory control over elimination. An ineffective response in any one of the systems can be an influencing factor of imbalance or disturbance in elimination.

The physiological mode of elimination will be examined according to five sets of theoretical relationships. The first four sets of relationships focus on adaptive regulatory responses of internal and external stimuli. The last set of relationships focuses on ineffective responses. The ineffective response will be examined according to regulatory behaviors, focal stimuli, manipulation of contextual stimuli and a brief discussion of residual stimuli.

First Set of Relationships

The first set of relationships is as follows: The magnitude of the internal and external stimuli will positively influence the magnitude of the physiological response of an intact system. This is predicated on the propositions indicated as 1.1 to 2.1, and 3.2 and 4.4 in Table 5.1.

Normal elimination takes place through both the internal gastrointestinal and urinary systems and the external integumentary system or skin. When the internal and external environment are altered beyond normal adaptive ability, the body regulatory system responds. Three methods of elimination will be discussed: urinary elimination, intestinal elimination, and elimination through the skin.

Elimination of urine involves two types of feedback, which are explained by both the osmotic and sodium theory (Guyton 1971). Osmotic theory implies that a rapid formation of glomerular filtrate causes a decrease in the osmolality of fluid. The dilute fluid causes constriction of the afferent arterioles which then decreases glomerular blood flow. The ultimate response is the formation of glomerular filtrate back to a normal level. Likewise stimuli causing a reduced formation of glomerular filtrate result in excess osmolarity of fluid. This response leads to dilation of the afferent areterioles and a subsequent rise in glomerular filtrate back to normal. The feedback mechanism attempts to regulate internal and external stimuli in an effort to maintain constant glomerular filtrate rate and constant renal perfusion. The feedback mechanism is renal autoregulation.

The second type of feedback involves sodium theory. The sodium theory indicates that too rapid a flow of glomerular filtrate through the tubules leads to an increased sodium concentration. The increased sodium concentration causes the afferent arterioles to constrict, thereby decreasing the glomerular filtrate rate back to a more normal level. Maladaptive problems would occur if the flow of glomerular filtrate was insufficient. Like osmotic theory, sodium theory results from autoregulation. The feedback mechanism of autoregulation takes places in each nephron (Guyton 1971).

Both types of feedback mechanisms enable the formation of urine as a byproduct of body metabolism. Urine volume varies and depends upon external and internal stimuli of kidney function, amount and type of fluids ingested, environmental temperature, fluid requirements of other organs, medications such as diuretics, and pressure or absence of draining wounds (Mitchell 1973). Internal and external stimuli also influence the color of urine. Urine that is pale may be due to excessively large intake of fluid, absorption of intestinal fluid, diabetes insipidus, or diabetes mellitus.

Intestinal elimination involves the incorporation of external stimuli such as food. Then internal stimuli act upon the ingested food, digest it, render toxic substances harmless, and absorb the necessary nutrients while eliminating others. The colon is a transport system that receives liquid chyme from the stomach via the small intestine, and transports it to the anus for elimination. While the liquid chyme is in the colon, water, sodium, and chloride are absorbed. Potassium and bicarbonate ions are excreted (Mitchell 1973). The movement of intestinal content through the colon is dependent upon the nature of the external stimuli, depending, for example, on the type of food ingested and the amount of residue produced. Internal stimuli, such as chemicals or infection within the colon, influence motility rate.

The skin is a significant part of the individual's sensory apparatus. The sensory fibers are responsible for receiving external stimuli such as pain, touch, and temperature changes. The stimuli are received and communicated by means of a complex dermal network. The dermis consists of connective tissue dividing the epidermis and cutaneous adipose tissue. The dermis contains blood vessels, nerves and nerve receptors, hair follicles, and sweat and oil glands. The skin provides a link between external and internal stimuli through numerous nerve receptors.

> The skin is rich with nerve receptors which help appraise the body of its external environment through pressure, pain, and temperature sensation. An intact integument is one of the most effective barriers between many of the pathogens in the environment and those parts of the body interior normally free of these organisms. [Innes 1973]

The sensory receptors enable awareness of environmental stimuli such as temperature changes. Cutaneous blood vessels and sweat glands are responsive to temperature changes. External stimuli of heat cause vasodilation of the cutaneous blood vessels. On the other hand, cold stimuli lead to the adaptive response of vasoconstriction of the small blood vessels.

The skin also functions as a barrier protecting the body from intrusion by harmful external stimuli. Although serving as a barrier, the skin is nevertheless easily permeated by gases, with the exception of carbon monoxide. Penetration of substances takes place faster when the skin temperature is increased or the epidermis has increased fluid. The epidermis provides the body with a protective layer to prevent the loss of fluid and electrolytes. It also provides a homeostatic internal environment for other intact organs (Luckmann and Sorensen 1974). The skin is also a mirror of internal events. Its color communicates blood flow changes or the amount of hemoglobin oxidation. Its turgor and elasticity reflects the hydration status of the individual.

Alterations in internal and external stimuli are received through receptors and communicated by means of the neural pathways. This process involves the second set of relationships.

Second Set of Relationships

In the second set of relationships, the intact neural pathways will positively influence neural output to effectors. This is predicated on the propositions labeled 3.1 to 2.1, and 4.4 in Table 5.1.

Neural input to the kidney and ureters takes place via the sympathetic and parasympathetic division of the autonomic nervous system. The vagus provides parasympathetic input to the kidneys. Sympathetic fibers originate from the thoracolumbar region. The afferent fibers from the kidney monitor internal stimuli such as changes in renal venous pressure and distention of renal pelvis and capsule. The bladder receives its neural input from three sources, namely, the sympathetic, parasympathetic, and somatic systems. Parasympathetic pathways provide the motor function of coordinated elimination of urine. Afferent parasympathetic fibers mediate the desire to void. Sympathetic afferents provide the individual with additional subjective awareness of bladder distention, pain, and the less specific discomfort of visceral distention (Perlmutter and Blacklow 1970).

Sensory receptors are important to neural communication and its influence upon elimination of urine. Sensory receptors have been isolated in the mucous membrane of the bladder. These receptors are responsive to painful stimuli within the mucous membrane. The sensory receptors within the urethra respond to flow, distention, and thermal sensation. Thermal sensation plays a role in the awareness or urination. Urinary elimination is therefore influenced by urethral sensation and traction in the bladder neck caused by bladder contraction.

Neural input to the gastrointestinal system arrives by means of the vagus, splanchnic, and pelvic nerves. These neural pathways provide communication between the central nervous system and the viscera. According to Peterson (1970),

> The parasympathetic efferent supply of the small bowel and the proximal third of the colon are supplied by the vagus and that of the remainder of the colon via the lower social segments of the spinal cord, through the pelvic nerves. The splanchnic nerves supply the sympathetic innervation. The afferent autonomic nerve distribution is also through the vagus, the splanchnic, and the pelvic nerves.

Peristaltic contraction of the small intestine is the responsibility of local mysenteric reflexes. Neural control in the bowel is the result of a balance between the adaptive forces of augmentation and inhibition. The mysenteric reflexes can be augmented by the vagus and pelvis efferent impulses. On the other hand, the same reflexes are inhibited by splanchnic efferent impulses. The latter is a sympathetic response. The small bowel's tone and peristaltic activity may be affected by impulses received through their extensive nerves.

Muscular activity of the large intestine differs from that of the small intestine. The large intestine exhibits automaticity and as a result can be stimulated by a number of stimuli. The mesenteric plexus represent the intrinsic nerve supply which is essential to normal bowel function. It should be pointed out that mobility of the gastrointestinal tract depends upon the extensive nervous system and the ability of muscle fibers to respond to internal stimuli. When the intrinsic nerve supply is altered, activity in the colon is effected. Any alteration in neuromuscular control of the intestine wall leads to changes in intestinal elimination (Mitchell 1973).

As previously mentioned, the skin contains sensory receptors and nerve networks that communicate external stimuli to the appropriate center. Needless to say the nerve network extends over the entire body. Therefore it serves to inform the individual of any external changes that need an immediate response. In many instances such as pain, the neural output to effectors is instantaneous.

Urinary elimination, intestinal elimination, and elimination through the skin is regulated by neural pathways that influence neural outcome. Sensory receptors in the bladder, bowel, or skin provide feedback regarding internal stimuli to void or defecate and external stimuli of pain, touch, or temperature changes. Therefore the intact neural system and its receptors influence neural output to effectors. If the neural system and its neural pathways did not positively influence neural output to effectors, the elimination from the bladder, intestine, and skin would reach a ineffective state of disequilibrium.

Third Set of Relationships

The second set of relationships and related propositions are a significant link to the third set of relationships. In the third set of relationships, chemical and neural inputs are postulated to influence normally responsive endocrine glands to hormonally influence target organs in a positive manner to maintain a state of dynamic equilibrium. This is predicated on the propositions labeled 1.1 to 3.2 in Table 5.1. This set of propositions seems to specify the interrelationship between the chemical and neural regulatory systems. Each system attempts to respond to alteration in the other to maintain a state of equilibrium.

The nephron's function is to remove from the blood plasma unwanted substances resulting from the production of protein metabolism. Chemical input involves metabolism. Metabolic processes result in urea, creatinine, uric acid, and sulfates. Nonmetabolic substances consist of sodium, potassium, and chloride. Metabolic processes provide the necessary energy for chemical reactions that cause transportation of the electrolytes so they will not accumulate to ineffective levels. As sodium is transported from the tubules the concentration of solutes in the tubular fluid decreases. The overall response is to increase tubular concentration of water.

The kidney's arterial system responds to neural input from sympathetic stimulation. Mild sympathetic stimulation of the kidney leads to constriction of the afferent and efferent arterioles. This constriction is done in equilibrium so that the glomerular filtration rate neither increases or decreases. The adaptive response makes possible a diverting of blood flow to other intact organs when a biological crisis occurs. The state of equilibrium between the afferent and efferent arterial system does not alter renal function. As the sympathetic stimulation increases, all arterioles are greatly constricted. The glomerular perfusion is thereby reduced, resulting in reduced glomerular filtration rate. Renal output or urinary elimination is reduced to almost zero (Guyton 1971).

Neurohormonal control of intestinal elimination is a combined effort of both chemical and neural input. A substance is released by the parasympathetic postganglionic fiber; the substance consists of acetycholine. Acetycholine functions to increase the tone and mobility of the intestine. Sympathetic postganglionic nerves release norephinephrine. Serotonin is found in the intestinal tract and its release is probably controlled by neural element in the intestinal wall. Serotonin helps to regulate peristaltic activity. This is accomplished through mediating pressure receptors in the mucosa. Potassium is another chemical that is significant to normal intestinal motor function through its effect upon nerves and muscle cells within the intestinal wall.

There are four types of sensations in the skin that are incorporated into the total body through chemical and neural input: pain, touch, cold, and warmth. According to Luckmann and Sorensen (1974),

Pain may be caused by physical, chemical, or mechanical stimulation. Touch stimuli are received from hair follicle and intervening skin. Itching arises from terminal nerve endings close to the skin surface. Temperature sense is probably gained through the free sensory nerve endings in the epidermis.

The nerve endings are therefore stimulated by external and internal stimuli.

Chemical and neural input affects urinary elimination, intestinal elimination, and elimination through the skin. Each system of elimination has its own chemical and neural system that seeks to maintain itself at an adaptive level. When the chemical and neural inputs are unable to positively influence the endocrine glands and subsequently the hormone's influence upon target organs then the system becomes disorganized. When this response occurs, the individual becomes aware of his own ineffective behavior.

Fourth Set of Relationships

A fourth set of relationships provides the transition between adaptive and ineffective behaviors. This set of relationships involves the body's response to external and internal stimuli and states that such stimuli will alter those external and internal stimuli. This is predicated on the propositions labeled 1.1 to 5.1 in Table 5.1.

Internal stimuli provide the individual with the information regarding the sensation of fullness in the bladder, contraction of the detrusor muscle, and relaxation of the sphincters. Stimuli communicating the need and desire to void are carried to the higher voluntary cortical micturation control center. As Mitchell (1973) points out,

> If the time for voiding is appropriate, the brain sends impulses to motor nerves in the sacral area of the spinal cord, causing parasympathetic efferent fibers of the pelvic nerve to stimulate the contraction of the detrusor muscle, relaxation of the sphincters, and voiding.

The specific mechanism of micturation initiation is unknown. It is believed that the conscious desire to void begins after the stimuli within the bladder cause it to contract.

The composition of urinary elimination can vary depending upon stimuli taken in such as type of food, medication, or fluids ingested, and internal stimuli indicating particular needs of the body. There are times when the body has an excess of fluid. Urinary elimination produces urine that is dilute in appearance. Likewise a body depleted of water will excrete a limited amount of urine whose appearance is a concentrated amber. While urinary elimination in this instance is reduced, the end products of protein metabolism and other substances are still removed. Hormonal influence such as is caused by large quantities of antidiuretic hormone will decrease the amount of urine output by its effect upon the pores of the distal tubules and collecting ducts. It should be noted that a feedback system exists between the distal tubules and afferent arterioles. Therefore conditions in the distal tubules controls blood flow through the afferent arterioles (Guyton 1971).

Intestinal elimination or defecation is due to internal stimuli providing input about the presence or absence of distention in the sigmoid colon and rectum. Physiologically normal intestinal elimination is a complex arrangement between voluntary and involuntary controls. A distended sigmoid and rectum causes stimulation of sensory nerves. The sensory nerves in turn send stimuli to the sacral nerves while other stimuli ascend the spinothalamic tract to the brain. The result is defecation. In addition to nervous stimuli, specific movements assist intestinal elimination. Fixing of the diaphragm and contraction of abdominal and chest muscles together with a relaxant of the anal sphincter all aid in elimination.

Alteration in external stimuli such as reduced residue in diet, decreased fluid intake, new medication, or increased caffeine consumption can change the mobility of fecal content in the intestinal tract. Likewise internal stimuli such as inhibition of the normal defecation reflexes can alter intestinal elimination. When intestinal elimination is reduced, the individual will increase external stimuli to augment defecation. The stimuli may consist of increased fluid intake, laxatives, exercise, residue in diet, or reduced stress. Likewise increased peristaltic activity leading to diarrhea force the individual to reduce or eliminate possible external stimuli causing the problem. There are times when internal stimuli causing increased mobility cannot be easily controlled. Intestinal infection, drugs altering intestinal flora, or toxic substances cannot be quickly eliminated to reestablish a state of dynamic equilibrium.

A diaphoretic individual is eliminating fluid through the skin as perspiration. The amount of diaphoresis depends upon the ability of other intact organs to eliminate fluids, external environmental temperature, and thermoregulatory functioning within the body. For the individual with congestive heart failure, chronic obstructive pulmonary disease, or renal failure the integumentary system becomes a vital output system. A cold environment causes vasoconstriction of blood vessels thereby reducing heat conduction or diaphoresis. Increased external environmental temperature and internal core temperature cause vasodilatation of the blood vessels. The result is an increased blood flow to the surface of the skin in an attempt to reduce temperature. Diaphoresis is the body's adaptive or regulatory way of compensating for increased body temperature.

External and internal stimuli—through regulation of elimination from the urinary system, gastrointestinal system, or skin—alter those external and internal stimuli. This regulatory process takes into account both negative and positive feedback. The body, when confronted with an alteration in elimination balance, seeks to positively adapt to the alteration by negating the potentially ineffective stimuli. The individual who experiences excess or deficit in elimination behaves in such a way as to restore balance. Therefore action upon internal and external stimuli causes elimination to be regulated at a level above or below that which contributed to the negative feedback. The entire process is considered to be adaptive. As pointed out earlier, other regulatory systems become involved.

The fourth set of relationships has an interadaptive quality signifying a linkage between adaptive and ineffective regulatory responses. There are times when the fourth set of relationships fails to successfully alter internal and external stimuli in an adaptive way. Instead the intact organ or system responds in a ineffective manner.

Fifth Set of Relationships

In the fifth set of relationships, the magnitude of the external and internal stimuli may be so great that the adaptive system cannot return the body to a state of dynamic equilibrium. This includes propositions 1.1 to 5.1 in Table 5.1.

When elimination imbalance exceeds the body's ability to restore equilibrium, regulatory mechanisms cannot be depended upon to resist further imbalance. External and internal stimuli may be so great that the body cannot return to equilibrium and instead experiences disequilibrium. An increase or decrease in elimination activates other systems which attempt to restore equilibrium. If the regulatory mechanisms fails, the result is disorganization and possible death.

The ineffective responses will be discussed under the headings of deficit or excess elimination. Each ineffective response within the general categories will be discussed according to regulatory behaviors, focal stimuli, and manipulation of contextual and residual stimuli.

Deficit in elimination

Urinary Elimination.   A deficit in urinary elimination is labeled urinary retention. The process involves a continued production of urine in the bladder; however, the bladder is unable to eliminate it. If urinary retention exceeds the bladder's ability to stretch, the epithelial wall becomes hypoxic. The hypoxia is caused by increased pressure in the arterial vessels.

REGULATORY BEHAVIORS.   In urinary retention the regulatory behavior depends upon the severity of bladder distention. The following regulatory behaviors are associated with urinary retention:

1. Severe discomfort
2. Distended bladder well above symphysis pubis
3. Sensitivity to palpation
4. Restlessness

5. Anuria
6. Oliguria
7. Infection

Obstruction in the urinary pathway therefore interfers with the flow of urine. Stasis of urine is accompanied by infection and/or stone formation.

FOCAL STIMULI. Several factors may cause urinary retention or reduced urinary output. The following focal stimuli contribute to urinary retention and the behaviors anuria or oliguria:

1. Urethral stricture
2. Benign prostatic hypertrophy
3. Urethral obstruction due to stones
4. Functional obstruction due to spinal cord tumor
5. Fever, diarrhea, or vomiting
6. Chronic renal failure
7. Acute tubular necrosis
8. Adrenal insufficiency

There may be other focal stimuli contributing to the ineffective response of urinary retention and resulting oliguria or anuria.

Intestinal Elimination.   A decrease in intestinal elimination leads to the ineffective response of constipation and eventual fecal impaction. In constipation defecation occurs after a prolonged period. The eliminated stool is hard and requires a tremendous use of voluntary muscles to expel it from the large bowel. Fecal impaction is the prolonged retention of fecal content in the sigmoid and rectum. The fecal mass can become a source of obstruction and irritation.

REGULATORY BEHAVIORS. The regulatory behaviors associated with decreased intestinal elimination depend upon the degree and duration of the constipation.

1. Fecal seepage due to bacterial action
2. Abdominal distention
3. Rectal pain
4. Everted anus
5. Hard mass in sigmoid flexture

Although there are other regulatory behaviors, these are the most significant ones.

FOCAL STIMULI. The focal stimuli that cause constipation can be categorized according to their neurogenic, muscular, and mechanical origin. The focal stimuli are therefore classified according to pathophysiological processes. See Table 8.1 (Peterson 1970). Although Table 8.1 is not an all-inclusive list it covers most of the many focal stimuli causing constipation. Regardless of the origin, intestinal mobility can be reduced to the point where intestinal elimination is severely altered.

Integumentary Elimination.   A deficit in integumentary elimination in the form of perspiration is called anhidrosis. This may lead to dryness of the skin. More importantly dryness can be caused by malfunction of the sebaceous glands. The sebaceous glands function to maintain the water content of the skin. When this function is altered, water is allowed to evaporate from the skin and dryness develops. Microorganisms can enter through

TABLE **8.1** Focal Stimuli in Constipation

Categories	Pathophysiologic Process
I. Neurogenic	1. Central nervous system lesions
	(a) Multiple sclerosis
	(b) Cord tumors
	(c) Traumatic spinal cord lesions
	2. Postganglionic disorders
	(a) Hirschsprung's disease
	(b) Opiate effect
	(c) Anticholinergic drugs
II. Muscular	1. Atony
	(a) Laxative abuse
	(b) Severe malnutrition
	2. Metabolic defects
	(a) Hypothyroidism
	(b) Hypercalcemia
	(c) Potassium depletion
	(d) Hyperparathyroidism
III. Mechanical	1. Bowel obstruction
	(a) Neoplasm
	(b) Diverticulitis
	2. Rectal lesions
	(a) Thrombosed hemorrhoids
	(b) Perirectal abscess

Source: Peterson, Malcolm. "Constipation and Diarrhea." In *Signs and Symptoms,* ed. Cyril MacBryde, and Robert Blacklow, p. 383. Philadelphia: Lippincott, 1970.

small openings caused by dryness. Because anhidrosis may have little or no clinical significance, regulatory behaviors and focal stimuli will not be discussed.

Excessive elimination

Urinary Elimination.   An excess in urinary elimination can involve either urinary incontinence or diuresis. Urinary incontinence is the inability of the urinary sphincter to withhold the elimination of urine from the bladder. Whether the patient experiences incontinence or excessive diuresis, the urine is assessed for evidence of pus, hematuria, odor, or color.

REGULATORY BEHAVIORS. The regulatory behaviors are very specific and mainly involve the inability to control the elimination of urine. The following is a brief list of possible regulatory behaviors:

1. Incontinence associated with laughing, coughing, or sneezing
2. Dribbling
3. Odor
4. Straw-colored urine with prolonged diuresis

FOCAL STIMULI. Like regulatory behaviors, focal stimuli causing urinary incontinence or excessive diuresis may be limited in numbers.

1. Reduced muscle strength due to multiparity
2. Reduced cerebral awareness indicating the need to void
3. Enlarged prostate
4. Urinary tract infection
5. Spinal cord injuries or trauma
6. Tissue damage to sphincter
7. Aging process
8. Medications such as diuretics

Focal stimuli associated with incontinence or diuresis involves pathophysiological, psychological, and developmental alterations. The aging process alone may alter muscle tone thereby causing incontinence.

Intestinal Elimination.   Increased intestinal elimination is labeled as diarrhea. Diarrhea is the rapid passage of liquid feces from the intestine. Another term associated with rapid expulsion of fecal content is dysentery. Dysentery is primarily associated with inflammation of the intestine characterized by the passage of mucus and blood.

REGULATORY BEHAVIORS. The regulatory behaviors associated with increased intestinal elimination may be caused by prolonged loss of fluid or nutrients.

1. Abdominal cramps
2. Poor tissue turgor
3. Weight loss
4. Weakness
5. Fatigue
6. General malaise

Additional regulatory behaviors such as increased temperature and arrhythmias result from severe fluid loss.

FOCAL STIMULI. The focal stimuli causing excessive intestinal elimination are many. The general pathophysiological processes associated with each category (Peterson 1970) are listed in Table 8.2. Restoration of adaptive intestinal eliminatory responses may be more difficult for individuals experiencing complex versus simple focal stimuli. The simple focal stimulus of anxiety, for example, is far easier to control than the more complex stimuli caused by neuromuscular maladaptive changes.

TABLE 8.2   Focal Stimuli in Excessive Intestinal Elimination

Categories	Pathophysiological Process

I. Malabsorption	1. Malabsorption of fats
	   (a) Lipase insufficiency
	   (b) Bile salt deficiency
	   (c) Defective path of absorption
	2. Malabsorption of carbohydrates
	3. Malabsorption of water
	   (a) Interference with absorption due to mucosal cell damage
	   (b) Excessive secretion

II. Neuromuscular	1. Autonomic system imbalance 2. Hormonal and pharmacologic influence
III. Mechanical	1. Incomplete obstruction 2. Fecal impaction 3. Muscular incompetency
IV. Inflammatory bases and direct irritants	1. Infections 2. Poisons

Source: Peterson, Malcolm. "Constipation and Diarrhea." In *Signs and Symptoms,* ed. Cyril MacBryde, and Robert Blacklow, p. 383. Philadelphia: Lippincott, 1970.

Integumentary Elimination.   An excess in integumentary elimination via perspiration is called diaphoresis. Perspiration is one mechanism through which the body is cooled. The moisture evaporates in an attempt to maintain or restore normal temperature.

REGULATORY BEHAVIORS. The regulatory behaviors associated with increased perspiration or diaphoresis may be attributed to underlying focal stimuli.

1. Moisture on forehead, palms, upper lip, and soles
2. Irritated skin with excessive moisture
3. Odor

Diaphoresis may be due to cardiac, pulmonary, metabolic, or neurological maladaptive problems. Therefore the above regulatory behaviors concern excess perspiration or diaphoresis without underlying pathophysiology.

FOCAL STIMULI. Focal stimuli causing increased perspiration and/or diaphoresis consist of the following:

1. Febrile state
2. Muscular activity
3. Increased environmental temperature and humidity
4. Increased metabolic rate
5. Disturbances in central nervous system
6. Stress and fear

Manipulating the stimuli

Given that the magnitude of the external and internal stimuli are so great that the adaptive systems cannot return the body to a state of dynamic equilibrium, the nurse intervenes by manipulating stimuli in an attempt to maintain or restore balance in elimination. In order to manipulate stimuli, the nurse assesses various influencing factors that contribute to the maladaptive responses. The influencing factors consist of focal, contextual, and residual stimuli. Focal stimuli were previously discussed in terms of pathophysiological maladaptive responses. Contextual and residual stimuli will be discussed in relationship to nursing intervention.

Contextual stimuli

The nurse alters ineffective regulatory responses from external and internal stimuli through manipulation of the following contextual stimuli: fluid, activity, nutrition, communication, aeration, and pain.

Fluid.   Fluid intake is balanced with fluid loss from the kidneys, intestine, and skin. As with other systems, fluid management involves assessment of sensible and insensible loss.

INTAKE. Intake involves physiological intake of oral and parenteral fluids as well as environmental intake. The amount of fluid intake depends upon the urinary and intestinal elimination. If the patient experiences increased urinary output and diarrhea, it may be necessary to increase the total fluid intake. Additional fluid intake may also be required for the patient who is constipated.

In evaluating the need for an increase or decrease in fluid intake, the nurse assesses the patient's skin turgor. Skin or tissue turgor indicates the amount of fluid surrounding the cells. When fluid volume is greatly depleted, the body's fluid is pulled from the peripheral tissue. The result is dry loose skin necessitating increased fluid intake. Edematous tissue leads to very taut tissue turgor. With extreme edematous states, the patient's skin becomes shiny and susceptable to breakdown. In this instance fluid intake should be limited.

Environmental intake involves protecting the patient from potential hazards and excessive temperature changes. Increased environmental temperature can contribute to an already existing febrile state or diaphoresis. Therefore the environment should be comfortable for the patient and his biological problem.

OUTPUT. Urinary elimination depends upon normal renal function, fluid intake, physiological status of other organs, dehydration or overhydration, or use of diuretics. The amount of urinary output is approximately 1500 cc per 24 hours. Less than 500 cc in a 24-hour period may indicate potential problems.

The color of urine is pale or amber and is attributed to the pigment urochrome. If the patient is receiving diuretics, the urine is pale. Other factors contributing to a pale color are reabsorption of interstitial fluid or edema, diabetes insipidus, or diabetes mellitus. When urine is a dark amber, it may indicate dehydration or the presence of urobilin. Red urine may be due to the presence of blood in the excretory system. This may be caused by urinary tract infection or disease.

Intestinal eliminaton may vary from individual to individual. Factors that influence elimination are liquids, positioning, enemas, laxatives, and medications. When physiologically possible, adequate fluid intake is desirable to prevent constipation.

Normal feces are a brown color due to bilirubin derivatives (sterobilin and urobilin) and the action of normal intestinal bacteria. A stool may be called acholic when there is an absence of bile entering the bowel. Therefore the white or clay-colored stool indicates biliary obstruction. Tarry stools signify some type of bleeding in the intestinal tract.

Increased intestinal output signifies diarrhea. Diarrhea leads to less absorption of vitamin B_{12}, thiamine, riboflavin, and vitamin K. Prolonged increased motility can lead to physiological problems associated with water, sodium, and potassium loss. Amino acids, carbohydrates, and fat reabsorption are also lost.

The skin is another source of output. The output takes the form of wetness or dryness and color. Diaphoresis represents an increased moisture on the skin and can be caused by temperature elevation, exercise, and increased environmental temperature.

Skin color varies from pallid to cyanotic. Pallor can be caused by vasoconstriction of the cutaneous blood vessels. The body's compensatory response is to conserve body heat or shunt blood to vital organs. The nurse may assess pallor in anemic patients. Reddened or flushed skin is caused by vasodilatation of cutaneous blood vessels, increased metabolism, and hyperthyroidism. The bluish tinged skin is called cyanosis and may be due to an excessive amount of deoxygenated hemoglobin in the cutaneous blood vessels.

With excessive urinary and intestinal output the patient can experience volume changes in body fluids due to hypoprotenemia. This can lead to interstitial edema and eventual tachycardia and hypotension. Increased temperature changes associated with dehydration also contribute to increased respirations.

Activity. The nurse can assess four major components of her patient's activity: physical activity, cardiopulmonary activity, metabolic activity, and mental activity.

Physical activity may need to be restricted for the patient who is hypovolemic due to excessive urinary and intestinal elimination. The patient with increased intestinal motility resulting in diarrhea may make frequent trips to the bathroom thereby increasing physical mobility. The weakened patient needs assistance to prevent physical injury.

Cardiac arrhythmias can result from electrolyte loss due to excessive fluid loss. Therefore until electrolyte balance is restored, the patient's cardiac status should be continually assessed.

As changes in acid-base balance occur, the patient's respiratory rate can also change. With metabolic acidosis, the pulmonary system compensates through increased ventilation thereby causing alkalosis.

It was previously mentioned that excessive urinary and intestinal elimination can contribute to metabolic changes. Depending upon the degree of fluid and electrolyte loss, the patient can experience metabolic acidosis or alkalosis. Electrolyte balance should be restored as quickly as possible. With electrolyte imbalance, calcium gluconate and sodium bicarbonate may be needed.

Changes in mental activity may reflect alterations in fluid status. Excessive elimination can lead to behavioral changes associated with electrolyte disturbances.

Nutrition.   If an increased intestinal motility leads to diarrhea, the nurse may assess the patient's dietary intake. Irritating foods or tube feedings high in protein or carbohydrates can contribute to diarrhea. In some instances antacids high in magnesium content can result in increased intestinal motility. The nurse's assessment includes determining the exact amount of urinary and intestinal loss or the presence of diaphoresis. The nurse attempts to replace the fluid loss via parenteral or oral fluids.

When diarrhea is caused by distrubed intestinal flora which sometimes occur with prolonged antibiotics, the patient's diet can include yogurt. Basically the goal of dietary intake is to replace fluids and electrolytes, thereby reducing the potential threat of hypovolemic shock and cardiac arrhythmias. To accomplish the goal, it may be necessary to administer hyperalimentation fluids.

Communication.   It is important for the patient to communicate his fear and concerns. This is especially true for the patient experiencing prolonged diarrhea and associated rectal pain. Because the patient may associate these symptoms with cancer, diagnostic studies should be done as quickly as possible to determine the origin of gastrointestinal changes. In addition the patient may have experienced weight loss resulting in body-image changes. Depending upon the physiological reason for the gastrointestinal change and weight loss, the patient needs reassurance that the alterations are temporary.

Aeration.   Aeration includes both psychological and environmental aeration. With psychological or emotional aeration, the patient is encouraged to verbalize his concerns, fears, or anxieties. The patient may need to be protected from an excessively warm environment. Such an environment may cause diaphoresis and fluid loss. Excessive sunlight entering the patient's immediate environment can contribute to an already febrile state.

Pain.   The patient may experience psychological pain due to an altered body image and the possibility of life-threatening illness. While psychological pain cannot be removed with narcotics, it can be treated with supportive care. For example, the patient with ulcerative colitis may need the supportive care of a psychiatrist. Prolonged illness can also lead to financial problems causing a burden to both the patient and his family. Therefore meaningful support from the health team is extremely important.

Residual stimuli

Residual stimuli may include a history of urinary, intestinal or skin disturbances; previous hospitalization for urinary tract or intestinal dysfunction; use of diuretics or laxatives; pain upon urination or defecation; or alteration in urinary or intestinal output pattern.

Example of Hypothesis for Practice

We have focused on the process of theorizing with the elimination physiological mode. Based on our theorizing with the elimination mode, we can postulate any number of hypothesis that can be tested. The theorizing encompasses the four sets of relationships and their related propositions. In addition the hypotheses can be used as a guide for practice. An example of a possible hypothesis will be discussed.

The hypothesis may be stated as follows: If the nurse helps the patient achieve an optimal level of urinary and intestinal elimination, the patient's eliminatory system will perform at a higher level. The reason for this hypothesis is drawn from the first set of relationships which are based on propositions. The reasons are shown below.

General Statement: The magnitude of the internal and external stimuli will positively influence the magnitude of the physiological response of an intact system.

Specific Statement: The magnitude of internal and external stimuli will positively influence the level of urinary and intestinal elimination.

The nurse utilizes the four sets of relationships to theorize regarding elimination. The theorizing permits hypothesis generation even when the nurse manipulates the contextual stimuli. If the nurse finds evidence of significance for a hypothesis, the nursing activity specified in the research protocol can become a prescription for practice in situations where nursing diagnosis warrants this intervention.

Summary

Elimination has been examined according to four sets of relationships which focus on adaptive regulatory responses. These responses take into account external and internal stimuli. The body attempts to adapt to chemical and neural inputs as they apply to elimination. However, ineffective responses occur when the magnitude of external and internal stimuli are greater than the body's ability to maintain a state of dynamic equilibrium. When the external and internal stimuli exceed the system's ability to adapt, the nurse assesses focal stimuli and regulatory behaviors, and manipulates contextual and residual stimuli. While doing so, the nurse generates hypotheses based upon the theorizing and propositions dealing with the elimination mode.

References and Additional Readings

Bertholf, Connie. "Protocol: Acute Diarrhea," *Nurse Practitioner,* (May-June 1978): 17–20.

Guyton, Arthur. *Textbook of Medical Physiology.* Philadelphia: Saunders, 1971.

Innes, Barbara. "Integumentary Status." In *Concepts Basic to Nursing,* ed. Pamela H. Mitchell. New York: McGraw-Hill, 1973.

Luckmann, Joan, and Karen Sorensen. *Medical Surgical Nursing: A Psychophysiological Approach.* Philadelphia: Saunders, 1974.

Mitchell, Pamela Holsclaw. *Concepts Basic to Nursing.* New York: McGraw-Hill, 1973.

Perlmutter, Alan, and Robert Blacklow. "Urinary Tract Pain Hematuria and Pyuria." In *Signs and Symptoms,* ed. Cyril MacBryde and Robert Blocklow. Philadelphia: Lippincott, 1970.

Peterson, Malcolm. "Constipation and Diarrhea." In *Signs and Symptoms,* ed. Cyril MacBryde and Robert Blacklow, p. 383. Philadelphia: Lippincott, 1970.

Porter, S. "Feeding Critically Ill Patients," *Nursing Times* , March 2, 1978, pp. 355–59.

Roberts, Sharon. "Skin Assessment for Color and Temperature," *American Journal of nursing,* 75, no. 4 (April 1975): 610–13.

CHAPTER **9**

Fluids
and electrolytes

The body fluids are highly significant to the individual's overall body function. Disturbances in body fluids and electrolytes can be the result of, or a variable contributing to, a maladaptive response or disease state. Therefore it becomes important to maintain body fluids and electrolytes in an adaptive state. Multiple systems throughout the body play a role in maintaining water and electrolytes at an adaptive level. This is accomplished through homeostatic regulation by means of the endocrine, gastrointestinal, renal, cardiovascular, nervous, and respiratory systems. These multiple systems have a regulatory control over water and electrolytes. More significantly they are the only controls over body fluids and electrolytes. Consequently a malfunction in any one of these systems can become an influencing factor of water and electrolyte imbalance.

The physiological mode of fluids and electrolytes will be examined according to five sets of theoretical relationships. The first four sets of relationships focus on adaptive regulatory responses of internal and external stimuli. The last set of relationships focuses on ineffective responses. The ineffective response will be examined according to regulatory behaviors, focal stimuli, manipulating contextual stimuli, and a brief discussion of residual stimuli.

First Set of Relationships

The first set of relationships is as follows: The magnitude of the internal and external stimuli will positively influence the magnitude of the physiological response of an intact system. This is predicated on the propositions indicated as 1.1 to 2.1, 3.2, and 4.4 in Table 5.1.

The normal fluid and electrolytes changes occurring in the internal environment are, as previously noted, regulated by multiple systems including the renal, respiratory, and acid-base buffer systems. When the internal and external environment are exposed to unusual stimuli from stressors, the body's regulatory systems react. The stress reactions causes endocrine, renal, circulatory, respiratory, gastrointestinal, and nervous response to neurohormonal stimulation.

According to Burgess (1979),

> The stress response includes three stages: (1) alarm reaction, (2) adaptation of countershock reaction, and (3) exhaustion. The former two stages are most intimately involved in the preparation of fluid and electrolyte changes which may return the organism to a state of equilibrium.

The alarm reaction is the result of adrenergic hormonal stimulation such as that caused by epinephrine and norepinephrine. Both hormones cause vasoconstriction of cerebral and visceral blood vessels. A decrease in circulating blood volume leads to reduced renal perfusion and a compensatory oliguria. Furthermore, reduced perfusion acts as an internal stimuli to the adrenal cortex causing it to secrete the mineralocorticoids.

The adaptive reaction follows in response to the alarm reaction stage. It is an attempt by the body to correct homeostatic disequilibrium of the organism with the internal and external environment. The adaptive reaction is controlled by adrenal cortical secretion of mineralocorticoids, glucocorticoids, and androgens. The mineralocorticoid response affects fluid and electrolyte balance. It is stimulated by a feedback system including adrenocorticotropin (ACTH) secretion, extracellular fluid volume, and serum concentration of potassium and sodium (Burgess 1979). The overall physiological goal is to keep body fluids at an adaptive level.

Body fluids have two basic functions. First, they provide a stable internal environment for cellular metabolic activity. Second, body fluids provide a transport system that brings nourishment to the cells and removes waste products (Harrington and Brener 1973). The transport system of fluid and electrolytes and its regulation is significant for comprehending ineffective responses such as edema, dehydration, circulatory overload, and water intoxication. The magnitude of internal and external stimuli in the form of intracellular and extracellular fluid positively influences the physiological response of the intact system, namely, fluids and electrolytes. The communication between these stimuli takes two processes into consideration. The first process consists of the transport of fluid and electrolytes between the intracellular fluid and extracellular fluid compartments.

The flow of fluid and electrolyte between the internal and external environment depends upon the osmolarity of the fluids compartment and the principle of active transport. Osmolarity controls water distribution between intracellular (ICF) and extracellular (ECF) fluid compartments. According to Luckmann and Sorensen (1974), "Should the ICF develop a greater osmolarity than the ECF, water will shift from the ECF into the ICF and the cells will consequently swell. Conversely, should the ECF develop a greater osmolarity than the ICF, water will shift from the cells into the ECF compartment, and the cells will shrivel. Thus, osmolar changes affect cell volume." Therefore osmolarity controls water distribution while osmolarity is regulated by water intake and output. The amount of water intake is controlled by thirst, and water loss is regulated by the antidiuretic hormone (ADH), the kidney nephrons, and the gastrointestinal tract.

Active transport applies to the work necessary to transport ions across a cellular membrane against chemical or electrical gradients. An important aspect of transport between the internal and external environment is that

cells are able to transport sodium and other positively charged osmotic particles across cell boundaries and into extracellular fluid where they balance the cell's anion, proteinate; the mechanism of this transport is called a "cation pump" or "sodium pump." [Luckmann and Sorensen 1974]

The second process consists of the transport of fluids between the interstitial fluid compartment and the vascular compartment. There are three major factors involved in the maintenance of blood volume, namely, blood hydrostatic pressure, colloid osmotic pressure, and filtration pressure. These influencing factors control the return of fluid to the vascular system. There are two factors that can contribute to the loss of water from the plasma: an increase in blood hydrostatic pressure and a decrease in colloid osmotic pressure. The magnitude of internal and external stimuli are influenced by the above factors and in turn influence the physiological response of fluids and electrolytes.

Alterations in internal and external stimuli are received through receptors and communicated by means of the neural pathways. This process involves the second set of relationships.

Second Set of Relationships

In the second set of relationships, the intact neural pathways will positively influence neural output to effectors. This is predicated on the propostions labeled 3.1 to 2.1, and 4.4 in Table 5.1. The overall function of the nervous system as a homeostatic regulator is to centrally control water and sodium intake together with excretion. The nervous system accomplishes this goal in three ways: (1) It manufactures and stores hormones; (2) it contains regulatory mechanisms for correcting changes in volume of body water; and (3) it contains regulatory mechanisms for correcting changes in the osmolarity of body water (Luckmann and Sorensen 1974).

First, the nervous system manufactures and stores antidiuretic and adrenocorticotropin hormone. The latter is a hormone that serves as a stimulus for the release of aldosterone from the adrenal cortex.

Second, the nervous system regulates the body's water volume.

The midbrain contains a volumetric monitoring system that responds to variations in extracellular fluid volume. This system evidently receives information about fluid volume from various receptors located in the walls of the great veins, the arteries, and the atria. From the volumetric monitoring system, information concerning blood volume is relayed to those control systems that govern ADH release, thirst, and the release of aldosterone. [Luckmann and Sorensen 1974]

Receptors in the hypothalamus stimulate the release of ADH while the thirst center located in the hypothalamus may be stimulated to turn off or on by changes in body fluid osmolarity. Therefore ADH release or inhibition can be a direct response to changes in body water volume such as hypovolemia or hypervolemia.

Third, the hypothalamus is the regulatory center for correcting changes in body osmolarity. According to Langley (1965),

The osmoreceptors are located in the hypothalamus. When the organism becomes dehydrated, the osmotic state of blood increases, and therefore the osmoreceptors in the hypothalamus respond. As a result, messages are sent to the posterior lobe of the hypophysis and a hormone, called the antidiuretic hormone or ADH, is released. ADH is carried by the blood to the kidneys where it acts to diminish the formation of urine.

The thirst center in the hypothalamus is also sensitive to the osmolarity of the body fluids. The thirst center is either stimulated or inhibited. Thirst is stimulated by low water intake, excessive solium intake, and excessive infusion of hypertonic solutions. On the other hand, thirst is inhibited by a large water intake, water retention within the body, a low sodium intake, and excessive infusion of hypotonic or isotonic solution.

In summary, central regulation of water and sodium homeostasis by the nervous system is accomplished by several factors. The intake of water is influenced by regulation of midbrain volume receptors and thirst osmoreceptors in the hypothalamus. Likewise excretion of water is regulated by volume receptors that stimulate water excretion when fluid volume is high and water retention when fluid volume is low; by osmoreceptors in the hypothalamus which releases ADH in response to hyperosmolarity and inhibit it in response to hypoosmolarity; and by midbrain and renal volume receptors that stimulate or inhibit aldosterone depending upon the volume and sodium level. Sodium intake and excretion is also regulated by the nervous system. Intake of sodium is regulated by a midbrain volume receptor which, by means of intact neural pathways, signals the adrenal cortex to release aldosterone. The intake of salt is either inhibited by a positive sodium balance or stimulated by a negative sodium balance. The excretion of sodium is regulated by both the midbrain and renal volume receptors. Decreased sodium leads to stimulation of aldosterone. Likewise increased sodium leads to inhibition of aldosterone. Therefore the intact neural system and its receptors influence neural output to effectors. If the neural system and its neural pathways did not positively influence neural output to effectors, the volume of body water and electrolyte levels would reach a ineffective state of disequilibrium.

Third Set of Relationships

The second set of relationships and related propositions become a significant link to the third set of relationships. In the third set of relationships, chemical and neural inputs are postulated to influence normally responsive endocrine glands to hormonally influence target organs in a positive manner to maintain a state of dynamic equilibrium. This is predicated on the propositions labeled 1.1 to 3.2 in Table 5.1. This set of propositions seems to specify the interrelationships between the chemical and neural regulatory systems. Each system attempts to respond to alteration in the other to maintain a state of equilibrium.

The electrolytes constitute a chemical framework for the stability of physical properties of extracellular fluids. According to MacBryde and Blacklow (1970),

The renal control of fluid balance is to a large degree under hormonal influence. The hormonal influence is excreted in the activity of the distal renal tubular cells and is concerned with the amount of water reabsorbed by the tubules and with the amount of certain solutes, particularly sodium and potassium, which are absorbed or excreted.

Chemical and neural inputs influence endocrine glands which in turn stimulate specific hormones. The hormones influence fluids and electrolytes to maintain dynamic equilibrium. The hormones of significance in the regulation of fluid and electrolyte metabolism are antidiuretic hormone or ADH, aldosterone, thyroid hormones, parathyroid hormone, and diuretic hormone.

Antidiuretic hormone serves the function of preventing the body from losing fluids. The release of ADH is initiated by three sets of receptors: the osmoreceptors in the hypothalamus, the stretch receptors in the great veins and atria, and the prereceptors in the atria (Langley 1965). According to Luckmann and Sorensen (1974), there are nine circumstances that can stimulate ADH production and release with resultant water conservation:

1. Water loss that causes an increase in ECF osmolarity
2. Reduced circulatory blood volume
3. Morphine sulfate injections
4. Pain
5. Barbituates
6. Anesthetics
7. Emotional stress
8. Surgical trauma
9. Accidental trauma

ADH stimulation can also be suppressed due to hypoosmolarity of the extracellular fluid or an increase in water load, increased blood volume, cold, acute alcohol ingestion, and diuretics. The physiological response is an increased urinary output.

Just as ADH becomes the body's regulator of water, aldosterone is the primary conserver of sodium.

Aldosterone is a mineralocorticoid secreted by the adrenal cortex in response to certain stimuli. Aldesterone influences the renal tubules to increase their reabsorption of sodium in exchange for excreting potassium. [Lancour 1979]

The aldosterone hormonal mechanism has a negative feedback nature. In the aldosterone-sodium control mechanism, increased sodium concentration leads to decreased aldosterone secretion. The result is a decreased sodium concentration. Therefore the response is negative to the initial increased sodium level. Likewise a decrease in sodium causes increased aldosterone secretion. This response becomes negative to the initiating stimulus. When aldosterone fails to respond appropriately to changes in sodium concentration, the response is positive feedback. The overall fluid and electrolyte response is ineffective and results in disorganization or disequilibrium.

Aldosterone can be regulated or controlled by six influencing factors (Luckmann and Sorensen 1974):

1. Sodium depletion is the greatest stimulus to aldosterone stimulation.
2. Alteration in ECF volume:
   (a) Increased ECF volume leads to decreased aldosterone secretion.
   (b) Decreased ECF volume (dehydration) leads to increased aldosterone secretion.
3. Alteration in blood volume:
   (a) Hemorrhage stimulates aldosterone.
4. Alteration in electrolyte composition of the plasma which increases aldosterone:
   (a) Increased sodium excretion
   (b) Decreased potassium excretion.
   (c) Increased potassium intake.
5. Constriction of carotid and renal arteries leads to increased secretion of aldosterone.
6. High doses of ACTH increases aldosterone secretion.

Besides antidiuretic hormone and aldosterone there are three other hormones that influence fluid and electrolyte in a positive manner to maintain a state of equilibrium: thyroid, parathyroid, and diuretic hormones. The stimulation of thyroid hormone causes an increase in renal blood flow which in turn contributes to increased glomerular filtration rate and urinary output. The diuretic hormone also increases diuresis. It acts directly by increasing urinary output.

The parathyroid hormone is also significant to regulation of fluids and electrolytes. The parathyroid hormone "is linked with the homeostatic regulation of calcium and phosphate ion concentration in body fluids. PTH acts mainly in the kidneys, bones, and gastrointestinal tract. Insufficient PTH can cause severe imbalance of calcium and phosphorus" (Luckmann and Sorensen 1974).

Chemical input in the form of electrolytes and neural input from the osmoreceptors of the hypothalamus positively influence the endocrine glands. The endocrine system, as a homeostatic regulator in response to chemical and neural inputs, stimulates hormones that regulate fluid and electrolytes at an adaptive level. When the chemical and neural inputs are unable to positively influence the endocrine glands and subsequently the hormone's influence upon target organs then the system becomes disorganized. When this response occurs, the individual becomes aware of his own ineffective behavior.

Fourth Set of Relationships

A fourth set of relationships provides the transition between adaptive and ineffective behaviors. This set of relationships involves the body's response to external and internal stimuli and state that such stimuli will alter those external and internal stimuli. This is predicated on the propositions labeled 1.1 to 5.1 in Table 5.1.

The previously discussed set of relationships involved both positive and negative feedback in response to external and internal stimuli. The exchange or feedback from external stimuli of fluid and electrolyte is accomplished by the gastrointestinal tract which then acts upon or alters internal stimuli. A major purpose of the gastrointestinal tract is the replenishment by absorption of the fluids and electrolytes lost to the external environment through the skin, respiratory tract, and kidney. Alteration of external and internal stimuli take into account four regulatory factors: regulation of extracellular volume, regulation of extracellular fluid osmolarity, regulation of electrolyte concentration, and regulation of acid-base balance.

The alteration of external and internal stimuli can initiate regulation of extracellular volume. "Volume regulation involves receptors which sense errors in volume, neural and humoral mechanisms which apprise the kidney of those errors, and renal mechanisms by which the kidneys compensate for them" (Pitts 1963). The volume receptors are sensitive to changes in the internal environment which is the extracellular fluid volume. According to Pitts,

> Changes in extracellular volume are sensed as changes in pressure or distention of the interstitial, venous, or arterial reservoirs or as changes in blood flow. . . . Several types of receptors responsive to as many stimuli probably activate a number of effector mechanisms and provide defense in depth.

The volume regulatory mechanism is independent of alterations in the regulator of extracellular fluid osmolarity.

Regulation of extracellular fluid osmolarity is accomplished by the osmoreceptor-antidiuretic hormone system. An increased extracellular fluid osmolarity acts as a stimulus to the hypothalamus which responds by sending nerve impulses to the neurohypophysis. The adaptive response is secretion of ADH which leads to increased water reabsorption and an overall reduced ECF osmolarity. Likewise a decreased extracellular fluid osmolarity causes osmosis of water into the fluid chambers of the osmoreceptors. The osmosis causes the osmoreceptors to swell, thereby decreasing their rate of impulse discharge. Therefore the body responds to alteration in osmolarity stimuli through chemical and neural feedback.

The third regulatory factor involves regulation of electrolyte concentration. As mentioned previously, electrolyte concentration must be carefully regulated because even small changes can lead to alterations in body function. Hypokalemia, for example, increases the electrical potential across nerve and muscle membranes. The ineffective response is paralysis. Furthermore, hypokalemia seems to elicit a negative feedback response that restricts aldosterone secretion. The goal is to maintain electrolyte balance. Therefore changes in the body's response to external intake of electrolytes and internal utilization of those same electrolytes will alter the external and internal stimuli.

A final regulatory factor to be considered is regulation of acid-base balance. The body attempts to prevent acidosis or alkalosis. To accomplish this goal, the body utilizes various control systems. All the body fluids contain buffer systems which seem to prevent unusual alterations in the hydrogen ion concentration. When the hydrogen ion concentration changes, the pulmonary system responds through pulmonary ventilation by altering carbon dioxide removal from the body fluid. The result is a shift of hydrogen ions towards normalcy. As the hydrogen ion concentration shifts towards normalcy, the kidneys excrete whatever is necessary to readjust hydrogen ion concentration, namely, an acid or an alkaline urine (Milhorn 1966).

External and internal stimuli, through regulation of extracellular volume, extracellular fluid osmolarity, electrolyte concentration, and acid-base balance, alter those external and internal stimuli. This regulatory process takes into account both negative and positive feedback. The body when confronted with an alteration in fluid and electrolyte balance seeks to positively adapt to the alteration by negating the potentially ineffective stimuli. The individual who experiences fluid and electrolyte deficit or excess behaves in such a way as to restore balance. Therefore action upon internal and external stimuli causes the fluid and electrolytes to be regulated at a level above or below that which contributed to the negative feedback. The entire process is considered to be adaptive. As pointed out earlier, other regulatory systems become involved.

The fourth set of relationships has an interadaptive quality and signifies a linkage between adaptive and ineffective regulatory responses. There are times when the fourth set of relationships fails to successfully alter internal and external stimuli in an adaptive way. Instead the intact organ or system responds in a ineffective manner.

Fifth Set of Relationships

In the fifth set of relationships, the magnitude of the external and internal stimuli may be so great that the adaptive system cannot return the body to a state of dynamic equilibrium. This includes propositions 1.1 to 5.1 in Table 5.1.

When fluid and electrolyte imbalance exceed the body's ability to restore equilibrium, regulatory mechanisms cannot be depended upon to resist further imbalance. External and internal stimuli may be so great that the body cannot return to equilibrium. Elevated or decreased fluid and electrolyte levels activate other systems which attempt to restore equilibrium. If regulatory mechanisms fail, the result is disorganization and possibly death.

The ineffective responses to be covered will be discussed under the heading of deficit or excess. Each ineffective response within the general categories will be discussed according to regulatory behaviors, focal stimuli, manipulation of contextual stimuli, and a brief discussion of residual stimuli.

Deficit in fluid and electrolytes

A deficit in fluid volume consists of dehydration whereby the body experiences a state of excessive fluid loss. The individual's biological being is dependent upon adequate performance by the body fluids of their functions of transportation of nutrient and excretory materials and of temperature and chemical regulation. Dehydration not only implies loss of fluid but of electrolytes as well. Electrolyte deficits include decreased sodium, potassium, calcium, and magnesium levels. Deficit in fluid and electrolytes will each exhibit specific regulatory behaviors.

Regulatory Behaviors. In dehydration the regulatory behaviors depend upon the severity of the fluid loss. MacBryde and Blacklow (1970) have identified three states and degrees of dehydration as shown in Table 9.1.

Just as dehydration has specific regulatory behaviors, deficiencies in electrolytes such as sodium, potassium, calcium, and magnesium also manifest specific behaviors unique to each as shown in Table 9.2. Sodium imbalance affects blood volume and blood pressure as well as the nervous system. Hypokalemia or potassium deficit affects cellular metabolism. The altered cellular metabolism affects other systems including the cardiovascular, renal, gastrointestinal, and respiratory systems. Calcium imbalance affects the bones, kidneys, and gastrointestinal tract. Lastly

TABLE **9.1**   Regulatory Behaviors in Dehydration

Stages	Regulatory Behaviors
1. Simple dehydration	Dry skin and mucous membrane
	Weight loss
	Thirst
	Nausea
	Fatigue
	Anorexia
	Oliguria
2. Moderate dehydration	Dry skin
	Weakness
	Faintness
	Fever
	Weak pulse
	Shock
	Coma
3. Severe dehydration	All previous regulatory behaviors
	Uremia
	Acidosis

TABLE **9.2**   Regulatory Behaviors in Electrolyte Deficiencies

Sodium	Potassium	Calcium	Magnesium
Weakness	Anorexia	Tonic muscle spasm	Tetany
Muscle cramps	Weakness	Tingling fingers	Hyperactive reflexes
Lassitude	Lethargy	Fatigue	Facial twitching
Apathy	Irritability	Trousseau's sign	Jerking
Anorexia	Flaccid paralysis	Positive Chvostch's sign	Convulsions
Hypotension	Arrhythmias	Convulsions	Hallucinations
Stupor	Congestive heart	Arrhythmias	Delusion
Confusion	failure	Laryngospasm	Combative behavior
Delusion	Paralytic ileus		

magnesium deficiency is characterized by increased neuromuscular and central nervous system irritability.

With an abnormal loss of sodium bicarbonate ($NaHCO_3$), the patient experiences acidosis. Metabolic and respiratory acidosis each manifest their own regulatory behaviors. These behaviors can be grouped as shown in Table 9.3.

TABLE 9.3 Regulatory Behaviors in Acidosis

Metabolic Acidosis	Respiratory Acidosis
Lethargy	Weakness
Kussmaul's respiration	Dyspnea
Stupor	Disorientation
Coma	Confusion
Death	Coma
	Death

Focal Stimuli.   There may be several factors operative in the production of dehydration. According to the analysis of MacBryde and Blacklow (1970), the following focal stimuli contribute to dehydration:

1. Failure of fluid intake
2. Failure of absorption
   (a) Diarrhea
   (b) Intestinal disorder
3. Loss from gastrointestinal tract
   (a) Vomiting
   (b) Diarrhea
4. Excess renal excretion due to renal factors
   (a) Failure of tubular reabsorption
5. Excess renal excretion due to prerenal factors
   (a) Disturbed body fluid chemistry
6. Excessive perspiration or vaporization
7. Loss from wounds or burns
   (a) Hemorrhage

Sodium deficiency is significant because its primary function is to control the distribution of water throughout the body. According to Roy's (1976) analysis, the focal stimuli contributing to a sodium deficit can be grouped into the following three categories:

1. Depletional hyponatremia: loss of sodium without a proportionate loss of water
   (a) Diuretics
   (b) Diarrhea, drainage, fistulas, and gastrointestinal suctioning
   (c) Adrenal insufficiency
   (d) Renal disease where tubules are unable to reabsorb sodium
2. Dilutional hyponatremia: water replacement without concomitant sodium replacement

(a) Excessive perspiration
(b) Excessive plain water enema
(c) Electrolyte free parenteral fluids
(d) Psychologic polydipsia
3. Conditions with unclear etiology
(a) Inappropriate ADH syndrome
(b) Congestive heart failure
(c) Cirrhosis of liver

Potassium deficiency affects the intracellular integrity and osmolarity. Because potassium is poorly conserved, its level in the body is dependent upon daily intake. According to Luckmann and Sorensen (1974) the focal stimuli contributing to potassium deficiency consist of the following:

1. Inadequate potassium intake
   (a) Nausea
   (b) Acute alcoholism
   (c) Dieting
   (d) Poor dietary intake
   (e) Parenteral fluids high sodium and low potassium
2. Loss through gastrointestinal tract
   (a) Diarrhea
   (b) Vomiting
   (c) Fistulas
3. Loss through therapeutic agents
   (a) Gastrointestinal suctioning
   (b) Steroid therapy
   (c) Diuretics
   (d) Colostomy and/or ileostomy
   (e) Excessive enemas
4. Hyperaldosteronism
5. Trauma
   (a) Burns
   (b) Crushing injuries
6. Renal disorders with deficit of tubular reabsorption

Calcium deficiency is significant because of its action upon bone structure and neuromuscular and cardiac activity. Specifically, calcium is necessary for normal blood coagulation, regulatory effect over nerve impulse, and influence over contractility and excitability of skeletal muscles. Focal stimuli contributing to a calcium deficit consist of the following:

1. Acute pancreatitis

2. Hypoparathyroidism
3. Vitamin D deficiency
4. Excessive administration of citrated blood
5. Alkalosis

Magnesium as an electrolyte is gaining more chemical attention. Magnesium is necessary for neuromuscular integration. A major deficit therefore causes central nervous system irritability leading to other regulatory behaviors. Focal stimuli contributing to a magnesium deficit consist of the following:

1. Low magnesium intake
2. Losses through gastrointestinal tract
3. Chronic alcoholism
4. Chronic nephritis
5. Severe diarrhea
6. Intestinal malabsorption
7. Hypoparathyroidism

The maintenance of hydrogen ion balance depends upon adaptive responses of the renal, pulmonary, and nervous system. When the body is exposed to a deficit of hydrogen ion, the physiological response is alkalosis. The two types of alkalosis to be considered are metabolic alkalosis and respiratory alkalosis.

With metabolic alkalosis there is a tremendous loss of nonvolatile hydrogen ion (H) from the body or an abnormal gain in bicarbonate (HCO_3) by extracellular fluid. Focal stimuli contributing to metabolic alkalosis consist of the following:

1. Excessive alkaline intake
2. Loss of gastric contents
   (a) Suctioning
   (b) Vomiting
3. Hypokalemia

Respiratory alkalosis can result from an excessive secretion of carbon dioxide. The stimulus that initiates carbon dioxide loss is hyperventilation. When carbon dioxide is greatly reduced, hydrogen ion concentration is also decreased. Focal stimuli contributing to respiratory alkalosis consist of the following:

1. Hyperventilation
   (a) Hysteria and anxiety reactions

(b) Severe exercise
(c) Anoxia at high altitudes
2. Overstimulation of respiratory center
   (a) Fever
   (b) Meningitis and encephalitis
   (c) Aspirin poisoning
   (d) Intracranial surgery

In summary, deficits in fluid and electrolytes include dehydration or decreased extracellular water volume; decreased sodium, potassium, calcium, and/or magnesium levels; and decreased hydrogen ion concentration leading to metabolic and respiratory alkalosis.

Excess in fluid and electrolyte

An excess in fluid is manifested as edema or increased extracellular water volume. Edema is the result of expansion of the extracellular fluid of the body. Edema can be defined as "any abnormal accumulation of extravascular extracellular (interstitial) fluid. The source of fluid is the blood plasma. All edema comes from the circulating blood and its composition is similar to that of plasma containing electrolytes, glucose, urea, creatinine, amino acids, and various other diffusible crystalloid substances" (Schroeder 1970). In edematous states, electrolytes such as sodium, potassium, calcium, or magnesium may be altered. There may also be changes in hydrogen ion concentration. Excess in fluid, electrolytes, and hydrogen ion will each exhibit specific regulatory behaviors and be caused by specific focal stimuli.

Regulatory Behaviors.   The major pathological effect of excess volume is an overloading of all fluid compartments with water and saline. It should be noted that with excess extracellular volume there is no change in the tonicity of body fluid or in the osmolarity of the cells. This includes the brain cells. The following are regulatory behaviors associated with edema or increased extracellular water volume.

1. Weight gain
2. Pitting edema
3. Pulmonary edema
   (a) Dyspnea
   (b) Cough
   (c) Sweating
   (d) Pinkish sputum

4. Puffy eyelids
5. Ascites

Just as edema or increased extracellular water volume has specific regulatory behaviors, an excess in electrolytes such as sodium, potassium, calcium, and magnesium also manifest specific behaviors. These are shown in Table 9.4.

Normally the body attempts to dilute excess hydrogen ions. For example, hydrogen ions can become excessively concentrated in a single tissue or area of the body. When hydrogen ions accumulate, the excess is removed by circulation and thereby distributed to other areas of the body. However, when this line of adaptive defense is stressed beyond its capacity, hydrogen ions accumulate, leading to two maladaptive responses. These responses are metabolic acidosis and respiratory acidosis.

Metabolic acidosis implies that excessive nonvolatile or metabolic hydrogen ions are being retained or HCO_3 is being lost at high rates via the kidneys. In respiratory acidosis, hydrogen ions are being retained in the body fluid as excess carbonic acid (H_2CO_3). Each type of acidosis has its own regulatory behaviors (see Table 9.3).

In summary, there are specific regulatory behaviors for each kind of excess, whether sodium, potassium, calcium, or magnesium levels; or increased hydrogen concentration. In addition each excess is caused by its own specific focal stimuli.

Focal Stimuli.   Edematous conditions or excess extracellular fluid

TABLE **9.4** Regulatory Behaviors in Excess of Electrolytes

Sodium	Potassium	Calcium	Magnesium
Confusion	Weakness	Bone pain	Hypotension
Dullness	Flaccid paralysis	Osteoporosis	Sedation
Apathy	Bradycardia	Osteomalacia	Respiratory
Coma	Cardiac arrest	Kidney stones	embarrassment
	Oliguria to anuria	Renal failure	Arrhythmias
		Diarrhea	
		Constipation	
		Anorexia	
		Nausea	
		Atony of	
		Intestinal tract	
		Lethargy	
		Confusion and	
		irritability	

volume may be caused by several focal stimuli. The following list may not include all possible stimuli:

1. Excessive parenteral fluid volume
2. Congestive heart failure
3. Renal failure
4. Hepatic disease
5. Cerebral disease
6. Increased ADH
7. Steroid therapy

An excessive amount of sodium (hypernatremia) can contribute to overhydration because sodium tends to retain water. The following focal stimuli contribute to hypernatremia:

1. Excess intake
   (a) Overtransfusion of hypertonic sodium-containing fluid
   (b) Excess oral intake of salt
2. Inability to excrete sodium
   (a) Hyperaldosteronism (Cushing's syndrome)
   (b) Excessive corticosteroids

Potassium excess or hyperkalemia leads to alteration of neuromuscular, cardiac, and cellular function. Kidney function is also disturbed with potassium disequilibrium since the kidney is the major organ of potassium excretion. The following focal stimuli contribute to hyperkalemia:

1. Decreased renal excretion of potassium
   (a) Oliguria or anuria
   (b) Azotemia
   (c) Addison's disease
   (d) Aldosterone antagonistic diuretics
2. Increased catabolism of endogenous proteins
   (a) Trauma
   (b) Burns
   (c) Untreated diabetic coma
3. Excessive administration of potassium

It was pointed out that calcium deficit primarily affects the neuromuscular system. Calcium excess or hypercalcemia tends to cause diffuse symptoms affecting many body systems. Focal stimuli contributing to hypercalcemia include of the following:

1. Hyperparathyroidism
2. Excessive mobilization and absorption of calcium
3. Decreased renal excretion of calcium
4. Excessive intake of vitamin D

Magnesium is responsible for neuromuscular integration. Therefore excess magnesium tends to act as a sedative to the neuromuscular system. The following focal stimuli contribute to excess magnesium:

1. Renal insufficiency
2. Overdose of magnesium
3. Enemas with magnesium sulfate
4. Use of antacids such as Gelusil

An excess of hydrogen ions takes the maladaptive form of metabolic acidosis and respiratory acidosis. With metabolic acidosis there is excessive loss of sodium bicarbonate ($NaHCO_3$) in conjunction with overproduction and retention of nonvolatile acids. In respiratory acidosis the primary cause is excess retention of CO_2. Both ineffective states are caused by specific, yet independent, focal stimuli (see Table 9.5).

TABLE **9.5** Focal Stimuli in Acidosis

Metabolic Acidosis	*Respiratory Acidosis*

1. Increased intake of hydrogen ions
2. Increased formation of hydrogen ions
  (a) Diabetes mellitus
  (b) Increased fat metabolism
3. Retention of hydrogen ions
  (a) Chronic renal failure
4. Increased loss of hydroxyl (OH) ions
  (a) Diarrhea
  (b) Ileostomy
  (c) Suctioning
  (d) Pancreatic fistula
	1. Hypoventilation
	2. Damaged respiratory center
	3. Chronic respiratory disease
	  (a) Emphysema
	  (b) Chronic bronchitis
	4. Hypothermia

Manipulating the stimuli

Given that the magnitude of the external and internal stimuli are so great that the adaptive systems cannot return the body to a state of dynamic equilibrium, the nurse intervenes by manipulating stimuli in an attempt to maintain or restore fluid and electrolyte balance. In order to manipulate stimuli, the nurse assesses various influencing factors which contribute to the ineffective responses. The influencing factors consist of focal, contextual, and residual stimuli. Focal stimuli were previously discussed in terms of pathophysiologically ineffective response. Contextual and residual stimuli will be discussed in relationship to nursing interventions.

Contextual stimuli

The nurse alters ineffective regulatory responses from external and internal stimuli through manipulation of the following contextual stimuli: fluid, activity, nutrition, communication, aeration, and pain.

Fluids. Fluid intake is balanced with fluid loss when the ability of the kidneys as a regulatory system is impaired. Therefore a primary nursing goal is the accurate measurement of fluid loss so that correct fluid replacement can be given. Fluid management involves assessment of sensible and insensible loss.

INTERSTITIAL EDEMA. Edema can be caused by increased capillary permeability, reduced colloid osmotic pressure of the blood, and decreased tissue perfusion. It is important to assess the mechanisms of interstitial edema caused by hypoproteinemia. The proteins are the only dissolved substances of the plasma that do not diffuse readily into the interstitial fluid. When small quantities of proteins do diffuse into the interstitial fluid, these are soon removed from the interstitial spaces by way of the lymph vessels. Therefore, the dissolved proteins of the plasma and interstitial fluids are responsible for the osmotic pressure that develops at the capillary membrane. Hypoproteinemia results in a decrease in serum osmotic pressure and movement of fluid out of the capillaries and into the body tissue.

The patient with maladapting kidneys is unable to excrete fluid and electrolytes. The result is cerebral, pulmonary, and peripheral edema as well as elevated sodium, potassium, calcium, and magnesium levels. The nurse is most concerned by the life-threatening problem of pulmonary edema. She assesses changes in her patient's behavior, blood gases, breath sounds, respiratory rate, and color. Internal interstitial edema creates excessive external stimuli in the form of skin breakdown. In addition, the skin becomes a vehicle for insensible loss of fluid. The nurse also keeps in mind that dry, flaky, itching skin can be caused by disturbances in calcium and phosphorus balance.

INTAKE. Intake involves physiological intake of oral and parenteral fluids as well as environmental intake. Because the body is unable to excrete fluids, oral intake may be restricted. The amount of oral restriction depends upon the degree of edema as determined by the physical appearance of the patient and by presence of weight gain. The patient who has oliguria or anuria should not receive abundant fluid administration as a means of compensation. Intake is based on the amount of fluid loss. The anuric patient may be limited to 1,000 cc per day. For the patient experiencing dehydration or a deficit of extracellular water volume, three goals of increasing fluid intake are significant: restoration of total body fluid volume to normal, restoration of electrolytes, and restoration of acid-base balance. To faciliate restoration of fluid to normal without reliance upon renal and gastrointestinal regulatory activity, the fluids given are similar to normal interstitial fluids. This is accomplished through parenteral fluids.

Parenteral fluid intake may be restricted or increased. There are instances in which the patient's total intake may be 1,200 to 1,500 cc a day, including both oral and parenteral fluids. If the patient is hyperkalemic, parenteral administration of 10 percent dextrose and water with insulin may be given. Insulin causes glucose to go into the cell. As glucose moves inside the cell, it takes potassium with it and reduces the serum potassium. Patients with debilitating problems such as renal failure can benefit from administration of hyperalimentation solution. Hyperalimentation is the infusion of basic nutrients in amounts large enough to achieve tissue synthesis and growth. Electrolytes are included in the hyperalimentation solution. Depending upon the patient's potassium level, potassium can be added to the solution. Potassium is needed for the transport of glucose and amino acids across the cell membrane. Calcium, magnesium, and phosphorus are given when needed.

The dehydrated patient may need to have his fluid and electrolyte intake increased. Restoration of total fluid volume including electrolytes can be accomplished through administration of isotonic sodium chloride. Isotonic sodium chloride is useful when two factors are present: renal function is normal, and potassium has not been withdrawn from the cells. When fluid deficit is primarily a water deficit with resulting hypernatremia, it may be imperative to give parenteral fluids containing no sodium chloride.

The nurse also assesses her pateint's environmental intake to protect her patient from potential hazards in his environment. The most significant environmental hazard besides stress is infection. The nurse assesses her patient for signs of infection. These include malaise, fatigue, increased heart rate, increased blood count, and rapid respiration. If the patient's resistance to infection is greatly reduced, he may need to be isolated from others to ensure his protection.

OUTPUT. Output consists of sensible loss such as urine, stool, and emesis; diagnostic procedures including blood pressure, pulse, respirations, temperature, specific gravity, daily weight, and central venous pressure; and laboratory tests such as serum electrolytes, BUN, creatinine, hemoglobin, hematocrit, uric acid, and white blood count.

Both sensible and insensible water losses are replaced with equal amounts of water in an attempt to maintain a state of balanced hydrations. Urinary output can safely range between 25 and 500 cc per hour. The nurse can report hourly output below or above these paramenters. In assessing renal status, the nurse realizes that urine output is a better guide than blood pressure to the state of blood supply to the kidneys. The expected urine output may vary with each patient and is dependent upon his overall extracellular volume status.

Besides assessing urine volume, the nurse also assesses its color and odor. Deep amber urine may indicate dehydration. Straw-colored urine may indicate the kidneys' inability to concentrate urine. Urine that is cloudy in appearance may indicate the presence of pus or proteins. A patient with nephrotic syndrome may be excreting large amounts of protein in his urine. Naturally urine should be somewhat odorless. The presence of precipitation in the urine, strong odor, or changes in color should alert the nurse that a potential problem exists.

Other sensible losses include stool, emesis, and blood. Intestinal hypermotility shortens the time for absorption of intestinal fluids and results in increased fluid loss in bowel movements. The nurse realizes that liquid stools contain water and electrolytes derived from secretions, from ingested food and fluids, and from extracellular fluid brought into the bowel to render ingested substances isotonic. The nurse should be alert for symptoms of volume depletion. Electrolytes lost through diarrhea and vomiting may alter other body systems. All losses derived from stool, emesis, or blood should be recorded and included in the total output.

Blood pressure variations are helpful in evaluating body fluid disturbances. Consequently arterial blood pressure can be taken frequently in order to determine whether there are real or potential water and electrolyte balance problems. If the patient is receiving antihypertensive drugs, the nurse will need to make frequent assessments of arterial pressure. Too rapid a decrease in arterial pressure may be harmful to renal function. Decreased blood pressure can lead to a drop in glomerular filtration rate, decreased renal perfusion, and further renal damage.

The patient's pulse can be evaluated in terms of rate, volume, and regularity. A weak pulse may indicate volume deficit and electrolyte imbalance. A bounding pulse may indicate volume excess. Because of alterations in potassium or calcium and digitalis therapy, the patient may develop arrhythmias. Therefore the patient's pulse can be assessed for regularity.

Respirations become important in assessing changes in body pH. The nurse realizes that the lungs play a major role in regulating body pH by varying the amount of carbon dioxide retention. The nurse assesses her patient's respirations for rate, depth, and regularity. Respirations change with metabolic acidosis and metabolic alkalosis. Respirations are assessed along with the patient's pulse rate and temperature. Besides rate the nurse assesses both depth and regularity.

Temperature is also assessed in conjunction with pulse and respirations. The frequency is determined by the absence or presence of fever. Fever causes an increase in metabolism, hyperpnea, and loss of body fluids. Likewise a decrease in temperature can indicate sodium depletion and/or fluid volume deficit. Temperature elevation may indicate excess fluid loss or dehydration. In validating dehydration, the nurse may observe her patient's hematocrit levels and assess skin turgor.

Specific gravity is another diagnostic procedure that provides the nurse with information regarding the kidney's ability to concentrate urine. Specific gravity reflects osmolarity which is determined by the presence in the urine of substances of low molecular weight such as urea, potassium, sodium, and glucose. A low specific gravity of 1.002 to 1.010 characterizes the oliguric phase. Other factors need to be assessed when a low specific gravity is discovered. It can be determined whether or not the patient is on a protein or sodium-restricted diet and if he has received a diuretic. Each of these factors is capable of producing a low specific gravity.

Daily body weights are necessary for determining the effectiveness of various therapeutic measures which alter fluid volume. Changes in daily weight reflect changes in fluid volume. A body weight that reaches stability over a period of days should not necessarily foster the nurse's sense of security. Fluids can pool in the body and create volume deficits not indicated by weight changes. Therefore a stable daily weight may not accurately reflect the internal instability of shifting fluid volume.

Central venous pressure is another diagnostic procedure to determine volume status of the patient. It provides momentary information regarding pressure in the right atrium of the heart. An increase beyond 12 cm can indicate problems such as hypervolemia, cardiac tamponade, and congestive heart failure. A decrease in venous pressure below the zero level can indicate possible hypovolemia. Daily weight, central venous pressure, and intake-output measurements are three diagnostic measures of significance in accurately determining the patient's fluid volume.

Laboratory tests of significance to the nurse measure serum electrolytes such as potassium, sodium, and calcium; substances derived from protein metabolism including BUN, creatinine, and uric acid; hemoglobin and hematocrit; and white blood count. Hyperkalemia can be caused by several related factors; namely, increased dietary intake of potassium, protein breakdown which releases intracellular potassium into the blood, acidosis, and hyponatremia. The nurse can also keep in mind the interrelationship between sodium and potassium. The distal tubule of the nephron secretes potassium and a high level of sodium enhances this process. However, low sodium levels, possibly associated with dietary restriction or diuretic therapy, lead to an increase in potassium. Hyponatremia can also occur through sensible loss of vomiting or diarrhea and insensible loss of sweating. Just as sodium and potassium are interrelated, calcium and phosphorus are also interchangeable. Low calcium levels are associated with an elevated phosphorus level.

Substances derived from protein metabolism are urea, creatinine, and uric acid. Urea, the end product of nitrogen metabolism, is formed in the liver and excreted by the kidneys. Blood urea levels (BUN) are usually elevated in uremia. Urea levels can be influenced by protein intake, rate of protein metabolism, and state of hydration. Creatinine is the end product of creatine metabolism. Because creatinine is related to muscle mass, it is less affected by external factors than BUN. Uric acid is the end product of purine metabolism. Purine is also a nitrogenous base. Uric acid is increased in maladaptive problems such as renal failure.

Patients with maladapting kidneys have a tendency to be anemic and susceptible to infection. The anemia is caused by lack of erythropoietic hormone which causes new blood cells to be produced by the bone marrow. The kidneys are normally responsible for secreting this hormone. However, in kidney failure the amount secreted is inadequate, causing the patient to become anemic. Furthermore, azotemia seems to depress the bone marrow. The nurse can observe her patient's red blood cell count including hemoglobin and hematocrit. Because of the patient's lowered resistance to infection, she must also be aware of change in white blood count.

Activity.   Because fluid and electrolyte alterations can lead to neuromuscular and other disturbances, the nurse needs to assess her patient according to four components: physical activity, cardiopulmonary activity, metabolic activity and mental activity.

Physical activity may need to be restricted for the patient with fluid excess or deficit and electrolyte imbalance involving neuromuscular changes. Furthermore, the patient with maladapting kidneys experiences anemia. The anemic patient responds to the demands of physical activity with a reduced energy level. Fatigue may be a sign of electrolyte imbalance. For the patient with increased uric acid levels and subsequent joint pain, physical activity may be painful. The nurse prepares her patient for ambulation by gently exercising his joints and maintaining muscle tone. Mobility also serves to encourage the patient because it indicates that his maladaptive fluid and electrolyte problem has stabilized. Fears of dependence and loss of personal dignity are replaced with feelings of independence and self-worth.

If the patient has a severe fluid and electrolyte imbalance resulting in arrhythmias, a cardioscope may become necessary. The cardioscope is a vehicle through which cardiac status can be consistently assessed. The nurse can also assess changes in behavior, vital signs, or color.

The patient's pulmonary status may vary in accordance with changes in acid-base balance. For example, if the patient experiences metabolic acidosis associated with renal failure or diabetes, his pulmonary system compensates. The response is pulmonary alkalosis. The nurse assesses Kussmaul's respiratory pattern with its rapid and deep breathing pattern.

Metabloic acidosis is associated with various maladaptive problems. One such problem is uremia. The uremic patient may have a serum bicarbonate level of 16 to 18mEq/l (normal 24 mEq/l). It may be difficult to return bicarbonate levels to within a normal range. The process may also precipitate tetany in the patient with decreased calcium. Consequently calcium gluconate may need to be given simultaneously with sodium bicarbonate.

The patient with fluid and electrolyte imbalance may experience psychological changes. The nurse may discover that her patient is lethargic, less mentally acute, and unable to concentrate. The confused patient needs to be protected from environmental injury. If the patient's biological ineffective response is uremia, his behavioral response may be paranoia or hallucinations.

Nutrition.   Protein is responsible for maintaining colloid osmotic pressure. Its loss creates volume shifts leading to ascites and edema. A patient with nephrotic syndrome may need a diet high in protein. On the other hand, a patient with renal failure will be placed on a low-protein diet. In renal failure the end products of protein metabolism are excreted at a decreased rate. Furthermore the diet must include calories to prevent the body's breakdown of protein for energy. If the patient is unable to eat because of nausea or anorexia, it may be necessary to provide the necessary nutrients through nasogastric feedings or parenteral hyperalimenation.

Potassium and sodium are two significant electrolytes that may need to be increased or decreased. If the patient is receiving diuretics or is in the diuretic phase of his renal disorganization, potassium is lost. Careful observation of serum potassium levels will indicate the necessary potassium intake. It is also important to assess sodium levels. Depending upon the biological problem, sodium may need to be greatly restricted. Patients with congestive heart failure, hypertension, or renal failure require a low-sodium diet.

Spiritual nutrition may also be important to the patient. Spiritual nutrition should be provided before the patient becomes too confused or lethargic to derive comfort. As soon as possible a minister, priest, or rabbi should be provided. Spiritual consolation may serve to comfort the depressed or discouraged patient.

Communication.   The patient needs to feel he can communicate his fears and concerns with someone in the environment. The individual most frequently within his environment is the nurse. She listens to his concerns or complaints and assesses changes in his behavior.

As the patient's fluid and electrolyte imbalance becomes more unstable or critical, his behavioral response may change. He may be oriented and alert one hour and disoriented or lethargic the next. The changes can reflect metabolic problems, blood gas changes, or electrolyte imbalance.

Aeration.   Psychological aeration implies that the patient be encouraged to ventilate his feelings regarding an ineffective body part, change in lifestyle, or future prognosis. Environmental aeration is an area in which the nurse can intervene. She protects her patient from distressing factors within his environment. The patient whose bed is close to the window may become diaphoretic. Diaphoresis may contribute to further volume depletion in the dehydrated patient, as he experiences greater insensible loss of water.

Pulmonary aeration is assessed according to the lungs' ability to compensate for metabolic acidosis. The lungs become a primary vehicle for stabilizing the body's pH. Through Kussmaul's breathing, excess carbon dioxide is exhaled. Because of the lungs' significance in maintaining a stable acid-base balance, they must be protected. Diseased lungs can inhibit acid-base balance because they become acidotic. When the kidneys are diseased, the result is metabolic acidosis with uncompensating respiratory acidosis. If the pulmonary system is ineffective in restoring the body's pH to a more normal level, sodium bicarbonate can be administered. Finally it may become necessary to utilize a volume respirator.

Pain.   Psychological pain cannot be alleviated with narcotics, analgesics, or tranquilizers. Such pain may originate because the individual feels his sense of personal integrity is being threatened. He may be forced to alter or completely change his life style. Psychological pain can be just as severe as physiological pain, even though it is less easily recognized. Behaviorally the patient may exhibit depression, tearfulness, or quietness.

Residual stimuli

Residual stimuli may include a history of fluid, electrolyte, and acid-base disturbances; previous hospitalization for cardiac and renal dysfunction; use of diuretics; pain upon urination; retention of fluid manifested as edema; and alteration in urinary output pattern.

Example of Hypothesis for Practice

We have focused on the process of theorizing with the fluid and electrolyte physiological mode. Based on our theorizing with the fluid and electrolyte mode, we can postulate any number of hypotheses that can be tested. The theorizing encompasses the four sets of relationships and their related propositions. In addition the hypotheses can be used as a guide for practice. An example of a possible hypothesis will be discussed.

The hypothesis may be stated as follows: If the nurse helps the patient maintain an optimal level of hydration, the patient will perform at a higher cellular level. The reason for this hypothesis is drawn from the first set of relationships which are based on propositions. The reasons are shown below:

General Statement: The magnitude of the internal and external stimuli will positively influence the magnitude of the physiological response of an intact system.

Specific Statement: The level of hydration achieved will positively influence the level of fluid and electrolyte balance.

The nurse utilizes the four sets of relationships to theorize regarding fluid and electrolytes. The theorizing permits hypothesis generation even when the nurse manipulates the contextual stimuli. With each component of the contextual stimuli, the nurse can hypothesize regarding patient care. If the nurse finds evidence of significance for a hypothesis, the nursing activity specified in the research protocol can become a prescription for practice in situations where nursing diagnosis warrants this intervention or interventions identified in the contextual stimuli section.

Summary

Fluid and electrolytes have been examined according to four sets of relationships that focus on adaptive regulatory responses. These responses take into account external and internal stimuli. The body attempts to adapt to chemical and neural inputs as they apply to fluid and electrolytes. However ineffective responses occur when the magnitude of external and internal stimuli are greater than the body's ability to maintain a state of dynamic equilibrium. The overall results leads to disequilibrium and disease.

When the external and internal stimuli exceeds the system's ability to adapt, the nurse assesses focal stimuli, regulatory behaviors, manipulation of contextual stimuli, and a brief discussion of residual stimuli. Lastly the nurse generates hypotheses based upon the theorizing and propositions dealing with the fluid and electrolyte mode.

References and Additional Readings

Burgess, Audrey. *The Nurse's Guide to Fluid and Electrolyte Balance.* New York: McGraw-Hill, 1979.

Freedman, Philip. "Acute Renal Failure," *Heart and Lung,* 4, no. 6 (November-December 1975): 873–78.

Grant, Marcia, and Winifred Kubo. "Assessing a Patient's Hydration Status," *American Journal of Nursing,* 75, no. 8 (August 1975): 1306–11.

Harrington, Joan, and Etta Brener. *Patient Care in Renal Failure.* Philadelphia: Saunders, 1973.

Hoops, Ellen. "Renal Function and Diuretics," *Critical Care Update,* 5, no. 2 (February 1978): 23–26.

Johnson, Katheryn. "Nursing Care of the Patient with Acute Renal Failure," *Nursing Clinics of North America,* 10, no. 3 (September 1975): 421–30.

Juliani, Louise. "Assessing Renal Function," *Nursing,* 8, no. 1 (January 1978): 34–35.

Kemp, Ginny, and Doug Kemp. "Diuretics," *American Journal of Nursing,* 78, no. 6 (June 1978): 106–110.

Kubo, Winifred. "Fluid and Electrolyte Problems," *Critical Care Update,* 6, no. 5 (May 1979): 5–14.

———. "The Syndrome of Inappropriate Secretion of Antidiuretic Hormone," *Heart and Lung,* 7, no. 3 (May-June 1978): 469–76.

Lancour, Jane. "ADH and Aldosterone: How to Recognize Their Effects," *Nursing,* (September 1978): 36–41.

Langley, L. L. *Homeostasis.* New York: Reinhold, 1965.

Luckmann, Joan, and Karen Sorensen. *Medical-Surgical Nursing: A Psychophysiological Approach.* Philadelphia: Saunders, 1974.

Luke, Barbara. "Nutrition in Renal Disease: The Adult on Dialysis," *American Journal of Nursing,* 79, no. 12 (December 1979).

MacBryde, Cyril, and Robert Blacklow, *Signs and Symptoms.* Philadelphia: Lippincott, 1970.

Milhorn, Howard. *The Application of Control Theory to Physiological Systems.* Philadelphia: Saunders, 1966.

Metheny, Norma, and William Snively. "Perioperative Fluids and Electrolytes," *American Journal of Nursing,* 78, no. 5 (May 1978): 840–45.

Oestreich, Sandy. "Rational Nursing Care In Chronic Renal Disease," *American Journal of Nursing,* 79, no. 6 (June 1979): 1096–99.

Pflaum, Sandra. "Investigation of Intake-Output as a Means of Assessing Body Fluid Balance," *Heart and Lung,* 8, no. 3 (May-June 1979): 495–98.

Pitts, Robert. *Physiology of the Kidney and Body Fluids.* Chicago: Year Book Medical Publishers, 1963.

Roberts, Sharon. "Renal Assessment: A Nursing Point of View," *Heart and Lung,* 8, no. 1 (January-February 1979): 105–13.

Roy, Sr. Callista. *Introduction to Nursing: An Adaptation Model.* Englewood Cliffs, N.J.: Prentice-Hall, 1976.

Schroeder, Henry. "Edema." In *Signs and Symptoms,* eds. Cyril MacBryde and Robert Blacklow. Philadelphia: Lippincott, 1970.

Sharer, JoEllen. "Reviewing Acid-Base Balance," *American Journal of Nursing,* 75, no. 6 (June 1975): 980–83.

Trunkey, Donald. "Review of Current Concepts in Fluid and Electrolyte Management," *Heart and Lung,* 4, no. 1 (January-February 1975): 115–21.

CHAPTER 10

Oxygen
and circulation

An individual's need for oxygen is a significant factor in his biological adaptive process. Oxygen is regulated in conjunction with related circulatory processes. The combined systems are responsible for delivering a sufficient amount of oxygenated blood to meet the body's need under a variety of conditions. It meets the body's metabolic needs by bringing oxygenated blood to all body tissue and subsequently removing the end products of metabolism. The entire process is a dynamic one which takes place during adaptive and ineffective responses.

Regulation of oxygen and circulation will be examined according to five sets of relationships which have been built upon a series on theoretical propositions. The fifth set of relationships will focus on ineffective problems associated with oxygen excess and deficits. Ineffective problems will be examined according to regulatory behavior, focal stimuli, manipulation of stimuli through nursing interventions that involve contextual stimuli, and a brief discussion of residual stimuli.

First Set of Relationships

The first set of relationships is as follows: The magnitude of the internal and external stimuli will positively influence the magnitude of the physiological responses of an intact system. This is predicated on the propositions indicated as 1.1 to 2.1, 3.2, and 4.4 in Table 5.1.

The respiratory center, located in the brainstem, adjusts the rate of alveolar ventilation to the demands of the body. The overall result is that the oxygen pressure of arterial blood (P_AO_2) and the carbon dioxide pressure of arterial blood (P_ACO_2) remains somewhat constant even during respiratory stress. Pulmonary ventilation is a process where gases are moved across the alveolar-capillary membrane. Therefore the rate of oxygen—carbon dioxide exchange depends upon metabolic and other physiological demands placed upon the individual.

Pulmonary ventilation is dependent upon external and internal stimuli. As the combined propositions indicate, the stimuli will influence the magnitude of physiological responses of the intact pulmonary system. External and internal stimuli can be categorized according to external and internal respiration.

Respiration is primarily concerned with the transport of oxygen from the external atmosphere to the cells. It also includes the transport of carbon dioxide and other cellular waste products from the cells back to the external atmosphere. According to Johnson (1966), external respiratory stimuli can be categorized into four major divisions:

1. Pulmonary ventilation: The volume and distribution of air ventilating the alveoli
2. Gas exchange: The transfer of oxygen and carbon dioxide between the alveoli and the blood
3. Transport: The carriage of oxygen and carbon dioxide by the blood and body fluids to and from the cells
4. Regulation: The control of the ventilatory and circulatory system by the response of specialized neuronal structure to changes in their environment

An intervening variable that links external and internal stimuli or external and internal environment is the transport of oxygen and carbon dioxide. The mechanism for transport is the cardiovascular or circulatory system. It is responsible for carrying the oxygen absorbed from the alveolar surface of the lungs to the tissues where it will be removed. The primary channel for this transport is the blood. The hemoglobin contained in the red blood cells enables the blood to carry large amounts of oxygen. Oxygen combines reversibly with hemoglobin and is transported in this form to the individual tissues of the body.

Internal respiration is the physiochemical and biochemical process of cellular metabolism in which oxygen is utilized and carbon dioxide is produced. Thus, the internal stimuli in oxygen regulation involve intracellular processes. It should be kept in mind that

> The internal distribution of carbon dioxide is managed by diffusion between compartments and by convection via circulation of blood. Interposed between the veins and the arteries in this convection system is a special mechanism, the lung, which forms the effective exchange surface between the organism and its external environment. [Yamamoto and Brobeck 1965]

Therefore external and internal respiration work together with the intervening variable of circulation to establish and maintain adaptive respiration. In adaptive respiration, the stimuli from external and internal respiration positively influence the physiological response of the intact respiratory-circulatory system. Altered external-internal stimuli are received and communicated via intact neural pathways. The neural communication brings us to the second set of relationships.

Second Set of Relationships

The second set of relationships states that intact neural pathways will positively influence neural output to effectors. This is predicated on the propositions labeled 3.1 to 2.1, and 4.4 in Table 5.1. The respiratory center is divided into three major areas: the medullary rhythmicity area, the apneustic area, and the pneumotaxic area. It is in the medullary rhythmicity area that the basic rhythm of respiration is established. When the individual is at rest, inspiration lasts approximately two seconds and expiration lasts three seconds. With increased respiration both processes are shortened. Likewise a decrease in respiration will lengthen the inspiration and expiration process. In the mechanism of rhythmicity controlled by the medullary area

> Two oscillating circuits are postulated: one for inspiration and one for expiration. However, the two circuits cannot oscillate simultaneously because they inhibit each other. Thus, when the inspiratory neurons are active the expiratory neurons are inactive, and the reverse effects occur when the expiratory neurons become active. Therefore, alteration occurs back and forth between inspiratory signals and expiratory signals, this process continuing indefinitely and causing the act of respiration. [Guyton 1971]

The apneustic area is located in the reticular substance of the pons. If the pons has been transected between the apneustic and pneumotaxic areas but remains connected to the medullary rhythmicity area, the pattern of respiration becomes prolonged inspiration and short respiration. This pattern is directly opposite to the pattern established by the medullary rhythmicity area. Likewise the pneumotaxic area is also located in the reticular substance of the pons. Stimulation of the pneumotaxic area can change the rate of respiration.

The respiratory center is influenced by motor neurons in the spinal cord and by the nuclei of some of the cranial nerves. Besides input from these neural pathways, the central respiratory center also receives input from the circulatory system. Therefore the respiratory center regulates the rhythm of the respiratory cycle and serves to integrate the input from other stimuli. For example, the neural impulses generated in the central respiratory center are transmitted to the motor neurons of the major thoracic respiratory muscles as well as to those of the sensory muscles.

A significant aspect of the neural communication center is the stretch receptor mechanism. Stretch receptors in the wall of the ascending aorta and the carotid sinuses send impulses to the medullary center which cause it to inhibit inspiration. Likewise when these same receptors are stimulated by a decrease in vascular wall tension, the result is an increase in minute ventilation (Sodeman 1968). The pulmonary stretch receptors are of significance in certain types of dyspnea.

An unpleasant acceleration of breathing can be produced by pulmonary vascular congestion or edema, diffuse interstitial processes or atelectsis. All these abnormalities reduce the compliance of the lung and sensitize the stretch receptors. [Sodeman and Sodeman 1968]

Furthermore there are receptors with both the small airways of the lungs and the vascular bed. The small airways are sensitive to external stimuli from chemical irritants. These airways are activated through vagal affects producing a cough and bronchoconstriction. On the other hand the receptors in the vascular bed are stimulated by embolism. The overall response is initial apnea, followed by the regulatory behavior of rapid shallow breathing, bradycardia, hypotension, and bronchoconstriction. It is believed that this reflex activity is mediated through both the vagi and the sympathetic afferents (Sodeman and Sodeman 1968).

Intact neural pathways connecting the respiratory center and the receptors positively influence neural output to effectors. Without the inhibitory-facilitating response of the respiratory system, the output in terms of rate and rhythm would be out of control. The controlling system or respiratory center responds to the many receptors to cause the appropriate response. The overall output of the controlling system is assessed to be the steady maintenance or balance between oxygen pressure and carbon dioxide pressure. If the neural pathways from the receptors fail to respond to the many feedback mechanisms, the individual's body and particularly his pulmonary system will reach a ineffective response level.

Third Set of Relationships

The third set of relationships and the theoretical propositions states that chemical and neural inputs will influence normally responsive endocrine glands to hormonally influence target organs in a positive manner to maintain a state of dynamic equilibrium. The specific theoretical propositions were labeled 1.1 to 3.2 in Table 5.1.

The respiratory system regulates carbon dioxide and oxygen levels through negative feedback; that is, a change in the CO_2 level or a decrease in the oxygen level brings about regulatory effects through ventilatory and circulatory parameters. According to Milhorn (1966),

> The controlling system receives three feedback signals and generates a single output which is alveolar ventilation. Alveolar ventilation, then, becomes the input to the controlled system, which generates three outputs (arterial CO_2 and O_2 partial pressure and H concentration). These outputs are then fed back to the controlling system.

The disturbances in the controlling system consist of carbon dioxide excess and oxygen deficiency or a combination of both.

The entire act of breathing is very complex with all its controls and regulations.

> The primary mechanisms of control and neural and chemical. Regulation and integration involve not only mechanisms initiated by the act of breathing, but also the chemical changes of respiration, chemical changes unrelated to the pulmonary segment of respiration, peripheral and central neuromuscular relations and purely voluntary cerebral modification. [Sodeman and Sodeman 1968]

The specific neural regulation achieved by respiratory neurons located in the medulla oblongata and lower pons has already been discussed under the second set of relationships.

Humoral regulation of respiration refers to the regulation of respiratory activity by changes in concentration of oxygen, carbon dioxide, or hydrogen ions in the body fluids. Carbon dioxide and hydrogen ions act upon the respiratory centers in the brain. Oxygen produces its effects almost entirely in the peripheral chemoreceptors which in turn affect the respiratory center.

It should be pointed out that humoral stimuli include modification in the physical or chemical properties of the circulatory blood that act on the respiratory center. Such stimuli can act in two ways: directly through the blood by its action on the central nervous system and indirectly by means of afferent fibers which originate peripheral to the central nervous system in baroreceptors or chemoreceptors.

A major humoral stimulus is carbon dioxide. An increase in arterial carbon dioxide tension leads to an increase in ventilation. Because carbon dioxide is one of the end products of metabolism, its concentration in the body fluids affects the chemical reaction of the cells. Therefore the tissue fluid carbon dioxide must be regulated exactly (Guyton 1971). It is also significant that the carbon dioxide stimulus plays a role in both normal and abnormal ventilatory pattern. During normal respiration, the major stimulus is the effect of carbon dioxide upon the central respiratory center. In abnormal situations where carbon dioxide is chronically increased, the overall effect of the carbon dioxide is more evident in the peripheral chemoreceptors.

In this situation the central nervous system is depressed and therefore the prime stimulus is at the peripheral level. The peripheral chemoreceptors are located in the carotid and aortic bodies. These receptors then have fibers that travel to the central nervous system and stimulate the respiratory system on that manner. [Beland 1975]

Additional humoral stimuli which affect ventilation are hydrogen ions. When hydrogen ions are increased the result is increased ventilation. Likewise a decrease in hydrogen ions will lead to a decrease in ventilation. The actual mode of action of the hydrogen ion stimulus is not exactly known. It is thought that hydrogen ions affect both the peripheral and the central ventilatory apparatus.

Beside the humoral stimuli of carbon dioxide, and hydrogen ions, blood pressure also acts as a stimulus for breathing.

The baroreceptors that respond to blood pressure have nerve endings that end near the respiratory centers, therefore they will often have an effect on ventilation. An increase in arterial blood pressure will cause hypoventilation or apnea by affecting the aortic and carotid sinus baroreceptors. A decrease in blood pressure will produce hyperventilation. [Beland 1975]

In addition to the direct sensitivity to humoral stimuli of the respiratory center itself,

Special chemical receptors located outside the central nervous system and called chemoreceptors are responsive to changes in oxygen, carbon dioxide, and hydrogen ion concentration. These transmit signals to the respiratory center to help regulate respiratory activity. These chemoreceptors are located primarily in association with the large arteries of the thorax and neck; most of them are in the carotid and aortic bodies. [Guyton 1971]

A decrease in arterial oxygen will stimulate the chemoreceptors. The chemoreceptors then stimulate the respiratory center to increase alveolar ventilation. In this respect the chemoreceptors provide a feedback mechanism to help maintain normal arterial oxygen concentration.

The primary mechanism for carrying the pulmonary gases is the blood. Significant to our discussion are two phases, namely, systemic circulation and pulmonary circulation. With systemic circulation, blood is propelled from the left ventricle through the arteries and arterioles to the capillaries. At the capillary level the substances carried are communicated to interstitial fluid and ultimately to the individual cells. The end products of metabolism are then transported back to the right atrium by means of the venules and veins. The lesser phase uses the pulmonary vessels and is labeled pulmonary circulation. Pulmonary circulation is significant because at the pulmonary capillaries the blood equilibrates with the oxygen and carbon dioxide in the alveolar air. The entire process is controlled by various regulatory systems that seek to maintain adequate blood flow to, and subsequently adequate oxygenation of body tissue.

The third set of relationships focuses on the target organ's ability to maintain a state of dynamic equilibrium when confronted with varying degrees of alterations in the external and internal stimuli. In this instance the target organs involved both the pulmonary and circulatory systems. From this set of relationships, we can conclude that, given the normal influential response of chemical and neural input upon hormonal effect as it pertains to the target organ, the target organ will maintain a state of dynamic equilibrium. When the chemical and neural inputs are unable to positively influence the endocrine glands and, subsequently, the hormonal influence upon target organs, the systems move towards ineffective responses.

Fourth Set of Relationships

A fourth set of relationships provides the transition between adaptive and ineffective behavior. This set of relationships involves the body's response to external and internal stimuli and state that such stimuli will alter those external and internal stimuli. This is predicated on the propositions labeled 1.1 to 5.1 in Table 5.1.

External stimuli affecting respiration involve the transport of oxygen from the external atmosphere to the cell. As briefly mentioned under the second set of relationships, they include pulmonary ventilation, gas exchange, transport, and regulation. (Guyton 1971).

Pulmonary ventilation is a mechanical process involving the muscular and elastic properties of the lung and thorax. Ventilation is only effective when the external atmosphere that is brought into the lungs can do the following: reach the alveoli for gas exchange to occur, be of sufficient volume to meet metabolic requirements, and have effective distribution throughout the alveoli with respect to blood flow (Wade 1977).

Whether the gases are able to reach the alveoli depends upon respiratory pressure, compliance, and pulmonary volume. Respiratory pressure refers to the intraalveolar pressure, or the fluid pressure in the intrapleural pressure. Pulmonary ventilation is dependent on the ability of the respiratory muscles to alternately compress and distend the lungs. This in turn causes the pressure of the alveoli to rise and fall.

Normally the pressure of the fluid in the intrapleural space is 10 to 12 mm Hg. According to Guyton (1971),

> When the chest cavity enlarges, this negative pressure causes the lungs also to enlarge. And when the chest cavity becomes smaller, the lungs likewise become smaller. The cause of the very negative intrapleural fluid pressure is the continued tendency of the pleural compliance to absorb fluid from the intrapleural spaces.

The recoil tendency of the lungs and intrapleural pressure is also a vital part of maintaining respiratory pressure. The lungs' ability to collapse and recoil is caused by two stimuli. First there are many elastic fibers throughout the lungs. These fibers are constantly stretched and shortened. Second, the surface tension of the fluid that lines the alveoli causes a continual tendency for the alveoli to collapse.

Compliance is another factor that facilitates the gases' ability to reach the alveoli. The expansibility of the lungs and thorax is called compliance. Compliance is influenced by lung tissue. Any condition that destroys lung tissue leads to an ineffective response. The tissue becomes fibrotic or edematous, the alveoli are blocked, and contraction causes decreased lung compliance. External stimuli such as deformities of the chest or other restraining conditions lead to a reduction in the expansibility of the lungs and subsequent reduction in pulmonary compliance.

Pulmonary pressure, the last component that affects the ability of gases to reach the alveoli, focuses on residual volume and vital capacity.

Residual volume refers to the air that cannot be removed from the lungs even by forceful expiration. Its function is to provide air in the alveoli to aerate the blood even between breaths. Without this function the overall concentration of oxygen and carbon dioxide in the blood would rise and fall markedly with each respiration. This could lead to ineffective regulatory behaviors. Vital capacity is influenced by the individual's position, strength of respiratory muscles, and distensibility of the lungs.

The second major external stimuli associated with external respiration is gas exchange. Once the alveoli are ventilated with external atmosphere air, the next process is diffusion of oxygen from the alveoli into the pulmonary bed and diffusion of carbon dioxide from the pulmonary bed into the alveoli. Diffusion as it pertains to the third set of relationships consists of diffusion of gases through the respiratory membrane.

Diffusion of gases through the respiratory membrane is dependent upon the permeability of the respiratory membrane, the thickness and surface area of respiratory membrane, and the diffusion capacity of oxygen and carbon dioxide. The influencing variable in the permeability of the respiratory membrane to gases is the rate at which the gases can diffuse through the water in the membrane. The rate of carbon dioxide diffusion in water is 20 times as rapid as the rate of oxygen diffusion.

Diffusion is also influenced by both the thickness and surface area of the respiratory membrane. When edema fluid collects in the interstitial space, the thickness of the respiratory membrane increases. As Guyton (1971) points out,

> Fluid may collect in the alveoli, so that the respiratory gases must diffuse not only through the membrane but also through this fluid. Finally, some pulmonary disease cause fibrosis of the lungs, which can increase the thickness of some portions of the respiratory membrane. Because the rate of diffusion through the membrane is inversely proportional to the thickness of the membrane, any factor that increases the thickness more than two to three times above normal can interfere markedly with normal respiratory exchange of gases.

Likewise the surface area of the respiratory membrane can be decreased due to removal of an entire lung or emphysema. Emphysema causes a dissolution of the septa between the alveoli. Even though the new chambers are larger than the original ones, the total surface area of the respiratory membrane is decreased. Under normal conditions the diffusion capacity for oxygen is 21 ml per minute. Carbon dioxide, on the other hand, diffuses through the respiratory membrane so rapidly that the average $P_A CO_2$ in the pulmonary blood is not very different from the $P_A CO_2$ in the alveoli—the difference is less than 1 mm Hg. The high diffusion capacity of carbon dioxide is significant when the intact organ moves from adaptive to maladaptive responses. When the respiratory membrane becomes damaged, its capacity for transmitting oxygen into the blood is always impaired enough to cause death long before impairment of carbon dioxide diffusion occurs. The only time when a low diffusing capacity for carbon dioxide causes difficulty is when lung tissue is compromised but oxygen is being maintained through oxygen therapy (Guyton 1971)

The third major external stimulus to be considered under external respiration is the transport of oxygen and carbon dioxide in the blood and body fluids. Oxygen is combined with hemoglobin in the red blood cells and transported from the lungs to the tissue capillaries where it is released for use by the cells. When the P_AO_2 is high, it is in the pulmonary capillaries, oxygen will bind with the hemoglobin. When P_AO_2 is low, as it is in the tissue capillaries, oxygen is released from the hemoglobin. The transport of carbon dioxide involves the reversible combination of carbon dioxide with water in the red blood cells under the influence of carbonic anhydrase. This means of transport accounts for 60 to 90 percent of all the carbon dioxide transported from the tissues to the lungs and is the most significant of all methods for CO_2 transport (Guyton 1971).

The final external stimulus, involving the regulation of respiration by means of the respiratory center, has already been discussed under the second set of relationships. Therefore the regulatory functions of external respiration will not be discussed.

The internal stimuli relating to internal respiration are concerned with how oxygen is utilized and how carbon dioxide is produced. Oxygen is continually being absorbed into the blood of the lungs, thereby permitting new oxygen to enter the alveoli from the atmoshpere. According to Guyton (1971),

> The more rapidly oxygen is absorbed, the lower becomes its concentration in the alveoli; on the other hand, the more rapidly new oxygen is brought into the alveoli from the atmosphere, the higher becomes its concentration. Therefore, oxygen concentration in the alveoli is controlled by, first, the rate of absorption of oxygen into the blood and second, the rate of entry of new oxygen into the lungs.

In terms of external stimuli, there are two factors that determine carbon dioxide partial pressure in the lungs: the rate of excretion of carbon dioxide from the blood into the alveoli, and the rate at which carbon dioxide is removed from the alveoli by alveolar ventilation. The internal stimulus of carbon dioxide alters internal stimuli. For example, stimulation of the respiratory center by carbon dioxide provides a feedback mechanism for regulation of carbon dioxide. This is accomplished in two ways: An increase in PCO_2 stimulates the respiratory center, and increased alveolar ventilation reduces the alveolar carbon dioxide. The overall result is to restore the tissue PCO_2 to normal.

Stimuli from external and internal environment can, as the propositions indicate, alter those external and internal stimuli. External stimuli involving pulmonary ventilation, gas exchange, transport, and regulation can greatly affect the internal stimuli of oxygen utilization and carbon dioxide production. When the external and internal stimuli fail to adaptively alter those stimuli, the physiological trend is towards ineffective behavior.

Fifth Set of Relationships

In the fifth set of relationships, the magnitude of the external and internal stimuli may be so great that the adaptive systems cannot return the body to a state of dynamic equilibrium. This includes propositions 1.1 to 5.1 in Table 5.1.

When the individual's pulmonary and/or cardiovascular disease process exceeds what either system is able to adaptively tolerate, the results are ineffective responses. These ineffective responses consist of respiratory insufficiency or failure and circulatory insufficiency or failure. Factors leading to failure of both systems will be listed rather than discussed. It should be kept in mind that the list is not an exhaustive one. Nevertheless it provides a framework for discussion of the regulatory behaviors. These behaviors include hypoxia and hypercapnea, each of which will be examined in terms of behaviors exhibited, focal stimuli, and nursing interventions designed to manipulate influencing contextual and residual stimuli.

Respiratory insufficiency means that respiratory function is ineffective to meet the body's need during exertion. Respiratory failure means that respiratory function is inadequate to meet the body's need even in the resting state. In both cases the lungs fail to maintain normal arterial blood gases. The different types of abnormalities that lead to respiratory insufficiency can be divided into three categories:

    I. Abnormalities that cause inadequate alveloar ventilation
        A. Paralysis of the respiratory muscles
        B. Diseases that increase the work of ventilation
            1. Increased airway resistance
               (a) Asthma
               (b) Emphysema
            2. Increased tissue resistance
               (a) Emphysema

(b) Pulmonary fibrosis

(c) Tuberculosis

3. Decreased compliance of the lungs and chest wall

(a) Silicosis

(b) Cancer

(c) Pneumonia

II. Diseases that decrease pulmonary diffusing capacity

A. Decreased area of the respiratory membrane

1. Removal of part or all of lung

2. Cancer

3. Emphysema

4. Pneumonia

5. Pulmonary edema

6. Atelectasis

B. Increased thickness of the respiratory membrane or alveolocapillary block

1. Pulmonary edema

2. Fibrotic conditions

C. Abnormal ventilation-perfusion ratio

1. Thrombosis

2. Emphysema

III. Abnormalities of oxygen transport from the lungs to the tissues

A. Blood flow changes

1. Anemia

2. Emphysema

Circulatory failure is defined as the inability of the circulation to maintain an adequate minute volume blood flow to supply the need of the tissue. Circulatory failure can be classified as acute or chronic. Among the factors that contribute to the maladaptive response of circulatory failure are the following:

1. Disturbances of blood volume

(a) Shock

(b) Hemorrhage

(c) Fluid overload

2. Obstruction of blood flow

(a) Thrombosis

(b) Embolism

(c) Infarction

3. Ischemia of heart muscle

(a) Angina pectoris

(b) Myocardial infarction

(c) Coronary insufficiency
4. Cardiac infectious process
   (a) Rheumatic heart disease
   (b) Subacute bacterial endocarditis
5. Hypertension

The respiratory and cardiovascular systems are able to tolerate a multitude of stresses, many of which were listed above. However a point is ultimately reached where both systems are unable to return the body to a state of dynamic equilibrium. Instead the system progresses towards dynamic disequilibrium. The state of dynamic disequilibrium is manifested as hypoxia and hypercapnia.

Hypoxia

Hypoxia refers to an inadequate supply of oxygen to the tissues for metabolic needs. Hypoxia can result from an imbalance of cardiac output, an inadequate amount of oxygen consumed by the metabolic process, or low hemoglobin levels (Wade 1977).

At onset, hypoxia manifests itself through subtle changes in the patient's condition. However, if the patient's airway becomes obstructed or if he experiences circulatory failure, the nurse assesses a rapid change in regulatory behaviors.

Regulatory Behaviors.   The regulatory behaviors vary from those caused by personality changes to those representing compensatory effects.

1. Restlessness
2. Impaired intellectual function
3. Confusion
4. Delirium
5. Impaired muscular coordination
6. Tachycardia
7. Tachypnea
8. Central cyanosis
9. Hypotension
10. Headache

Unless interventions are taken to prevent further hypoxia, external and internal stimuli are unable to return the individual to a state of equilibrium. The ultimate ineffective response is unconsciousness and death.

TABLE **10.1** Focal Stimuli in Hypoxia

Category	Precipitating Factor	Possible Cause
Hypoxic hypoxia	Reduction in inspired oxygen concentration	High altitude Asthma
Hypemic hypoxia	Reduction in the oxygen carrying capacity of the blood	Anemia Carbon dioxide
Histotoxic hypoxia	Reduction in ability of cells to utilize oxygen	Alcohol Narcotics Cyanide
Stagnant hypoxia	Reduction in cardiac output	Decreased coronary perfusion Congestive heart failure Shock

Focal Stimuli.   Hypoxia can be classified into four general categories (Roy 1976). Each category has specific focal stimuli which lead to the ineffective state and can be grouped according to their predisposing factor (see Table 10.1). The above categories, precipitating factors, and possible causes are not all-inclusive yet they do identify several focal stimuli that contribute to ineffective responses.

Hypercapnia

Hypercapnia or hypercarbia is defined as an increase in carbon dioxide at the cellular level. It should be pointed out that hypercapnia occurs in association with hypoxia only when it is caused by either hypoventilation or circulatory deficiency.

Regulatory Behavior.   The major effect of high levels of carbon dioxide in the body fluid is depression of the central nervous system. The patient with hypercapnea will exhibit the following regulatory behaviors:

1. Headache
2. Drowsiness

3. Inability to concentrate
4. Confusion
5. Irritability
6. Twitching
7. Hypertension

The regulatory behaviors manifested by changes in the central nervous system may occur quickly, thereby going unnoticed. Therefore, any time the patient with a pulmonary or cardiovascular dysfunction exhibits alteration in central nervous system status, hypercarbia may be the nursing diagnosis.

Focal Stimuli.   The specific focal stimuli that contribute to the ineffective response of hypercapnia include hypoventilation and/or ventilation-perfusion disorders.

Manipulating the stimuli

Given that the magnitude of the external and internal stimuli are so great that the adaptive systems cannot return the body to a state of dynamic equilibrium, the nurse intervenes by manipulating stimuli in an attempt to maintain or restore oxygen and circulation. In order to manipulate stimuli, the nurse assesses various influencing factors which contribute to the maladaptive behaviors. The influencing factors include focal, contextual and residual stimuli. Since focal stimuli have already been discussed in terms of pathophysiological causes of ineffective responses, we shall turn to contextual and residual stimuli.

Contextual stimuli

The nurse alters ineffective regulatory responses from external and internal stimuli through manipulation of the following contextual stimuli: fluid, activity, nutrition, communication, aeration and pain.

Fluid.   Fluid considerations include interstitial edema, intake, and output. The patient with pulmonary and circulatory dysfunction is confronted with the problem of interstitial edema. The nurse's goal in altering external and internal stimuli is to decrease capillary venous pressure and pulmonary venous pressure. Mobilization of edema fluid in congestive heart failure involves potential hazards for the patient in cardiopulmonary disequilibrium. Edema fluid is not merely water—it contains much metabolic debris which is toxic. Too rapid a mobilization of extensive edema may lead to profound intoxication and add injury to an already seriously injured myocardium. The nurse can promote a decrease in capillary venous pressure and pulmonary venous pressure by allowing the patient to sit up with his feet on a chair for support. This intervention promotes pooling of fluid in the abdominal cavity and extremities. The nurse realizes that interstitial edema resulting from pedal dependency can lead to skin breakdown. The patient will need to have his position changed frequently to prevent additional skin breakdown due to pressure and poor tissue integrity.

Movement of fluids into serous cavities, where infringement on respiration and/or cardiac function may occur, must be removed by thoracentesis. Caution is taken to avoid too rapid a removal of intrathoracic fluid. The nurse assesses her patient for evidence of pain, dyspnea, or color changes during this procedure. Mechanical removal of fluid has two advantages over mobilization of fluids through diuresis. First, diuresis requires the heart to move all the fluid via the circulation to the kidneys. Second, diuresis may cause systemic intoxication subsequent to the movement of edema fluid from cavities to the bloodstream (Sharpe and Stieglitz 1954).

Intake includes both oral and parental fluids, medication; and environmental intake. The type and amount of intravenous fluid depends upon the hydration level of the patient. The hydration status of the patient is assessed by comparing the relationship of total intake and output, by looking at skin turgor and mucous membranes, by comparing changes in his daily weight, and by watching changes in vital signs, particularly body temperature. Optimal hydration will help to liquify bronchopulmonary secretions thereby making their removal easier. The patient with tenacious secretions is encouraged to have a high fluid intake, providing his circulatory status can handle an increase in fluid intake.

Intravenous solution may infuse simply to keep the vein open in case of cardiopulmonary complications. In addition it may be used for the purpose of providing medication to lower blood pressure, facilitate cardiac output, or reduce pulmonary embarrasment. The nurse must keep in mind that intravenous fluids need to be administered slowly to eliminate the danger of hypervolemia with congestive heart failure and pulmonary edema. The specific type of intravenous solution depends on the patient's unique problem. The nurse's responsibility is to administer the proper amount in the proper period of time without overhydrating or underhydrating the patient.

If the amount of fluid to be received over a 24-hour period includes both parenteral and oral fluids, the nurse can carefully arrange her patient's oral intake to occur during meals and administration of medications. The hypoxic or hypercapnic patient who is already irritable may resent the need for curtailment of his fluids. Therefore the nurse can carefully explain the reasons behind the restriction. The specific kinds of fluids offered to the patient can be taken into consideration. If the patient has a Foley catheter, the nurse may choose to offer cranberry juice. Cranberry juice serves to maintain an acid pH of urine in the bladder thus preventing urinary calculi. Other juices offered, if possible, are orange and grape juice both of which elevate the patient's potassium level.

The administration of medication is another significant aspect of fluid intake. A full discussion of specific medications is not possible here, so they will only be mentioned. Among the medications used to treat patients with pulmonary dysfunction are antihistamines, antimicrobiols, bronchodilators, cough medications, respiratory stimulants, vasoconstrictors, and decongestants. Medications that serve to maintain or restore cardiovascular function are antihypertensives, diuretics, digitalis, nitroglycerin, antiarrhythmic agents, and anticoagulants.

The last aspect of intake is environmental intake. The patient is taken from a familiar environment and placed into the unfamiliar world of a busy hospital. The environment may be frightening because it contains all the environmental props that remind him of his illness. These props often include ventilators, intravenous and oxygen tubing, and cardioscopes. Furthermore, there may be a restriction on visitors. The patient is also concerned about his future biological status. Death may seem very close to the patient who has severe respiratory insufficiency. As a result of his fear and anxiety, the patient's intake may be greatly reduced. He may fail to hear explanations regarding his progress and care. Therefore he may unintentionally disobey orders. The nurse needs to accurately assess the origin of her patient's behavior. Confusion may be due to hypoxia or hypercapnia. The goal is to provide the patient with support and encouragement. He needs assurance that his biological integrity is stabilizing.

Output as it relates to pulmonary and cardiovascular dysfunction takes several forms. It includes emesis; urinary output and specific gravity; vital signs including pulse, respiratory rate, temperature, arterial blood pressure, venous pressure; weight; and information derived from laboratory studies.

The patient with cardiac dysfunction such as myocardial infarction or congestive heart failure may experience nausea and vomiting. The amount and content of emesis can be recorded. Frequent emesis together with diuresis can contribute to the patient's dehydration and electrolyte imbalance. Vomiting may also increase the workload of the patient's heart leading to the possible extension of his myocardial infarction. Vomiting may present unique problems to the patient with pulmonary dysfunction. Vomiting is produced by a sudden spasm of the diaphragm which momentarily halts respiration. Persistant vomiting or retching necessitates immediate relief procedures because the breathing becomes irregular and rapid, and aspiration can occur. The nurse intervenes to assess the origin of her patient's emesis, to support him during the episode, and to administer treatments to reduce its occurrence.

Urinary output is an important indication of adequate circulatory function. Beside assessing the amount of urinary output, the nurse also assesses its color, odor, and specific gravity. Reduced urinary output coupled with concentrated urine can indicate dehydration. The nurse may need to assess the relationship between her patient's total volume intake and output including emesis, urine, and incidental factors. The nurse can independently assess the specific gravity of her patient's urine. Specific gravity provides information regarding the patient's level of hydration and the ability of his kidneys to remove wastes.

A second major component of fluid output consists of vital signs. The patient's pulse provides feedback regarding his cardiocirculatory integrity and internal changes associated with pulmonary irregularities. An increase in pulse rate may indicate hypoxia, the need to be suctioned, the presence of infection, impending cardiac failure due to pulmonary capillary hypertension (cor pulmonale), or shock from reduced cardiac output of blood loss. In addition, an increased heart rate may indicate airway obstruction. Therefore the nurse assesses other patient parameters such as blood pressure, urine output, neck vein distention, and respiratory rate.

The patient's respirations are another significant aspect of his output system. In assessing her patient's respirations, the nurse pays particular attention to their rate, rhythm, regularity, and skin color. Assessment of subtle changes in breathing patterns provides advance warning of impending trouble. The impending problem can often be controlled by immediate interventions such as suctioning, oxygen administration, or ventilation assistance.

Temperature is an important patient parameter. Elevation of the patient's temperature can be an early sign of infection. This becomes a serious complication for patients who have cardiopulmonary dysfunction. An increase in the patient's temperature leads to an increase in metabolism, increased need for oxygen, increase in workload of the heart, and a greater demand for pulmonary ventilation.

Arterial blood pressure is a reflection of left ventricular contraction, blood volume, blood viscosity, and elasticity of artery walls. Factors that contribute to an increase in arterial pressure by increasing cardiac output and arteriolar constriction are stress, anxiety, and worry. The nurse also realizes that chronic hypoxia from impaired ventilation causes a rise in arterial blood pressure. Chronic hypoxia causes hypervolemia resulting in an increased cardiac output. Another condition that leads to a decreased arterial pressure is congestive heart failure with a reduced cardiac output; reduced blood volume; and vasodilation. The nurse assesses what is a normal arterial blood pressure for her patient and evaluates potential hazards if deviations from his normal should develop.

Venous pressure is a reflection of how well the right ventricle is able to empty, thus reducing or increasing pressure in the right atrium. It represents a dynamic relationship between cardiac output, blood volume, and venous tone. A rise in central venous pressure is due to right-sided heart failure. Other factors leading to an increase in venous pressure are pleural effusion, emphysema, and extensive pneumonia. If direct measurement of central venous pressure is not possible, the nurse can assess for neck vein distention.

The patient's weight is a good indicator of the effectiveness of diuretic therapy. To assure accurate measurement of the patient's weight, he should be weighed in the same scale and at the same time each day. Weight is a good index of fluid reduction or loss, tissue catabolism, and renal function.

Laboratory studies are the last component of fluid output. A lengthy discussion of each laboratory study as it pertains to pulmonary or cardiovascular function is not possible. The pertinent laboratory studies test for arterial blood gases, serum electrolytes, serum enzymes, complete blood count (CBC), and prothrombin time. Arterial blood gas measurements reflect ventilation efficiency, the ability of hemoglobin to carry oxygen and carbon dioxide, the rate of cellular metabolism, and the state of the buffer system. The PO_2 level gives an indication of the amount of oxygen that has diffused through the alveoli into the arterial blood. The PCO_2 measures carbon dioxide in arterial blood. It reflects how well the lungs are able to ventilate.

Serum electrolytes and serum enzymes are significant to the patient with pulmonary or cardiovascular dysfunction. Because the patient may be receiving diuretics, his serum electrolytes (calcium, potassium, chloride, sodium, and phosphorus) should be closely monitored. Likewise serum enzymes such as SGOT, LDH, CPK and HBD are also assessed with patients who have cardiovascular problems. Complete blood count measures both of white blood cells (WBC) and red blood cells (RBC). The latter count is significant because it represents the patient's hemoglobin and hematocrit level. Hemoglobin represents the amount of respiratory pigment protein available to combine with oxygen and carbon dioxide. Hematocrit represents the relative volume of cells and plasma in the blood.

Activity.   Nursing care of the patient with pulmonary and cardiovascular dysfunction involves four activity components: physical activity in general, and cardiac, pulmonary, and mental activity.

Rest is an important, although an often ill-used, form of therapy of cardiac illness. The patient's biological problem must be assessed in regard to complications derived from bed rest. Naturally the patient with severe pulmonary dysfunction will not have the energy to get out of bed.

It must be kept in mind that before the nurse attempts to ambulate her patient, she assesses the stability of his cardiac rhythm, quality of heart sounds, pulse, and stability of blood pressure. Early ambulation of the patient is to his physiological and psychological advantage. With prolonged bed rest the patient begins to feel hopeless about his progress. In this respect ambulation signifies improvement.

Cardiac monitoring of the patient with acute cardiovascular dysfunction is essential to detect early cardiac arrhythmias. It is also helpful when digitalis toxicity is suspected. The nurse uses her patient's cardioscope as a means of cardiac assessment. It may be necessary to regulate the patient's cardiac activity by means of a pacemaker. If the patient experiences angina, he should be advised to curtail his activities and reduce his rate of performance. While curtailing some activities, he is encouraged to keep physically fit within the limits of his cardiac tolerance.

Pulmonary activity is assessed through chest x-ray, altered by changes in position and assisted by use of a ventilator. A chest x-ray is helpful in obtaining direct visualization of the patient's chest. Assessment of the chest for infiltrations of fluid or secretions can be made with x-rays.

The position assumed by the patient affects his ventilation. The sitting position permits gravity to move fluid to the dependent parts and prevents the pooling of blood in the pulmonary vascular structure. If the patient has difficulty exhaling, he has a tendency to lean forward in an attempt to compress the chest. However such a position may cramp the patient's chest and thus his pulmonary inflation will be limited. Besides position changes to maintain adequate ventilation and circulation, the patient also needs sleep. This is especially true for the patient who tires easily, who works hard to breathe, and whose metabolism is affected by decreased oxygen. The nurse attempts to position her patient comfortably, to promote a quiet environment, and to facilitate his sleep state.

The patient's pulmonary activity may be ineffective in supplying oxygen for metabolism and removing carbon dioxide produced by metabolism. In such instances the patient's faltering pulmonary system may need to be supported by a respirator. Intermittent positive pressure breathing (IPPB) machines serve to alter the quality of respirations by delivering a volume of air or oxygen under increased pressure to the airway at a set rate. With the IPPB machine, ventilation is either assisted or controlled. The nurse must be familiar with the type of ventilator, amount of pressure, and response of her patient.

Mental activities are a significant treatment mode for the cardiac and pulmonary patient. Mental or diversional activities are the best means of stimulation. The patient's mental activity and his need to learn, express, and relate should be considered. Any change in mental activity such as confusion, restlessness, irritability, or paranoia should alarm the nurse. Such regulatory behaviors may signify biological maladaptation.

Nutrition.   The patient with a respiratory ailment may have a poor appetite due to the unpleasantness of sputum production. Appetite may be impaired because of dyspnea, fatigue, nausea, or other unpleasant symptoms. Small and frequent servings of food are more effective than larger meals. The cardiac patient may be placed on a low-salt diet. A diet too restrictive in sodium coupled with use of diuretics, which cause increased sodium and chloride excretion, can lead to hypochloremic alkalosis. The nurse must assess the patient's daily electrolyte panel. The diet, because it deviates from the patient's normal diet, may not be looked upon as palatable. Therefore, whenever possible, the patient should be permitted to make choices within the existing restrictions. A dietitian can be of value to the patient and his nurse.

Nutritional status of the patient does not refer solely to his ability to ingest or digest. It also implies a need for spiritual nutrition. Spiritual needs of the patient are as significant as dietary needs. The patient who fears that death is forthcoming needs the counsel of his minister, priest, or rabbi. Such counsel must be provided in order to give holistic care.

Communication.   Communication is a dynamic concept. It involves biological communication through surgical or mechanical intervention, environmental communication, and human-to-human communication. Many cardiovascular diseases once thought to be hopeless are now corrected through surgery. Coronary artery blood flow is returned to the myocardium through surgical intervention of coronary artery bypass. Diseased valves leading to the maladaptive response of congestive heart failure are replaced with artificial valves. The breakdown of biological communication with the patient's pulmonary system is more difficult to correct. Respirators have helped sustain pulmonary function when the individual could not spontaneously or independently sustain himself.

Environmental communication implies communication between the patient and his equipment or treatment procedures, environment in general, and diversional activities. The nurse assesses that communication exists between the patient and his cardioscope, arterial line, IV, Foley catheter, respirator, nasal-gastric tube, or air mattress. The patency of tubes must be frequently assessed to ensure openness of flow and communication. In creating a protective environment, the nurse protects her patient from infection, particularly if his ineffective response has lowered his resistance to infection.

The human-to-human communication that exists among patient, family, and nurse is most important. The patient looks to his nurse for support, understanding, and compassion. The nurse maintains her patient's sense of worth and dignity by personalizing his care. The patient needs to feel that he is more significant than the equipment which surrounds him. Besides providing a personalized external environment, the nurse encourages internal personalization by allowing the patient to express his fears. Anxiety and fears alter the depth and rate of respiration. The patient's fears of being a cardiac or respiratory cripple need to be discussed with both nurse and existing family members.

Diversional activities can consist of T.V., radio, books, or family visits. These are provided when appropriate and realistic. They serve the purpose of reducing anxiety by momentarily diverting the patient's attention from the immediate problem.

Aeration.   Aeration involves aeration of the patient's lungs as well as his feelings. Oxygen and humidification are important aspects of aeration. Oxygen therapy is indicated in the acute state of left ventricular failure. In cases where failure may involve the right side such as cor pulmonale, oxygen may be dangerous and cause death from carbon dioxide narcosis. Moreover, oxygen administration may not be practical over a long period of time. When indicated, oxygen can be administered by mask, nasal catheter, or nasal prongs. Humidification means provision of additional moisture to the inspired air. One goal in treating the pulmonary patient is the prevention of dryness in the mucous membranes and their secretions.

The patient needs an opportunity to aerate his feelings. Aeration of feelings not only alleviates his fears but it also reduces the possibility of respiratory acidosis. As the patient talks he is removing excess carbon dioxide. It is worth mentioning that stress increases the secretion of mineralocorticoids with subsequent retention of sodium and water. Therefore the nurse's goal is to identify and reduce the patient's stress.

Pain.   The patient with a pulmonary or cardiac dysfunction experiences two types of pain—physiological and psychological. Physiological pain is more definitive. It includes pain associated with an acute myocardial infarction or angina, headaches due to hypertension, and chest discomfort associated with pulmonary distress. Regardless of its origin, pain can be exhausting to the patient. It takes energy he needs for the purpose of breathing or ambulating.

Psychological pain is equally as significant as physiological pain to the patient. Dyspnea, curtailment of activity, fatigue, and dependency are factors that contribute to psychological pain. Changes in lifestyle and financial loss due to hospitalization can also lead to psychological pain. Psychological pain may be more diffuse and less definitive than physiological pain but it nevertheless exists and can be alleviated.

Residual stimuli

Residual stimuli include a history of previous pulmonary and/or cardiovascular problems; previous or no prior experience with hospitalization, obesity, consumption of 2 or more packs of cigarettes a day, or long hours of work with little physical activity. Depending upon the patient and his particular ineffective response, the nurse may assess additional residual stimuli that need to be manipulated.

Example of Hypothesis for Practice

We have focused on the process of theorizing with the oxygen and circulatory physiological mode. Based on our theorizing with the oxygen and circulatory mode, we can postulate any number of hypotheses that can be tested. The theorizing encompasses the four sets of relationships and their related proposition. In addition the hypotheses can be used as a guide for practice. An example of a possible hypothesis will be discussed.

The hypothesis may be stated as follows: If the nurse helps the patient achieve an optimal level of oxygenation and circulation, the patient's alveolar-capillary system will perform at a higher level. The reason for this hypothesis is drawn from the set of relationships which are based on propositions stated earlier. The reasons are shown below.

General Statement: The magnitude of the internal and external stimuli will positively influence the magnitude of the physiological response of an intact system.

Specific Statement: The level of alveolar-capillary exchange and perfusion will positively influence the level of oxygenation and circulatory balance.

The nurse utilizes the four sets of relationships to theorize regarding oxygen and circulation. The theorizing permits hypothesis generation even when the nurse manipulates contextual stimuli. With each component of the contextual stimuli, the nurse can hypothesize regarding patient care. If the nurse finds evidence of significance from a hypothesis, the nursing activity specified in the research protocol can become a prescription for practice in situations where nursing diagnosis warrants this intervention or interventions identified in the contextual stimuli section.

Summary

Oxygen and circulation have been examined according to the four sets of relationships which focus on adaptive regulatory responses. These responses take into account external and internal stimuli. The pulmonary and cardiovascular system attempts to adapt to chemical and neural inputs. However, ineffective responses occur when the magnitude of external and internal stimuli are greater than the body's ability to maintain a state of dynamic equilibrium. The overall result leads to disequilibrium and disease.

When the external and internal stimuli exceed the system's ability to adapt, the nurse assesses focal stimuli, regulatory behaviors, and manipulates the contextual stimuli, and assesses residual stimuli. While doing so, the nurse utilizes the propositions to generate hypotheses for nursing practice.

References and Additional Readings

Alspach, JoAnn. "The Patient with Chest Trauma," *Critical Care Update,* 6, no. 7 (July 1979): 18–26.

Barstow, Ruth. "Coping with Emphysema," *Nursing Clinics of North America, 9,* no. 1 (March 1974): 137–45.

Beland, Irene, and Joyce Passos. *Clinical Nursing: Pathophysiological and Psychosocial Approaches.* New York: Macmillan, 1975.

Brannin, Patricia. "Oxygen Therapy and Measures of Bronchial Hygiene," *Nursing Clinics of North America, 9,* no. 1 (March 1974): 111–21.

Engberg, Sandra. "Understanding Blood Gases," *Critical Care Update,* 6, no. 7 (July 1979): 5–15.

Guyton, Arthur. *Textbook of Medical Physiology.* Philadelphia: Saunders, 1971.

Hudelson, Evelyn. "The Continuously Ventilated Patient," *Critical Care Update,* 6, no. 9 (September 1979): 26–27.

Johnson, Paul. "The Dynamics of Respiratory Structures." In *Physiology,* ed. Ewald Selkurt, p. 427. Boston: Little, Brown, 1966.

Kirilloff, Leslie, and Ruth Maszkiewicz. "Guide to Respiratory Care in Critically Ill Adults," *American Journal of Nursing,* 79, no. 11 (November 1979).

Lagerson, Joanne. "Nursing Care of Patients with Chronic Pulmonary Insufficiency," *Nursing Clinics of North America, 9,* no. 1 (March 1974): 165–79.

Milhorn, Howard. *The Application of Control Theory to Physiological Systems,* Philadelphia: Saunders, 1966.

Moody, Linda, and Betty Bunke. "Pulmonary Care Update," *Critical Care Update,* (July 1978).

Roy, Sr. Callista, *Introduction to Nursing: An Adaptation Model,* Englewood Cliffs, N.J.: Prentice-Hall, Inc., 1976.

Selkurt, Ewald. *Physiology.* Boston: Little, Brown, 1966.

Sharpe, George, and Edward Stieglitz. "Cardiac Decompensation." In *Geriatric Medicine,* ed. Edward Stieglitz. Philadelphia: Lippincott, 1954.

Sodeman, William, and William Sodeman, Jr. *Pathologic Physiology: Mechanisms of Disease.* Philadelphia: Saunders, 1968.

Wade, Jacqueline. *Respiratory Nursing Care.* St. Louis: C. V. Mosby, 1977.

Yamamoto, William, and John Brobeck, eds. *Physiological Controls and Regulations.* Philadelphia: Saunders, 1965.

CHAPTER 11

Temperature

The human person as a living open system maintains body temperature independent of, and yet in relationship to, his external environment. The internal regulator mechanism attempts to maintain a near constant body temperature. This is accomplished through a highly organized adaptive system based upon neural and chemical input, feedback, and effectors or responses which bring about the final adaptive or ineffective output. The temperature-regulating mechanism is influenced by both internal and external stimuli. Consider, for example, input in the form of intense external stimuli such as high temperature in an older person whose adaptive mechanism is already compromised. While the internal regulatory mechanism voluntarily attempts—through negative feedback—to remain constant, the final output may be heat stroke. Ineffective behavior may be so severe that entropy in the form of death becomes the final response.

A series of theoretical propositions will be applied to the temperature regulating subsystem. The propositions presented as sets of relationships build from adaptive response to ineffective ones in which the regulatory system is no longer able to cope. More specifically there are five sets of relationships.

First Set of Relationships

The first set of relationships is as follows: The magnitude of the physiological responses of an intact system. This is predicated on the propositions indicated as 1.1 to 2.1, 3.2, and 4.4 in Table 5.1.

Temperature as a vital sign is one condition that is hemostatically controlled. This is accomplished by an exchange of stimuli between nerves, hormonal, and circulatory systems. Although body temperature is regulated, the temperature of the external environmental stimuli affects the ease with which this is accomplished. The magnitude of both internal and external stimuli will influence the system's ability to physiologically respond.

Input of internal and external stimuli takes two forms. In discussing body temperature regulation, one usually means the temperature in the interior. Therefore, input from internal stimuli is described as core temperature. The inner core temperature is accurately regulated, varying under normal conditions from the mean by not more than 1 °F. Input of external stimuli is referred to as surface temperature. Surface temperature signifies the skin's ability to lose heat to the surroundings. Therefore surface temperature rises and falls dependent upon stimuli from the environment. Such thermal information is picked up by the body's temperature sensors. These consist first of the warmth receptors which respond maximally to temperature above body temperature. Second, there are cold receptors which likewise respond maximally to temperature below body temperature. Therefore a change in the magnitude of external environmental stimuli can influence the physiological responses of the body. Because surface temperature is more variable, it is more sensitive to alterations in the magnitude of stimuli.

Alterations in internal or external stimuli are received through receptors and communicated via the body's neural pathways. This brings us to the second set of relationships.

Second Set of Relationships

In the second set of relationships, the intact neural pathways will positively influence neural output to effectors. This is predicated on the propositions labeled 3.1 to 2.1, and 4.4 in Table 5.1. The effector system in thermoregulation consists of the following activities: increasing metabolic heat production, increasing or decreasing peripheral blood flow, and increasing heat loss by evaporation. Skin temperature affects thermoregulatory responses. The preoptic hypothalamic tissue is significant in regulating internal body temperature. In addition there are other temperature-sensitive areas in the central region of the body that respond to changes in internal body temperature. This can occur without sensory input from other areas of the body (Huckaba and Downey 1973).

It should be pointed out that receptors activate the intact nerves and, as a result, messages are communicated via neural pathways to the brain. These messages inform the individual of external temperature so that he can respond. Furthermore the messages initiate a sequence of events that oppose changes in external temperature in an attempt to maintain the constancy of internal temperature (Langley 1965). Temperature regulation via intact neural pathways is accomplished by the nervous feedback mechanism located in the hypothalamus. According to Beland and Passos (1975),

> Despite a lack of knowledge of the number of circuits involved in the nervous control of body temperature, it behaves as if it were a closed-loop negative feedback system. Information is fed into the hypothalamus by the temperature of the blood circulating through it and / or by sensory receptors in other parts of the body. In the hypothalamus the information is interpreted and converted into neural impulses that initiate behavior that increases or decreases rate of heat loss and heat production.

For the feedback mechanisms to function appropriately there must also exist temperature detectors or receptors to determine when the body temperature varies too greatly from the normal. The hypothalamus, which functions as a central thermoreceptor area, integrates sensory information from three sources. First are the thermal receptors located in the periphery. As Matzke and Foltz (1972) state

> Information from peripheral temperature receptors is transmitted inward over the lateral spinothalamic tract of the spinal cord, which carries impulses of pain and temperature to the thalamus, where automatic responses are integrated and initiated. Fine discrimination and intiation of voluntary responses occur only if and when messages reach the cerebral cortex.

Second, there are thermal sensitive cells in the hypothalamus which are extremely significant receptors for control of body temperature. Many special heat-sensitive neurons are located in the preoptic area of the anterior hypothalamus. These neurons increase their impulse output as the temperature rises and decrease their output when the temperature decreases.

> Messages from the hypothalamus are conveyed to the surface of the body by the sympathetic, or thoracolumbar, division of the autonomic nervous system. It innervates both the sweat glands and the peripheral blood vessels. Although the postganglionic fibers supplying the sweat glands are cholinergic, they respond to stimulation of the sympathetic nervous system. [Beland and Passo 1975]

The last thermoreceptors are the core receptors located in deep body tissue.

In order for the individual to respond to internal and external stimuli there must be intact neural pathways. As we have discussed, these neural pathways positively influence neural output. This is accomplished by means of the neural pathways going from the hypothalamus to thermal effector organs within the body. The overall output of the controlled systems is assumed to be the temperature of the body as it is represented by the temperature of the hypothalamus. If the neural pathways from the hypothalamus to the thermal effectors fail to respond to the many feedback mechanisms, the individual's body approaches an ineffective response.

Third Set of Relationships

The second set of relationships and related propositions are a significant link to the third set of relationships. In the third set of relationships, chemical and neural inputs are postulated to influence normally responsive endocrine glands to hormonally influence target organs in a positive manner to maintain a state of dynamic equilibrium. This is predicated on the propositions labeled 1.1 to 3.2 in Table 5.1. This set of propositions seems to specify the interrelationships between the chemical and neural regulatory systems. Each system attempts to respond to alterations in the other to maintain a state of equilibrium.

Neural input was specifically discussed as it pertains to the second set of relationships. Of significance here are the nerve receptors that transmit cold and warmth sensations. The nerve receptors play a contributory role in regulating internal body temperature. They accomplish this by causing an emotional drive which seeks warmth, by communicating nerve impulses to the CNS so that the hypothalamic thermostat can be altered, and by stimulating local cord reflexes which affect skin blood flow. The skin blood flow attempts to help maintain normal body temperature. Neural as well as chemical input has an influence on several systems. According to Hardy (1965), cells can furnish input and outputs that simultaneously serve several systems. The sympathetic nervous system controls circulation through the skin's blood vessels. This function serves as a major factor in the control of the flow of heat from muscles and internal organs to the environment through the skin (Hardy 1965).

Neural and chemical balance is measured according to heat production and heat loss. Factors responsible for heat production include rate of metabolism of all cells in the body, increased rate of metabolism caused by muscle activity, increase in metabolism caused by effect of thyroxine in cells, increase in metabolism caused by effect of norepinephrine and sympathetic stimulation in cells, and increase in metabolism caused by increased temperature of body cell (Guyton 1971).

Chemical input influences the normally responsive endocrine system to produce the appropriate hormones. The hormonal system influences heat production and salt retention. The latter causes an increase in water retention which facilitates the transfer of heat from the interior of the individual's body to the external environment. The temperature that is being controlled or regulated is that of the deeper or core tissue of the body.

Other chemical stimuli include epinephrine and norepinephrine. For example, either sympathetic stimulation or norepinephrine and epinephrine circulating in the blood can cause an immediate response that brings an increase in the rate of metabolism. This effect is called chemical thermogenesis. Chemical thermogenesis results from the ability of epinephrine and norepinephrine to uncouple oxydature phosphorylation. As a result more oxidation of foodstuffs takes place, which then produces the necessary amount of high-energy phosphate compound needed for normal body function. The overall response is an increase in cellular metabolism.

Another hormone also plays a significant role in heat production. An increase of the neurosecretory hormone thyrotropin-releasing factor can be initiated by cooling the preoptic area of the hypothalamus. An intact neural and chemical system causes the hormone to move by way of the hypothalamic portal veins to the adenohypophysis where it stimulates the secretion of thyroxin. The increased thyroxin then increases the rate of cellular metabolism throughout the entire body.

The temperature-regulating mechanism, taking into account both the neural and chemical inputs upon the hormonal system, attempts to maintain a state of dynamic equilibrium. Changes in external and internal stimuli bring about changes in the dynamic state. For example, "when the temperature receptors of the skin are strongly stimulated, impulses from these interact with the hypothalamic temperature regulatory mechanism to reset the control levels of the hypothalamus thermostat slightly" (Guyton 1971). While there may exist strong external stimuli leading to overheating of the skin, the thermostatic center responds to the situation. Such a response is initiated before the excessive heat can be transmitted from the exterior or skin to the interior of the body. Likewise cooling the skin would lead to a similar set of responses. The temperature regulatory mechanism, together with neural and chemical input and feedback, strives to maintain equilibrium.

The third set or relationships focuses on the target organ's ability to maintain a state of dynamic equilibrium when confronted with varying degrees of change in internal and external stimuli. In this case the target organ is the temperature-regulating system. From this set of relationships, we can conclude that, given the normal influential response of chemical and neural input upon hormonal effect as it pertains to the target organ, the target organ will maintain a state of dynamic equilibrium. Such dynamic interplay occurs without the individual's awareness because these propositions involve normal adaptive responses. It is only when the chemical and neural inputs are unable to positively influence the endocrine glands and subsequently the hormone's influence upon target organs that the system becomes disorganized. When this response occurs, the individual becomes aware of his own ineffective behavior.

Fourth Set of Relationships

A fourth set of relationships provides the transition between adaptive and ineffective behaviors. This set of relationships involves the body's response to external and internal stimuli and states that such stimuli will alter those external and internal stimuli. This is predicated on the propositions labeled 1.1 to 5.1 in Table 5.1.

The above set of relationships involve both positive and negative feedback in response to external and internal stimuli. The exchange or feedback from temperature changes in the environment, for example, act upon internal stimuli. Likewise internal stimuli acts upon external stimuli that in return alter internal stimuli. Alterations of external and internal stimuli take into account three factors, namely, skin receptors, heat conservation, and response to heat loss. Each factor consists of adaptive responses that seek to maintain a state of normalcy.

The alteration of external and internal stimuli can be initiated by skin receptors. The body contains a set of skin receptors that respond rapidly to changes in temperature. Input received through skin receptors indicating a cold environment stimulates an increase in metabolic processes by means of increased muscle activity. Consequently a series of chemical reactions takes place each time a muscle contracts, and a byproduct of this process is heat—a normal adaptive response. The adaptive processes continue when the individual is placed in an environment that deviates from the normal. The skin receptors sense a cold external environment. The input received is communication via sensory nerves to the brain. Here impulses are transmitted by motor nerves to the muscles. The response leads to shivering and ultimately to an increase in heat production.

In order for the body to protect itself from undue loss of heat from the blood as it flows through exposed areas of the skin, it reduces blood flow through the skin. Cold external stimuli alter internal stimuli by vasoconstriction of the arterioles through which blood flows to the skin's capillaries. According to Langley (1965),

The cold air causes the skin receptors to fire, messages are transmitted by sensory nerves to the brain which in turn sends messages over motor nerves to muscles of the walls of the arterioles, and as a result, they constrict. Blood flow to the skin is therefore impeded.

The feedback mechanism involves the countercurrent heat exchange system. Internal body temperature is maintained through the process of vasoconstriction and countercurrent heat exchange system. The former limits blood flow to the body's skin surface. The latter serves to rewarm the blood. Both processes can increase body temperature a fraction of a degree in cold weather. Therefore the principle mechanisms of shivering, vasomotor control, and sweating are considered to be independent regulating systems in that each operates over a range of temperature.

A second example of altered external and internal stimuli involves heat conservation, which is a normal adaptive response. Heat conservation takes place through means already partially discussed. These include vasoconstriction, piloerection, and shivering. Vasoconstriction of the skin is a result of sympathetic stimulation leading to adrenergic vasoconstriction. Therefore heat is conserved. Piloerection is a second means by which heat is conserved—when the hypothalamus is cooled, the hairs stand on end. Lastly, shivering increases heat production through increased muscle activity. In terms of system theory, shivering results from feedback oscillation of the muscle spindle stretch reflex mechanism.

The third factor that can be associated with the fourth set of relationships is heat loss. According to Milhorn (1966),

> Heat is continually being produced by the body as a by-product of metabolic reaction. On the other hand, heat is continually being lost to the surroundings. Some feedback control system, therefore, is necessary to regulate the heat loss or heat production so that the body temperature remains constant.

Body temperature is maintained by a balance between heat production and heat loss. This is accomplished by three processes: radiation, which is the transfer of heat by means of waves; convection, which is movement of heat from one site to another by currents of air or fluid; and evaporation, which implies that water is converted to steam.

> The transfer of heat from the tissue to the blood and from the blood to the tissue illustrates one of the laws of thermodynamics; that is, energy travels from an area of greater energy to an area of lesser energy; that is, heat moves from the warmer to the cooler tissue. [Beland and Passos 1975]

Another facet of the body's response to alteration of internal and external stimuli is that heat is not always lost to the external environment.

Heat in the individual's extremities can be transmitted from the arteries to the cooler blood within the veins. This is accomplished by means of the countercurrent heat exchange mechanism. As circulating blood is increased through the skin, heat is lost. Heat is also lost by increasing the amount of skin surface exposed to the environment and enhancing the capacity of air around the body to assume heat or moisture. These latter events become significant for the nurse who manipulates ineffective stimuli.

External and internal stimuli by means of skin receptors—factors involved in heat conservation or heat loss—alter those external and internal stimuli. We implied that this was accomplished through negative feedback. The body, when confronted with an alteration in temperature regulation, seeks to adapt to the alteration by negating the potentially maladaptive stimuli. The individual who experiences a fever behaves as if his temperature-regulating center were reset at a higher level. In other words, action upon internal and external stimuli causes the body temperature to be regulated at a level above normal. This is still considered to be adaptive behavior. Naturally other subsystems become activated. Increased metabolism, increased heart rate, and increased respiratory rate are just a few of the possible effects.

The first four sets of relationships focused on normal adaptive temperature regulatory processes. The various propositions examined the following key concepts: internal and external stimuli, intact neural pathways, chemical and neural inputs, and feedback that permits the body to respond to external and internal stimulation. Each was examined in terms of their normalcy or adaptive response. As previously mentioned, the fourth set of relationships seems to have an interadaptive quality. This implies that there are instances when the fourth set of relationships fails to successfully alter internal and external stimuli in an adaptive way. The result begins the physiological trend towards ineffective behavior.

Fifth Set of Relationships

In the fifth set of relationships, the magnitude of the external and internal stimuli may be so great that the adaptive system cannot return the body to a state of dynamic equilibrium. This includes propositions 1.1 to 5.1 in Table 5.1.

When temperature exceeds 41 °C or 106 °F, regulatory mechanisms cannot be depended upon to resist further rise. External and internal stimuli may be so great that the body cannot return to equilibrium. Excessively high temperature can severely alter adaptive systems by inactivating essential enzyme systems and by producing permanent damage to the structure of body proteins. These two maladaptive responses alone lead to disequilibrium, disorganization, and potential death. Each maladaptive response will be discussed according to behavior exhibited, stimuli influencing ineffective regulation, and nursing interventions.

Hyperthermia

Hyperthermia is defined as a body temperature elevation above 41 °C or 106 °F. As this state approaches disorganization, the individual's body metabolism continues to produce heat. Even though heat is produced, very little heat is dissipated from the body. The patient is unable to perspire and his superficial blood vessels fail to dilate; consequently, his temperature continues to rise. The response is such that normal adaptive physiologic regulation can no longer overcome the rapid rate at which heat is produced. The overall result is that the patient's cooling mechanism is inadequate and death will result.

Regulatory Behavior.   Several of the behavioral manifestations associated with hyperthermia are the result of an increased metabolic rate. Regardless of their origin, the following behavioral responses are significant to the nurse in her assessment of the patient:

1. Headache, nausea, and vomiting
2. Rapid respirations and rapid bounding pulse which is probably the result of increased metabolic processes
3. Weakness and muscle flaccidity
4. Seizures
5. Delirium
6. Chills
7. Sweating

The latter two behaviors are of significance to the nurse attempting to intervene at the maladaptive level. As the patient chills, his skin becomes pale, cyanotic, and covered with goose flesh. The most common cause of a chill is the introduction of a foreign substance into the blood stream—either living infectious agents or their products, bacterial pyrogens. Extraneous substances such as lymphoma and hypernephroma can also cause chills. Regardless of its cause, the nurse should recognize that the behavior is indicative of a potentially serious problem.

Sweating is the counterpart of the chill. Sweating facilitates heat loss and tends to produce a rapid fall in temperature. It is usually combined with an increased circulation to the skin which thereby permits rapid dissipation of heat by vaporization. The nurse keeps in mind that sweating is a common behavior in diseases associated with intermittent fever such as tuberculosis and rheumatic fever. When the magnitude of external and internal stimuli exceeds the thermoregulatory center's ability to adapt there is an absence of sweating. The absence of sweating may signify to the nurse that CNS damage has occurred.

Focal Stimuli.   Focal stimuli in the fifth set of relationships involve temperature imbalance and are represented by disease states. These disease states place a strain upon normal temperature regulatory mechanism, thereby contributing to a maladaptive state. The focal stimuli can be grouped into twelve categories.

1. Diseases of the central nervous system
   (a) Head injury
   (b) Cerebral vascular accident
   (c) Neurologic hyperthermia
   (d) Spinal cord injury
   (e) Brain tumor
2. Neoplasms
   (a) Lymphoma
3. Blood diseases
   (a) Anemias
   (b) Leukemias
4. Embolism
5. Heat stroke
6. Disturbance in fluid balance
   (a) Dehydration
7. Diseases affecting the heart
   (a) Congestive heart failure
   (b) Subacute endocarditis
8. Drug fever
9. Fever of unknown origin
10. Thyroid disease
11. Liver disease
12. Tissue trauma

It should be kept in mind that the above list of categories is not an exhaustive one.

Manipulating Stimuli.   Given that the magnitude of the external and internal stimuli are so great that the adaptive system can return the body to a state of dynamic equilibrium, the nurse intervenes by manipulating stimuli that contribute to the maladaptive or disorganized state.

Manipulation of focal stimuli lies within the physician's domain. The nurse can nevertheless utilize her physical assessment skills in an attempt to alter the regulatory behavior. In this respect, the nurse intervenes by manipulating external and internal stimuli to increase heat loss. Such manipulation includes altering environmental temperature; reducing physical activity, thereby conserving metabolic processes; administering antipyretic drugs; taking direct measures to reduce hyperthermia; and administering dietary and fluid intake. Such manipulation involves the contextual stimuli.

The patient's environmental temperature needs to be monitored for its appropriateness to his particular problem. For example, an environment that is too warm will only act to increase metabolic processes and thereby increase temperature. Furthermore, a warm environment will cause the patient to experience irritability, malaise, and restlessness. If the hyperthermic patient is near a sunny window, the nurse can either move the patient to a less sunny location or pull the curtains. When possible, environmental air may be cooled by means of an air conditioner.

When temperature is elevated, measures may be taken to manipulate those stimuli increasing the metabolic rate. Such stimuli include chilling, increased mobility, and infection. When the patient chills, his temperature can increase anywhere from 2° to 7°. Chilling increases the metabolic rate, causing a further rise in temperature. Therefore, the patient's temperature can be taken frequently during and after the chill. When feedback fails to negate those stimuli altering the thermoregulatory center and causing high temperature, a rectal probe may be inserted to continually monitor the patient's temperature. A rectal probe reduces the constant stimulation of the patient caused by repeated insertion of a thermometer. It also provides a more accurate reading of body temperature.

During the chill episode there is a tendency to cover the patient with several blankets. This seems to be an appropriate intervention. The blankets serve as an insulator of body heat. The result may be a further contribution to elevated body temperature immediately after the chill episode. Therefore the nurse, realizing that the chill episode is a temporary event, may better assist her patient by applying fewer rather than more blankets. The goal is to avoid placing additional stress upon the already stressed thermoregulatory system.

Physical activity leads to an increase in body metabolism, thereby increasing body temperature. It should be kept in mind that regulatory behaviors such as increased cardiac and respiratory rate are the result of increased metabolism due to high temperature. A compensatory response is dilation of the peripheral-blood vessels, causing the patient to feel flushed.

Vascular changes, including tachycardia, can place an additional burden on cardiac reserve leading to the ineffective response of cardiac failure. Furthermore the patient's other adaptive systems may be weakened or threatened so that resistance to infection, for example, is lessened. Therefore the patient should be confined to his bed with little physical activity. Because a febrile state causes fatigue, the patient may not have the energy for mobility. If the patient is comatose, his nurse should facilitate movement through frequent turning. The patient whose skin breaks down from immobility is a candidate for infections which lead to increased metabolic processes.

Protection from infection should be a major nursing goal regardless of the underlying focal stimuli necessitating hospitalization. It becomes even more critical for patients with high body temperature.

Direct manipulation of focal stimuli can be accomplished with antipyretic drugs. Antipyretic drugs act upon hypothalamic centers. Their effectiveness is accomplished through the reduction of the thermoregulatory center's sensitivity and the production of diaphoresis. Antipyretic drugs are useful in treating temperature elevation caused by the action of pyrogens in the thermoregulatory center. There are hyperthermic situations that do not respond to antepyretic drugs. According to Luckmann and Sorensen (1974), "These drugs are of little or no value in treating hyperthermias resulting from hypoxia, heat stroke, or injured thermoregulatory center, e.g. from CVA, cerebral trauma, or following head injury or brain surgery." The nurse assesses whether or not the drug is effective in reducing the patient's temperature. Inability of the drug to reduce temperature caused by focal stimuli normally responsive may indicate a further maladaptive problem.

In addition to administering antipyretic drugs, the nurse may need to utilize direct cooling measures. When the thermoregulatory center is injured so that the adaptive systems are unable to return the body to a state of dynamic equilibrium, the only effective measures are those that increase heat loss through an increase in the temperature gradient between the skin and the external environment. The nurse accomplishes this goal by increasing the evaporation of moisture from the patient's skin, thus enabling heat to move from the patient's tissue to the surrounding environment. A measure to enhance evaporation is to cool the patient's skin with water or alcohol. During an alcohol or water bath the skin is massaged to enhance circulation. The measure is continued until the patient's temperature begins to decline.

When cooling by an alcohol or water bath fails to decrease the patient's temperature it may be necessary to utilize a hypothermia blanket. The hypothermia blanket causes heat loss by two processes, namely conduction and convection. Heat is transferred from the body surface to the cooling blanket. Throughout the entire cooling process, the nurse assesses any regulatory behavior indicating potential complications. These regulatory behaviors include sudden changes in temperature, shivering, changes in cardiac rate, or arrhythmias.

Lastly the nurse seeks to administer fluids and facilitate appropriate dietary intake. Fluid intake is decreased or increased depending upon the underlying focal stimuli. A patient with a neurological dysfunction may better adapt with a decreased fluid intake. On the other hand, the patient whose metabolic rate increases also experiences an increase in sweating. The overall result is a loss of as much as three liters of water each day. Furthermore salt is also lost. It becomes imperative for the nurse to extrinsically maintain a fluid balance through replacement of lost fluids. This is accomplished through careful administration of intravenous and oral fluids.

Just as increased metabolism leads to increased fluid and salt loss, it also contributes to an increase in utilization of calories and protein catabolism. Carbohydrate and protein intake needs to be increased in proportion to the degree of temperature elevation to prevent or control weight loss. The nurse can independently assess the patient's daily weight and amount of dietary intake. If both seem to be in deficit, she can communicate her assessment to the appropriate individual.

Hypothermia

Hypothermia can result from either accidental or intentional stimuli. The patient may have suffered from prolonged exposure to extremely cold environmental stimuli. Whether intentional or induced, hypothermia is the controlled reduction of body temperature from 89.6° to 78.8 °F.

The body can tolerate, within limits, temperatures above or below what is considered to be normal. According to Guyton (1971),

> Once the body temperature has fallen below 85 °F, the ability of the hypothalamus to regulate temperature is completely lost, and it is greatly impaired even when the body temperature falls below approximately 94 °F. Part of the reason for this loss of temperature regulation is that the rate of heat production in each cell is greatly depressed by the low temperature. Also, sleepiness and even coma are likely to develop which depress the activity of the central nervous system heat-control mechanism and prevent shivering.

For example,

> The rate and moisture associated with cooling are critical factors in determining whether or not tissue injury results. With fast moist cooling, ice crystals form that damage capillary endothelium, thus increasing capillary permeability. Intravascular fluid leaks into interstitial spaces, erythrocytes concentrate and clump in the capillaries, blood flow is obstructed, and tissue destruction ensues. [Beland and Passos 1975]

Regulatory Behaviors. A maladaptively low body temperature can result in behavioral manifestations indicative of a lowered metabolic rate. The regulatory behaviors of significance are the following:

1. Increased cardiac rate
2. Decreased respiratory rate
3. Cardiac arrhythmias
4. Hypotension
5. Oliguria
6. Piloerection
7. Pale to cyanotic skin
8. Numbness in extremities
9. Shivering
10. Possible loss of consciousness

Just as the patient with impending hyperthermia can experience shivering, the patient with hypothermia can also demonstrate the same regulatory behavior. As previously mentioned, shivering is accompanied by an increase in the production of heat and by changes decreasing heat loss. When the mechanisms are adequate, body temperature is maintained at a normal level. When there is greater insulation due to fat or clothing, lowered environmental temperature will increase heat production. Body weight also enhances heat conservation. If cold environmental stimuli continue, shivering ceases; however heat production is sustained by enzymatic activity of muscles, liver, and other organs.

Focal Stimuli. The focal stimuli influencing a maladaptive state leading to hypothermia cannot be specifically categorized as those leading to hyperthermia. However, we can state that, in general, the following can cause hypothermia:

1. Extremely cold environment
2. Artificial induction through use of hypothermia blanket
3. Depression of CNS by drugs such as morphine and barbituates
4. Cool temperature which damages the hypothalamus

Once again the above list is not an exhaustive one. It simply provides a framework for considering possible focal stimuli that could cause or be caused by hypothermia.

Manipulating the Stimuli. The nurse attempts to manipulate those stimuli that influence maladaptive temperature regulation, namely hypothermia. The contributing focal stimuli are not all within the nurse's domain. Instead she makes assessments and interventions by manipulating contextual stimuli.

Manipulation of contextual stimuli includes rewarming the hypothermic patient through passive or active rewarming techniques. Passive rewarming consists of placing the patient in an environment slightly warmer than his own body temperature. This process prevents additional heat loss while allowing heat production to increase core body temperature. The nurse manipulates environmental stimuli by placing the patient at normal room temperature. Furthermore she covers him with light bed covering. The patient's temperature should be monitored frequently in order to determine its gradual increase of 1° to 2°F every hour. While rewarming the patient, the nurse realizes that any attempt to bring about an adaptive state can simultaneously overstress other systems.

As the patient warms, he is in danger of developing hypovolemic shock as his arterioles dilate. To prevent this complication the physician may prescribe intravenous fluids. They should be administered slowly because rapid infusion of fluids may overload the circulatory system. [Beland and Passos 1975]

While rewarming the patient, the nurse takes particular care not to overheat the sensitive skin of the hypothermic patient. Any external heat is therefore applied very carefully. The skin of the hypothermic patient should be frequently inspected.

The second technique utilized by the nurse to manipulate contextual stimuli is active rewarming of the hypothermic patient. Active rewarming is accomplished by altering the internal or external environment of the patient. Manipulation of external stimuli involves placing the patient in hot water or between thermal blankets. Such an intervention can lead to undesirable stimuli such as rewarming shock caused by peripheral vasodilation. Manipulation of internal stimuli is accomplished by applying heated fluids directly to the core organs in greatest danger of injury from hypothermia. This process involves peritoneal dialysis, cardiopulmonary bypass, and thoracotomy with lavage of the mediastinum.

Regardless of which technique is utilized to bring about an adaptive state of normal body temperature, the nurse assesses the patient's vital signs including central venous pressure. Besides the threat of rewarming shock, the patient is susceptible to arrhythmias such as ventricular fibrillation and cardiac arrest. The arrhythmias can result from metabolic acidosis which in return is the result of anaerobic metabolism. Therefore the patient can be connected to a cardioscope so that life-threatening arrhythmias can be recognized, recorded, and reported.

Residual stimuli

Regardless of the maladaptive thermoregulatory problem, the nurse realizes that the residual stimuli are numerous. The residual stimuli may include age, educational background, previous experience with illness, and knowledge regarding current illness.

The patient may or may not have difficulty understanding the external and internal stimuli that contribute to an ineffective response of either hyperthermia or hypothermia. If, for example, the patient's hyperthermia is due to heat stroke, he should be educated as to the hazards of an extremely warm environment. Likewise the aged patient with peripheral vascular insufficiency should be instructed to avoid extremely cold environmental stimuli thereby causing a compensatory peripheral vasoconstriction. This regulatory response can further compromise an already compromised peripheral blood flow which could end with the loss of a limb.

Example of Hypothesis for Practice

We have focused on the process of theorizing with the temperature physiological mode. Based on our theorizing with the temperature mode, we can postulate any number of hypotheses that can be tested. The theorizing encompasses the four sets of relationships and their related propositions. In addition the hypotheses can be used as a guide for practice. An example of a possible hypothesis will be discussed.

The hypothesis may be stated as follows: If the nurse helps the patient maintain a temperature level for normal physiological functioning, the patient's cellular activity and body metabolism will perform at a more optimal level. The reason for this hypothesis is drawn from the set of relationships which are based on propositions stated earlier. The reasons are shown below.

General Statement: The magnitude of the internal and external stimuli will positively influence the magnitude of the physiological response of an intact system.

Specific Statement: The amount of input in the form of heat will positively influence the temperature regulatory system.

The nurse utilizes the four sets of relationships to theorize regarding temperature regulation. The theorizing permits hypothesis generation even when the nurse manipulates contextual stimuli. With each component of the contextual stimuli, the nurse can hypothesize regarding patient care. If the nurse finds evidence of significance for a hypothesis, the nursing activity specified in the research protocol can become a prescription for practice in situations where nursing diagnosis warrants this intervention. The theorizing also applies to interventions identified in the contextual stimuli section. Therefore several different hypothesis can be generated for the temperature mode.

Summary

Temperature regulation has been examined according to four sets of relationships. The propositions and theorized relationships focus on external and internal stimuli that influence normal physical process in thermoregulation. The thermoregulatory center attempts to adapt to chemical and neural inputs. Ineffective responses occur when the magnitude of external and internal stimuli are greater than the body's ability to maintain a state of dynamic equilibrium. The result leads to disequilibrium, and acute or chronic illness.

When the temperature-regulating mechanism is ineffective, the nurse intervenes by assessing and manipulating the influencing factors—focal, contextual, and residual stimuli—as they apply to hyperthermia and hypothermia. While doing so, the nurse can draw upon the theorizing and related propositions to generate hypotheses regarding any aspect of temperature regulation.

References and Additional Readings

Beland, Irene, and Joyce Passos. *Clinical Nursing Pathophysiological and Psychosocial Approaches.* New York: Macmillan, 1975.

Castle, Mary, and Jane Watkins. "Fever: Understanding A Sinister Sign," *Nursing,* 9, no. 2 (February 1979): 26–33.

Felton, C. L. "Hypoxemia and Oral Temperatures," *American Journal of Nursing,* 78, no. 1 (January 1978): 56–57.

Guyton, Arthur. *Textbook of Medical Physiology.* Philadelphia: Saunders, 1971.

Hardy, J. D. "The Set Point Concept in Physiological Temperature Regulation." In *Physiological Controls and Regulation,* ed. William Yamamoto and John Brobeck. Philadelphia: Saunders, 1965.

Huckaba, Charles, and John Downer. "Overview of Human Thermoregulation." In *Regulation and Control in Physiological System,* ed. A. S. Iberall, and A. Guyton. Pittsburg: Instrument Society of America, 1973.

Langley, L. L. *Homeostasis.* New York: Reinhold, 1965.

Luckmann, Joan, and Karen Sorensen. *Medical-Surgical Nursing: A Psychophysiologic Approach.* Philadelphia: Saunders, 1974.

Matzke, Howard, and Floyd Foltz. *Synopsis of Neuroanatomy.* New York: Oxford University Press, 1972.

Milhorn, Howard. *The Application of Control Theory to Physiological Systems.* Philadelphia: Saunders, 1966.

Swift, Nancy. "Helping Patients Live with Seizures," *Nursing,* 8, no. 6 (June 1978): 24–31.

Zenk, Karin. "Drugs Used for Neurological Disorders," *Critical Care Update,* 6, no. 9 (September 1979): 19–24.

CHAPTER 12

The senses

The sensory system enables the human person to receive inputs from the external and internal environment. These inputs are necessary for interactive purposes. Individuals have a tendency to take their relationship with the sensory environment for granted. The sensory stimuli received through the various sensory modalities stimulate the regulatory processes and bring about adaptation.

The senses can be separated into general and special types. The separation is based on the causative stimuli.

> General senses are those aroused by stimuli acting in and within the body. These energy changes are mainly mechanical in nature. We usually think of special senses as those which are aroused by stimuli originating at a variable distance from the body, as, for example light and sound waves. [Gardner 1969]

Even when the stimuli are at a variable distance they nevertheless must be close enough to interact with the receptors. For example, sound waves must reach the ear in order to be heard. On the other hand, taste cannot occur at a distance. Special senses therefore refer to "sensory qualities dependent upon receptors in the cranial region, whose afferent paths are over cranial nerves and which may allow perception of distant objects (Gardner 1969).

Input to the nervous system of sensory stimuli such as touch, sound, light, and taste is provided through sensory receptors. The sensory modalities or special senses can be classified according to external modalities and internal modalities. The external modalities are auditory, visual, gustatory, olfactory, and tactile. The internal modalities, on the other hand, are kinesthetic-visceral. The sensory modalities of greatest significance are visual, auditory and tactile. Ineffective responses in any one of the mentioned target systems can become an influencing factor for sensory deprivation and sensory overload.

The visual, auditory, and tactile sensory modes will be discussed according to the five sets of theoretical relationships. The first four sets of relationships focus on adaptive regulatory responses of internal and external stimuli. The last set of relationships focuses on ineffective responses. The ineffective response will be examined according to regulatory behaviors, focal stimuli, manipulation of contextual stimuli, and a brief discussion of residual stimuli.

First Set of Relationships

The first set of relationships is as follows: The magnitude of the internal and external stimuli will positively influence the magnitude of the physiological response of an intact system. This is predicated on the propositions labeled 1.1 to 2.1, 3.2, and 4.4 in Table 5.2.

Adequate stimuli are stimuli of a magnitude necessary to generate electrical potential in the specific sensory receptor. Stimuli external to the individual generate a response in the modes to be discussed, namely, visual, auditory, and tactile. Internal stimuli generates responses in the visceral and kinesthetic sensory modes. Stimuli from internal and external sources contribute to the overall sensory information which the brain then interprets in an attempt to make the correct response. Changes in the magnitude of environmental stimuli can alter the sensory input to the brain. It should be kept in mind that the stimuli received are quite specific for the sensory receptors. For example, one does not see a noise or hear a light. Therefore the process of sensory perception is initiated by an external or internal stimuli. External stimuli influence the intact visual, auditory, and tactile sensory systems.

The visual sensory system is highly complex and consists of the cornea, the lens, the pupil, the muscular following system for tracking, and its signal-processing capability. The cornea and the lens act together to form images on the retina. External visual stimuli are received through the pupil. The pupil sharpens the image through the process of accommodation. The pupil also acts as part of a feedback loop that controls a stimuli such as light entering the eye and subsequently striking the retina (Milhorn 1966). The magnitude of the incoming visual stimulus is controlled by the ability of the lens to accommodate or adapt to that stimulus. As the magnitude of the light increases, the pupil responds by constricting. Likewise a decrease in magnitude of light causes the pupil to respond by becoming less constricted.

The auditory system is a mechanoreceptive sensory mode, in which the ear responds to mechanical vibrations of sound waves in the air. The ear contains a structure called the organ of Corti. This intact organ contains a series of mechanically sensitive hair cells. The hair cells are the receptive end organs that generate nerve impulses in direct response to sound vibration. As the magnitude of external auditory stimuli such as sound vibrations increases, the intact receptive end organs or hair cells augment nerve impulses. According to Guyton (1971),

> The transduction mechanism for detecting sound by the cochlear of the ear illustrates still another method for separating gradations of stimulus intensity. When sound causes vibration at a specific point in the basilar membrane, weak vibration stimulates only those hair cells in the very center of the vibrating point.

The ear also contains cochlear nerve fibers for the receptive areas of the basilar membrane terminating in a corresponding area of the cochlear nuclei. The intensity and pitch of sounds activate specific neurons. Such a response is the result of signal being received from the auditory tract in the brain stem in conjunction with signals from the auditory receptive field in the cerebral cortex.

The tactile system contains the pacinian corpuscle which is responsive to the external stimuli of compression or touch. Compression of the corpuscle causes the central core of the nonmyelinated nerve fiber to become elongated, shortened, or deformed. The response is dependent upon the magnitude of external stimuli. Sudden external pressure applied to the skin will excite the pacinian corpuscle receptor for a few seconds. While the external stimulus continues, the excitation of the receptor terminates. "In other words, the pacinian corpuscle is exceedingly important in transmitting information about constant pressure applied to the body (Guyton 1971).

Deformation of the central core of the nerve fiber with the pacinian corpuscle causes a sudden change in membrane potential. The change in local membrane potential leads to a local circuit of current flow which spreads along the nerve fiber. The magnitude of stimuli determines the magnitude of generator potential response. As Guyton (1971) points out,

At low stimulus strength, very slight changes in stimulus strength increase the generator potential markedly; whereas at high levels of stimulus strength further increases in generator potential are very slight. Thus, the pacinian corpuscle is capable of accurately measuring extremely minute changes in stimulus strength at low intensity level and is also capable of detecting much larger changes in stimulus strength at high intensity levels.

Therefore tactile sensation is the result of external stimuli in the tactile receptors which are found in the skin and in the layer of tissues directly beneath the skin.

Alterations in internal and external stimuli are received through receptors and communicated by means of neural pathways or nerve fibers. This process involves the second set of relationships.

Second Set of Relatiionships

In the second set of relationships, the intact neural pathways will positively influence neural output to effectors. This is predicated on the propositions labeled 3.1 to 2.1, and 4.4 in Table 5.1. The specific sensory receptor receives input and transmits the neural input to the brain. The neural input may directly synapse with areas of the brain or with sensory nerve tracts in the spinal cord. The visual sensory system can be categorized according to visual control, receptor cells of the retina, the conducting pathways, and the primary receptive and association parts of the cerebral cortex.

The visual control system consists of accommodation, pupillary aperture, eye movement, and the retina. Accommodation, which is essential for visual acuity, is the result of contraction or relaxation of the ciliary muscle. Contraction leads to increased strength of the lens system. On the other hand, relaxation causes a decreased strength in the same receptor. According to Milhorn (1966), "Accommodation is regulated by a negative feedback mechanism that automatically adjusts the focal power of the lens for the highest degree of visual acuity." The pupillary aperture is decreased due to excitation of the pupillary sphincter by the parasympathetic nerves. Likewise the pupillary aperture is increased when the radial fibers of the iris are stimulated by sympathetic nerves. The third component of visual control is eye movement or visual associative area. The visual associative area receives visual, positional, and eye positional information. Once the information is received, it is transmitted to the occulomotor center where an output command such as movement is accomplished. Lastly the retina functions as a facilitator of information between light received and nervous impulses to the central nervous system. The visual pathway and visual cortex act on the retinal output in such a manner as to provide a visual image. Furthermore the visual pathway and visual cortex relay information to the already mentioned associative areas.

The receptor cell of the retina consists of the rods and cones. The rods and cones are the photosensitive elements of differential sensitivity and distribution.

> The general arrangement of retinal cells is such that rods and cones connect with bipolar cells, which in turn synapse with ganglion cells. The axons of the ganglion cells course toward the back of the eye; at the optic disk they collect to form the optic nerve. [Gardner 1969]

Each type of receptor is sensitive to the particular stimulus for which it is designed. It is nonresponsive to normal intensities of other types of sensory stimuli. For example, the receptive cells of the rods and cones are responsive to light but nonresponsive to heat, cold, or pressure on the eye.

The auditory pathways will positively influence neural output to effectors. Guyton describes four significant points relating to the auditory pathway. First, stimuli from either ear are transmitted through the auditory pathways of both sides of the brainstem with only slight transmission in the contralateral pathway. Second, many collateral fibers from the auditory tracts pass directly into the reticular activating system of the brainstem. Third, the pathway for transmission of sound stimuli from the cochlea to the cortex consists of at least four neurons and sometimes as many as six. Some of the tracts are more direct than others. Therefore some sound stimuli reach the cortex sooner than other sound stimuli even when they originate at the same time. Lastly, there exist significant pathways from the auditory system into the cerebellum. The pathways come directly from the ischlear nuclei, the inferior colliculi, the reticular substance of the brain stem, and the cerebral auditory areas (Guyton 1971).

The tactile sensory mode involves neural pathways from the node of Ranvier which lies inside the pancinian corpuscle. The local stimuli leading to current flow will initiate the action potentials in the nerve fiber. In other words, the stimuli through the node of Ranvier depolarize it with the output being transmission of action potential along the nerve fiber to the central nervous system. The body also contains special tactile receptors in the fingertips, lips, and skin which allow the individual to discriminate spatial characteristics of tactile stimuli. This type of receptor is called Meisser's corpuscle, an encapsulated nerve ending whose function it is to excite a large myelinated sensory nerve fiber. The areas of the body that contain Meissner's corpuscles are responsible for providing a steady-state signal that permits the individual to assess continuous touch of objects against the skin (Guyton 1971). Touching the body's hair stimulates nerve fibers encompassed in the hair's base. The hair end organ is a specialized receptor that adapts to movement of objects on the body's surface.

The osmoreceptor of the supraoptic nuclei in the hypothalamus is activated when tactile stimuli become strong enough to damage the tissue. When the tissue becomes too deformed, the ability of the pacinian corpuscle to emit its local current is depressed. The resulting output is decreased nerve fiber firing.

The intact neural system and its receptors influence neural output to receptors. If the neural system and its neural pathways did not positively influence neural output to effectors, the sensory modalities—visual, auditory, and tactile—would reach an ineffective state of disequilibrium.

Third Set of Relationships

The second set of relationships and their propositions are an important building block to the third set of relationships. In the third set of relationships, chemical and neural inputs are postulated to influence the normally responsive sensory system to hormonally influence target organs in a positive manner to maintain a state of dynamic equilibrium. This is predicated on the propositions labeled 1.1 to 3.2 in Table 5.1.

According to Mitchell (1973),

> The thalamus, hypothalamus, and reticular activating system (RAS) all play roles in assembling and integrating income and outgoing data. The input is relayed to the cortex, where it is interpreted, and conscious awareness of sensation occurs. Firing of neurons within the cortex itself can activate the reticular system and influence or alter the perception of external stimuli.

The input from sensory stimuli goes through the reticular activating system from the hypothalamus and the classical sensory tracts. Stimulation of the reticular activating system leads to an aroused state. Likewise a decrease of incoming stimuli leads to drowsiness. In the latter instance, the individual seeks stimuli that will restore equilibrium. When sensory stimuli exceed the optimal magnitude, the individual will seek ways to reduce input.

There are neural feedback mechanisms which consist of nerves from the brain to the retina. The feedback mechanism seeks to alter retinal behavior. Specifically the feedback control from the brain tends (1) to keep the overall light intensity in the retina constant by varying the pupillary opening, (2) to keep the image in sharp focus on the retina by varying the optics of the eye, (3) to keep the image steady upon the retina by varying the contraction of the extraocular muscles so as to hold fixed the direction of gaze (Lipetz 1973). The input is conducted via the visual pathway and visual cortex to act upon the retinal output which responds by providing a conscious visual image and relays information to the associative areas. The visual associative areas receive the neural input and send an output command to the oculomotor center to cause movement. The oculomotor purpose is to receive and interpret the information received so that the appropriate muscle commands can take place.

Neural fiber input from the ear terminates in the auditory areas of the brain. Regardless of the type of auditory stimulus that excites the nerve ending, it first causes a local flow of current in the neighborhood of the nerve ending. The current generated in turn excites action potentials in the nerve fibers. The second mechanism for causing local current involves specialized receptor cells. These specialized cells can be found adjacent to the nerve endings. According to Guyton (1971), "when sounds enter the cochlea of the ear, the hair cells that lie in the basilar membrane emit electrical circuits that in turn stimulate the terminal nerve fibrils itself or from a specialized receptor cell."

It should be kept in mind that each nerve tract terminates at a specific point in the central nervous system. The type of sensation experienced when the nerve fiber receives a stimulus is dependent upon the specific area in the nervous system to which the fiber leads. If for example, the touch fiber is stimulated through excitation of a touch receptor, the individual will perceive touch. This is because the touch or tactile areas in the brain have received neural input. The thalamus receives tactile stimuli and relays information received to the cortex.

Chemical input can also influence the sensory system's ability to maintain a state of dynamic equilibrium. Changes in temperature and chemical composition in the blood flow which circulates in the retina can cause alterations in it's behavior. The alterations require periods of several minutes before they become evident (Lipetz 1973). Nevertheless chemical input can also lead to alterations in receptor potentials.

> For instance, in the rods and cones of the eye it is known that changes in certain intracellular chemicals in exposure to light alter the membrane potential, resulting in the receptor potential. In this case, the basic mechanism causing the receptor potential is a chemical one in contrast to mechanical deformation that causes the generator potential in the pacinian corpuscle. [Guyton 1971]

When the chemical and neural inputs are unable to positively influence the sensory system and its hormonal influence upon target organs, the system becomes disorganized. When disorganization begins, the individual becomes aware of his own ineffective responses.

Fourth Set of Relationships

A fourth set of relationships provides the transition between adaptive and maladaptive behavior. This set of relationships involves the body's response to external and internal stimuli and state that such stimuli will alter those external and internal stimuli. This is predicated on the propositions labeled 1.1 to 5.1 in Table 5.1.

Receptors that adapt quickly are not used to transmit a continuous signal because these receptors are stimulated only when the external and internal stimuli strength changes. The receptors will respond strongly while an alteration is taking place. The external and internal stimuli once received will not become psychologically meaningful until the stimulus undergoes organizaton. Factors that will influence the selection of internal and external stimuli include intensity, size, charge, and repetition of stimuli. For example, the intensity of sound, light, or touch stimuli influences the individual's attention. The more intense the stimuli, the greater the body's tendency to attend to the stimuli. Furthermore repeated stimuli have a greater tendency towards reception than do infrequently repeated stimuli.

There are also poorly adapting receptors. The receptors that adapt slowly also do not adapt to extinction. Instead they continue to transmit impulses to the brain as long as the external and internal stimuli are present. The brain is therefore continually apprised of the status of the body and its relationship to the environment. Other examples of poorly adapting receptors include receptors of the macula in the vestibular apparatus, the sound receptors, and the pain receptors. The poorly adapting receptors are called tonic receptors because they can communicate information for many hours. It is possible that many of the poorly adapting receptors would adapt to extinction if the intensity of the external or internal stimuli remained absolutely constant for a prolonged period of time (Guyton 1971).

Reception is therefore the biological aspect of the sensory process. For example, the receptors of the semicircular canals in the vestibular system of the ear have the unique ability to detect the rate at which the head begins to turn when running around a curve. Likewise visual experience occurs through receptors of the eye. Various types of disturbances will alter external and internal stimuli. Dyplopia, myopia, cataracts, or detached retina are among the disturbances that impede the visual process. Depending upon the intensity or severity of the visual disturbances, the individual's sensory process may not be able to respond to external and internal stimuli. As Guyton (1971) points out,

> Adaptation of receptors seems to be an individual property of each type of receptor in much the same way that development of a generator or receptor potential is an individual property. For instance, in the eye, the rods and cones adapt by changing their chemical compositions.

Just as reception is the biological aspect of the sensory system, perception is the psychological aspect of the same sensory system. The individual is able to perceptually adapt when looking at an object either at a distance or close at hand. In this respect, the individual selects and organizes the psychologically meaningless retinal images into something meaningful.

The fourth set of relationships has an interadaptive quality and signifies a linkage between adaptive and ineffective regulatory responses. There are times when the fourth set of relationships fails to successfully alter internal and external stimuli in an adaptive way. Instead the intact organ or system responds in an ineffective manner.

Fifth Set of Relationships

In the fifth set of relationships, the magnitude of the external and internal stimuli may be so great that the adaptive systems cannot return the body to a state of dynamic equilibrium. This includes propositions 1.1 to 5.1 in Table 5.1

When the level of imbalance in the sensory system and any one of its external or internal modes exceeds the body's internal ability to restore equilibrium, regulatory mechanisms cannot be depended upon to resist further imbalance. External and internal stimuli may be of a magnitude that the body cannot return to equilibrium; instead it experiences disequilibrium. Sensory deprivation and sensory overload become ineffective responses associated with the sensory system. If a regulatory mechanism such as sensoristasis fails, the result ranges from the disorganization of confusion or hallucination to psychotic behavior.

Ineffective responses to the visual, auditory, and tactile sensory modes revolve around the regulatory mechanism called *sensoristasis*. When sensory stimuli fall below the optimal level, the individual will seek alternative stimuli or alternative ways of carrying the stimuli. According to Schultz (1965),

> Sensoristasis can be defined as a drive state of cortical arousal which impels the organism (in a waking state) to strive to maintain an optimal level of sensory variation. There is, in other words, a drive to maintain a constant range of varied sensory input in order to maintain cortical arousal at an optimal level. Conceptually, this sensory variation based formulation is alien to homeostasis in that the organism drives to maintain an internal balance, but it is a balance on stimulus variation to the cortex as mediated by the RAS (Reticular Activating System).

When the external and internal stimuli exceeds the ability of the visual, auditory, and tactile sensory modes to adapt, the ineffective response includes sensory deprivation and sensory overload. Sensory deprivation and sensory overload will each be examined in terms of regulatory behaviors, focal stimuli, and manipulation of contextual and residual stimuli.

Sensory deprivation

Sensory deprivation is defined as "an absolute reduction in variety and intensity of sensory input, with or without a change in pattern. An environment of silence and darkness, for example, would be considered an instance of sensory deprivation" (Worrell 1971). The experience of sensory deprivation can be described as a situation in which reception or perception of external or internal stimuli is blocked or altered. With sensory deprivation there is a reduction in the quality of input with or without a change in pattern. Sensory deprivation involves a reduction in the intensity of stimulation; in the meaningfulness of stimulation; and in the patterning of stimulation of the visual, auditory, and tactile sensory modalities. Sensory deprivation exhibits specific regulatory behaviors.

Regulatory Behaviors. The regulatory behaviors associated with sensory deprivation can result from stimulus reduction to a single or multiple modality. In other words, restricted sensory input may take place in one or all three sensory modes discussed. Behavioral responses associated with reduced external or internal sensory input include the following:

1. Acute anxiety
2. Delusions
3. Hallucinations
4. Confusion
5. Disorientation
6. Nervousness
7. Anger

Each individual differs in his or her specific behavioral response to deprivation. Furthermore the duration and intensity of deprivation can influence the overall rapidity in onset of the ineffective regulatory behaviors.

Focal Stimuli. When one modality is affected by a decreased input, other modalities become sensitive to stimuli. A reduction in visual stimuli may enhance auditory stimuli. There are various influencing factors that contribute to ineffective response of the visual modality. The following focal stimuli bring about reduction in visual stimulation:

1. Eye trauma
   (a) Foreign body
   (b) Toxic chemicals
   (c) Penetrating wounds
   (d) Lacerations

2. Infection
   (a) Conjunctivitis
3. Strabismus
4. Glaucoma
5. Retinal detachment

Reduction in stimulation, meaningfulness, and patterning can be further influenced by other events. The age of the individual, the onset of visual alteration, and the severity of the alteration—whether it is partial or complete—will affect the person's adaptive response. For example, an individual who suddenly experiences blindness due to an injury, illness, or accident has little time to psychologically adapt to the loss.

Like the visual mode, the auditory modality can experience deprivation through reduced input of stimuli. The following focal stimuli lead to altered auditory input:

1. Foreign bodies
2. Otitis media
3. Mastoiditis
4. Ocosclerosis
5. Neural Damage
   (a) Toxic drugs
   (b) Head injury
   (c) Viral infection
6. Ruptured eardrum

Reduced auditory input to a maladaptive level is influenced by age of onset and degree of hearing loss.

Input of tactile stimuli can be reduced or totally eliminated depending upon the type of instigating focal stimuli. Many neurological illnesses decrease tactile perception and sensation. Neurological and other focal stimuli can be classified as follows:

1. Neurological disease
   (a) Guillain-Barré disease
   (b) Cerebrovascular accident
   (c) Cerebral tumor
   (d) Cerebral infarction
2. Spinal cord injury
3. Burns
4. Peripheral Neuropathy

Individuals with reduced or absent tactile stimulation lose perception of their body boundaries, body parts, and body schema. The body schema integrates perceptual and cognitive processes. These processes contribute to the individual's ability to locate new sensations and decide how the body will respond. Deprivation of the visual, auditory, and tactile modes disorganizes the spatial schema and ultimately disrupts the body schema.

Sensory overload

According to Lindsley (1965), the centrifugal control of afferent sources permits the level of activity aroused in the cortex and the reticular formation to regulate the sensory input. It may be that as the number of stimuli increases in frequency and intensity, the centrifugal cortical system is unable to regulate the amount of incoming stimuli. Too many stimuli enter the patient's internal environment too rapidly, creating behavioral responses and changes.

Sensory overload implies that two or more modalities are in action simultaneously at levels of intensity greater than normal, and that the combination of stimuli is introduced suddenly. Sensory overload involves multisensory experiences. Too many incoming stimuli confuse the patient. According to Lindsley (1965), an excess of stimulation from two or more sense modalities, especially a sudden, intense barrage from afferent and corticofugal sources, as in surprise or fear, may block the reticular formation, and behavioral immobilizaton and general confusion may result. It seems that it might not be the "quality of change in sensation that the brain requires for normal functioning, but a continuous, meaningful contact with the outside world. It may well be this lack of meaningful stimuli which contributes to the behavioral manifestations in a situation of sensory overload" (Worrell 1971).

Regulatory Behaviors.   The regulatory behaviors associated with sensory overload are similar to those of sensory deprivation. Both sensory maladaptive responses are the result of altered incoming external and internal stimuli. The difference between sensory deprivation and sensory overload is the rapidity of onset in stimuli. The following are several regulatory behaviors which are due to sensory overload:

1. Extreme alertness
2. Restlessness
3. Delusions
4. Paranoia

5. Irritability
6. Confusion
7. Disorientation
8. Hallucinations

For sensory overload, the onset may occur so quickly that the individual is unable to adapt.

Focal Stimuli.   Sensory overload may originate from excessive environmental stimuli or physiological disease which causes stimuli to be distorted. Individuals experiencing excessive environmental stimuli are bombarded with all types of meaningful stimuli. The anxious individual reacts with tunnel vision and perceptual distortion. Images that enter his environment are blurred, sounds are muffled and indistinguishable, and excessive tactile input become annoying.

Physiological influencing factors can also contribute to sensory overload. Some inflammatory diseases involving the central nervous system can alter the normal inhibition of background stimuli. The normal sensory environment overstimulates cortical arousal, thereby causing sensory overload. Individuals with neurological diseases such as encephalitis or meningitis respond with agitation or nervousness. They become disturbed by such environmental stimuli as normal daylight, bright colors, or voices. Neurological disorders also affect meaningful input of tactile stimuli.

Regardless of their origin, a reduction in incoming stimuli can lead to sensory depression, and excessive incoming stimuli can lead to sensory overload. These sensory maladaptive responses of the visual, auditory, or tactile mode can therefore cause a once normal individual to achieve a level of disequilibrium and disorganization.

Manipulating the stimuli

Given that the magnitude of the external and internal stimuli are so great that the adaptive systems cannot return the body to a state of dynamic equilibrium, the nurse intervenes by manipulating stimuli in an attempt to maintain or restore sensory balance. In order to manipulate stimuli, the nurse assesses various influencing factors which contribute to the maladaptive responses. The influencing factors consist of focal, contextual and residual stimuli. Focal stimuli were discussed in terms of pathophysiological maladaptive responses. Contextual and residual stimuli will be discussed in relationship to nursing interventions.

Contextual stimuli

The nurse alters ineffective regulatory responses from external and internal stimuli through use of the assessment hierarchy. The nurse assesses the visual, auditory, and tactile mode for reduction or overload of stimulation, meaningfulness, and patterning. She intervenes to enhance stimulation, to provide meaning, and to alter patterning. Her overall goal is to maintain optimal cortical arousal.

Visual Sensory Mode.   Before utilizing the assessment hierarchy, the nurse assesses her patient's visual acuity level. This reflects the optimal distance necessary for a particular patient to see without the use of glasses. The assessment may reveal that without the use of glasses the patient's vision is so greatly restricted that it is difficult for him to view either objects, events, or people in the immediate environment.

Whether the altered stimulation is reduced or enhanced, the nurse has the greatest latitude in creating an environment that is conducive for optimal visual arousal. Immobilization can reduce visual stimulation because the individual's visual field may be limited. Therefore the nurse intervenes by frequently changing her patient's position. Visual stimulation can be enhanced by placing cards, colorful posters, drawings from children or grandchildren, or family pictures in the patient's immediate environment. Excessive visual stimuli caused by unnecessary environmental clutter or too frequent territorial intrusions by several members of the health team can be controlled so as not to cause sensory overload.

The nurse in providing an optimal level of visual stimuli realizes that the stimulus should have meaning so that it can be integrated into his cognitive structure. The nurse controls physiological and environmental factors contributing to reduced meaningful visual stimuli. The patient needs physiological feedback regarding diagnostic studies. The nurse can explain the significance, findings, and specific implications for the patient of diagnostic tests. The explanation given can arouse cortical interest. Too much explanatory information creates sensory overload. Likewise too little information tends to oversimplify the patient's problem thereby contributing to a false sense of security. Territorial intrusion is controlled by limiting the number and frequency of staff who enter the patient's environment.

As familiar stimuli are reduced or temporarily eliminated the nurse needs to offer meaningful explanations in their place. The patient may not understand why his personal belongings are replaced by hospital environmental props which he associates with illness.

The patterning of visual stimuli should also be varied. The nurse facilitates this by varying the lighting effect, rearranging the location of environmental props, and providing variation in personal props such as cards or pictures.

Auditory Sensory Mode.　The baseline assessment of the auditory modality becomes a means of comparison for later assessment. The nurse assesses the intensity of auditory stimuli necessary before the patient receives a verbal message or nonverbal sound such as the ticking of a watch. Just as visual assessment is made without glasses, auditory assessment is made without use of a hearing aid.

Physiological factors that may reduce auditory stimuli include drug toxicity, inflammation of the middle ear, and physiological alterations associated with aging process.

Interventions directed at altering the intensity of auditory stimuli include making sure the patient is wearing his prosthetic hearing device, encouraging autostimulation through talking or singing, and directly conversing with the patient at a level appropriate for hearing.

Meaning should be attached to the various environmental sounds. The sounds emitted from the supportive equipment and the hospital in general should be identified individually for the patient so that he can differentiate, for example, between the alarm of his respirator and the alarm of the cardiac monitor. It is important to translate technical language into words that have meaning for the individual. Where English is a second language, a translator may be needed. Diversional activities such as television or radio should provide as much meaning as possible. When possible, tape recordings of favorite music could be encouraged as a means of including meaning and familiarity in the environment.

The patterning of auditory stimuli can be controlled by reducing certain environmental sounds to emphasize others; closing the patient's door, thereby exluding extraneous noises; increasing the volume of the television to override noises from supportive devices; and encouraging verbal communication with family members.

Tactile Sensory Mode.　The baseline assessment of the patient's tactile acuity level is accomplished by determining whether or not the patient desires to be touched; whether there are body regions such as arthritic joints where touch would be considered a noxious stimuli; and whether there are cultural factors influencing the need for greater or lesser physical contact.

If the patient has experienced a previous or current neurological alteration such as a cerebrovascular accident (CVA) or Guillain-Barré Syndrome, the nurse assesses those regions capable of receiving tactile stimulation. Having accomplished this, she provides tactile stimulation to the nonaffected area and usually reacquaints the patient with his nonsensory body part. Likewise, the nurse avoids noxious tactile stimulation to those individuals experiencing arthritic pain from prolonged immobility by first gently exercising the affected extremity. In addition, she protects the patient with peripheral neuropathy from unnecessary stimulation. The nurse also assesses whether or not drugs are reducing her patient's sensitivity to tactile stimulation. If so, either the drug can be eliminated or another one substituted at a later time.

Environmentally the nurse can remove restraints and assist the patient in reacquainting himself with the previously restrained body part. For example, the patient may carefully examine his hand as if to reassure himself of its continued existence. Furthermore, the body part covered with dressings should be stimulated with stroking from touch or a washcloth when the dressing is removed. The family or staff can be encouraged to stroke the patient's face or forehead in an attempt to provide tactile stimulation to those areas capable of sensory input. Besides touching the patient, the nurse can provide other texture stimulation. A sheepskin can be placed under the patient not only to protect his skin from breakdown but to provide another textural stimulation. For the patient immobilized in bed, a footboard can provide another source of tactile stimulation.

The nurse attempts to help the patient derive meaning from explanations regarding alteration in tactile stimulation. For the patient with a pulmonary dysfunction superimposed on a neurological problem, priorities of care need to be established. The patient's attention is focused on the body part that cannot be altered, namely his paralyzed arm or leg. While this is his primary focus, concern needs to be directed to the reason for his being hospitalized. The reasons can be explained in ways that have meaning to the patient.

Environmentally, the nurse attempts to link tactile stimulation with positive reward or reinforcement that has significance. In so doing, she attempts to break noxious chains of negative stimuli. If intrusive procedures are attempted, they can be done in a positive manner. The nurse also realizes that it is difficult to make touch meaningful during a painful or traumatic procedure. Whenever possible, meaningless tactile stimuli should be replaced by meaningful stimuli from the health team, family, or friends.

Residual stimuli

Residual stimuli include a history of sensory disturbances; previous hospitalization for surgical correction of sensory maladaptive responses; use of prosthetic devices such as glasses, hearing aid, dentures, walker, limb, or crutches; and use of medication or eye drops.

Example of Hypothesis for Practice

We have focused on the process of theorizing with the sensory physiological mode. Based on our theorizing with the sensory mode, we can postulate any number of hypotheses that can be tested. The theorizing encompasses the four sets of relationships and their related propositions. In addition the hypotheses can be used as a guide for practice. An example of a possible hypothesis will be discussed.

The hypothesis may be stated as follows: If the nurse provides optimal sensory input, the patient will achieve an optimal level of cortical arousal. The reason for this hypothesis is drawn from the set of relationships which are based on propositions stated earlier. The reasons are shown below.

General Statement: The magnitude of the internal and external stimuli will positively influence the magnitude of the physiological response of an intact system.

Specific Statement: The amount of sensory input via each sensory modality will positively influence the level of cortical arousal.

The nurse keeps in mind that one sensory modality may be so damaged (e.g. blindness) that the optimal level of cortical arousal needs to be achieved through other sensory modalities. The nurse utilizes the four sets of relationships to theorize regarding the sensory modalities. The theorizing permits hypothesis generation even when the nurse manipulates contextual stimuli. With each component of the contextual stimuli, the nurse can hypothesize regarding patient care. If the nurse finds evidence of significance for a hypothesis, the nursing activity specified in the research protocol can become a prescription for practice in situations where nursing diagnosis warrants this intervention. The same hypotheses generation and research protocol development applies to interventions in the contextual stimuli section. Therefore several different hypotheses can be generated for the sensory mode.

Summary

The sensory system enables us to interact with our environment. When one sensory modality is altered, other modalities compensate. The sensory apparatus has receptors and effectors that are sensitive to ineffective responses. A communication system transmits information obtained through the receptors to centers for interpretation and then to effector cells.

The visual, auditory, and tactile sensory modalities have been examined according to four sets of relationships that focus on adaptive regulatory responses. These responses take into consideration external and internal stimuli. The body through receptors and effectors attempts to adapt to chemical and neural inputs as they pertain to specific sensory modalities. However, ineffective responses occur when the magnitude of external and internal stimuli are greater than the body's ability to maintain a state of dynamic equilibrium.

When the external and internal stimuli exceeds the sensory sytem's ability to adapt, the nurse assesses regulatory behaviors and focal stimuli, and manipulates contextual and residual stimuli. While doing so, the nurse generates hypotheses based upon the theorizing and propositions discussed earlier. This adds to the body of knowledge regarding the sensory physiological mode.

References and Additional Readings

Adams, Margaret. "Psychological Responses in Critical Care Units," *American Journal of Nursing,* 78, no. 9 (September 1978): 1504–12.

Dodd, Marilyn. "Assessing Mental Status," *American Journal of Nursing,* 78, no. 9 (September 1978): 1500–1503.

Gardner, Ernest. *Fundamentals of Neurology.* Philadelphia: Saunders, 1969.

Guyton, Arthur. *Textbook of Medical Physiology.* Philadelphia: Saunders, 1971.

Lindsley, Donald. "Common Factors in Sensory Deprivation, Sensory Distortion and Sensory Overload." In *Sensory Deprivation,* Cambridge, Mass.: Harvard University Press, 1965.

Lipetz, Leo. "The Vertebrate Eye: Difficulties in Describing an Information Processing System Even Under Favorable Circumstances." In *Regulation and Control in Physiological System,* ed. A. S. Iberall, and A. Guyton. Pittsburg: Instrument Society of America, 1973.

Milhorn, Howard. *The Application of Control Theory to Physiological Systems.* Philadelphia: Saunders, 1966.

Mitchell, Pamela Holsclaw. *Concepts Basic to Nursing.* New York: McGraw-Hill, 1973.

Schultz, Duane. *Sensory Restriction: Effects on Behavior.* New York: Academic Press, 1965.

Worrell, Judith. "Nursing Implications in the Care of the Patient Experiencing Sensory Deprivation." In *Advanced Concepts in Clinical Nursing,* Philadelphia: Lippincott, 1971.

CHAPTER **13**

The endocrine system

The endocrine system is one of the most complex adaptive processes in the body. Furthermore its various subsystems or organs are highly interrelated. Therefore an alteration in one subsystem leads to subsequent changes in other endocrine subsystems. In this respect the entire body becomes involved.

It should be remembered that the body has two agencies whose responsibility is to communicate information between body parts. The agencies consist of the nervous and endocrine systems. Whether it be through direct or indirect means, the endocrine system is controlled by the nervous system. At the same time, the amount of circulating hormone can affect how the central nervous sytem functions. Because the endocrine glands form chemical substances that are communicated throughout the body, they have their effect upon target tissues or organs which then respond. Malfunction in one target organ can become an influencing stimulus for hypersecretion or hyposecretion of various hormones.

The physiological mode of the endocrine system will be discussed according to five sets of theoretical relationships. The first four sets of relationships focus on adaptive regulatory responses of internal and external stimuli. The last set of relationships focuses on ineffective responses. The

according to regulatory behaviors,
 ̖tual stimuli, and a brief discussion of

 ̤ips

The f.   relationships is as follows: The magnitude of the internal
and ex̖   ̖l stimuli will positively influence the magnitude of the
physiological response of an intact system. This is predicated on the propositions indicated as 1.1 to 2.1, 3.2, and 4.4 in Table 5.1.

The endocrine system consists of the hypothalamus, pituitary,
thyroid, parathyroid, adrenals, pancreas, and sex glands. Each subsystem
contributes to the overall regulatory function of the total endocrine system.
The normal endocrine changes occuring in the internal environment are
regulated through hormonal action. When the internal and external environment is exposed to environmental stimuli, the entire endocrine system
may become involved.

The multitude of stimuli have the potential of altering the activity of
the endocrine glands. Alteration in both the internal and external environment instigates factors that lead to changes in the output of hormones in an
attempt to maintain the internal environment within the boundaries com-
patable with life itself. The endocrine system attempts to maintain the internal environment, including for example the body fluids, at a constant level
with respect to volume and concentration. The stimuli which ultimately influence the output of a particular hormone may be transmitted through
neural channels, hormonal influence, or integration of both, namely,
neurohumoral channels.

The hormones themselves influence reactions that aid in the
maintenance of a constant internal environment. This includes the regulation of rates whereby carbohydrates, fats, proteins, electrolytes, and water
are either deposited in or removed from the body tissue. Changes in the internal environment, such as in the body tissues themselves, influence the
central nervous system and thereby begin the cycle of hormone activity. According to Sodeman and Sodeman (1968),

> The central nervous system, by way of neurohumoral pathways from the
> hypothalamus, influences the anterior pituitary gland to alter its production
> and/or release of a tropic hormone, which affects the target gland so that it
> changes its production and/or release of a tissue-affecting hormone, which
> brings about an adjustment in the body tissue.

When the internal environment is exposed to noxious stimuli such as a frac-

ture, burn, infection, operation, or drug reaction, a series of a
docrine responses occur. The noxious stimuli resulting from the local tiss
damage act upon the central nervous system.

> The central nervous system . . . , in turn causes release from the anterior pituitary gland of ACTH; ACTH stimulates the adrenal cortex so that there is an increase in the production of "sugar" hormone (cortisol), which then inhibits the anabolism of protoplasm in the nondamaged parts of the body tissue, and thus floods the damage site with materials for tissue repair. [Sodeman and Sodeman 1968]

External stimuli include any environmental stressors, such as exposure to warm or cold temperature as well as stressful events themselves. Spencer (1973) describes how environmental situations can influence the response of the endocrine system:

> Stress is a powerful stimulus to thyroid function, affecting cerebral centers in the brain (the hypothalamus) and pituitary TSH production. Other factors that stimulate the thyroid include prolonged exposure to moderate cold or to rapidly altering heat and cold. Among the depressant influences are excess of certain dietary substances; drugs, such as sulfonamides, salicylates, phenoylbutazones, and paraaminosalicyles acid; and exposure to prolonged heat.

The internal and external stimuli that activate the endocrine system are both varied and extensive. A common characteristic of these diverse stimuli is that all represent abrupt alterations of the internal and external environment which impose demands for somatic or visceral responses. Once a particular hormone has been stimulated and accomplishes its unique physiological function, its rate of secretion will begin to decrease. Each endocrine subsystem, in its adaptive role, has a tendency to oversecrete its particular hormone. However, once the normal physiological effect of the hormone has responded to stimuli and achieved the desired response, feedback is transmitted to the secretory gland to terminate further secretion. Likewise, if the gland undersecretes, the physiological effects of the particular hormone decreases. The result is a decreased feedback to the involved intact subsystem. The intact subsystem responds by secreting adequate quantities of the hormone. Consequently the rate of secretion for each hormone is controlled according to the specific need for the hormone.

Alterations in internal and external stimuli are received through receptors and communicated by means of the neural pathways. This process involves the second set of relationships.

Second Set of Relationships

In the second set of relationships, the intact neural pathways will positively influence neural output to effectors. This is predicated on the propositions labled 3.1 to 2.1, and 4.4 in Table 5.1. The anterior pituitary gland has been described as the master gland. As the master gland it is the target of various stimuli, both neural and humoral. Such stimuli can either inhibit or stimulate the gland's activity. According to Moore (1966),

> The supreme control of the endocrine system resides within the central nervous system, but this regulation is not expressed via secretomotor fibers to these glands. It is expressed rather through the secretion of mediator substances released by nerves of the hypothalamus which stimulate the release of the respective trophic hormones from the pituitary.

Therefore the hormonal system of the body is subject to nervous control. The anterior pituitary or master gland maintains its influence upon other endocrine subsystems by means of trophic hormones. The result is that the target glands then produce tissue-affecting hormones.

The hypothalamus can be influenced by nervous input from various areas of the body. Intact neural pathways are a vital communication system from the body. As Smith (1965) points out,

> The medial tuberal region of the hypothalamus contains neurons which secrete a corticotrophic releasing factor (CRF). The hypothalamus is accessible to humoral and neural stimuli of diverse origin and its dense meshwork of fibers and small cells serves to organize the numerous inputs into a neural signal of definite intensity and sign which then acts upon the CRF neurons. The pool of CRF neurons forms the final common pathway for the pituitary-adrenocortical system.

Therefore the hypothalamus receives signals or input from all possible sources in the nervous system. A few examples of this process include exposure to pain; exciting or depressing thoughts in which a portion of the signal is transmitted to the hypothalamus; olfactory stimuli, representing pleasant or unpleasant odors, which transmit strong signals via the amygdaloid nuclei into the hypothalamus; and the concentration of nutrients and electrolytes in the blood. The hypothalamus therefore receives and collects information regarding the individual's biological well-being. The information is used to control secretion in the master gland.

An additional example of how the intact neural pathway will positively influence neural output involves the influence of the hypothalamus on the thyroid regulating system.

> The hypothalamus is capable of secreting its own hormone which is called a neurohumor because it is secreted by the nerve cells. This neurohumor stimulates the hypophysis to secrete more TSH. There is some evidence that thyroxin inhibits the secretion of the neurohumor. [Langley 1965]

The intact neural system and its receptors influence neural output to receptors. If the neural system and its neural pathways did not positively influence neural output to effectors, this endocrine system including the various subsystems would reach a maladaptive state of disequilibrium.

Third Set of Relationships

The second set of relationships and their related propositions are an important building block to the third set of relationships. In the third set of relationships, chemical and neural inputs are postulated to influence normally responsive endocrine glands to hormonally influence target organs in a positive manner to maintain a state of dynamic equilibrium. This is predicated on the propositions labeled 1.1 to 3.2 in Table 5.1. This set of propositions seems to imply the interrelationships between the chemical and neural regulatory systems. The third set of relationships will be examined according to the specific hormones secreted by the anterior pituitary gland, the feedback mechanism, and hormonal control including chemical and neural controls.

The anterior pituitary secretes six hormones whereas the posterior pituitary only secretes two hormones. Each hormone is necessary for maintaining adaptive biological responses. According to Coughran and Liggett (1976), the six anterior hormones can be described as follows:

1. Somatropic hormone (STH), also called growth hormone (GH): Affects both nutritive metabolism and growth of the skeletal system.
2. Adrenocorticotropic hormone (ACTH): Stimulates the adrenal cortex which then secretes the necessary adrenal steroid.
3. Thyrotropic hormone, (TSH): also called thyroid stimulating hormone. Helps maintaining an adequate metabolic rate.
4. Follicle-stimulating hormone (FSH): Stimulates the development of the ovarian follicles. Together with the luteinzing hormone it stimulates the growth and development of the male testes and spermatogenesis.

5. Luteinzing hormone (LH): Besides working in combination with FSH in the above manner, it also has a role in ovulation and development of the corpus luteum.

6. Luteotropic hormone (LTH), also called prolactin: Stimulates the mammary glands for the production of milk. In addition it initiates and maintains secretion of progesterone from the corpus luteum during the menstrual cycle.

The two hormones secreted by the posterior pituitary consist of oxytocin and antidiuretic hormone (ADH). Oxytocin serves the function of contracting uterine muscles as well as enhancing milk secretion by the lactating mammary gland. Vasopressin is the antidiuretic hormone. Its primary function is to affect renal reabsorption of water.

The feedback mechanism is particularly significant for the endocrine system. In the adaptive state of health, the level of each hormone is maintained within certain physiological boundaries of normalcy. Furthermore each is maintained in a state of equilibrium with all other hormones. This process is accomplished by two types of regulatory mechanisms. The first type is a negative feedback relationship between the regulator and the target gland.

> In negative feedback, there is regulatory relationship between two factors or elements in which the increase in one results in an increase in the activity of the second, but the increase in the activity of the second results in a decrease in the activity of the first. [Beland and Passos 1975]

In the second type, no feedback relationship between the glands has been seen. Instead stimulation or depression of the hormones' secretion results from the level of glucose, water, or sodium in the blood.

Negative feedback can be demonstrated in the relationship of the anterior pituitary to the adrenal cortex. When ACTH is increased by stimulation of the anterior pituitary, the level of adrenal glucocorticoid also increases. Once the glucocorticoids rise above a normal level, secretion of ACTH is depressed. Similarly, as glucocorticoids decrease below normal, ACTH secretion increases. The overall release of ACTH as well as of other hormones requires stimulation of the releasing factor from the hypothalamus. When a feedback mechanism does not exist, the rate of hormone production is assessed to be controlled by a mechanism at the site of the formation of the hormone itself. Such a mechanism may involve nervous, chemical, or physical factors.

In summary,

> The hypothalamus stands in a key position between the nervous and endocrine

systems. Either directly or indirectly the hypothalamus serves as a center for the exchange of messages between higher centers in the nervous system and endocrine glands. The hypolthalamus receives and relays messages from the higher centers to the appropriate endocrine gland. It also sends messages to the higher centers apprising them of conditions within the organism. [Beland and Passos 1975]

Hormonal regulation by chemical and neural controls is a significant aspect of the third set of relationships. It is thought that the stimulating hormone acts at the membrane of the target cells. It does so by combining with a specific receptor for that particular hormone. A hormone's effect upon a particular target cell is dependent upon the specificity of the receptors. In terms of their chemical nature, hormones have been classified by Luckmann and Sorensen (1974) as follows:

1. Amines: epinephrine and norepinephrine
2. Amino acids: thyroxine
3. Peptides: vasopressin or ADH
4. Proteins: pituitary, growth hormone and parathyroid
5. Steroids: aldosterone, cortisol, estrogen, progestrone androgenic hormones

Chemical stimuli include two responses: a decreased blood level of particular hormones, and alteration in the blood levels of other specific substances. With decreased blood level of hormone,

biochemical activity which is generally specific for the organ, may involve complex mechanisms. Thus a low level of thyroxine causes thyroid stimulating hormone (TSH) production by the pituitary, which in turn enables the thyroid to produce more thyroxine. A high level of thyroxine inhibits TSH production, leading to a secondary inhibition of thyroid gland activity. This type of self-regulating system called a negative feedback system tends to produce an equilibrium. [Spencer 1973]

The second type of chemical stimulation can be demonstrated through the example of blood sugar level upon insulin production. Normally individuals who have an increased blood sugar level will have a subsequent increase in insulin production. Likewise a decrease in blood sugar leads to lowered insulin level. Chemical stimuli controlling hormonal blood levels are controlled by negative feedback.

Neural stimuli result from stress and are mediated by both the autonomic and central nervous system. The central nervous system reacts to stimuli of all types from external and internal environments. The reactions are communicated to the hypothalamus which sends the stimuli to the pituitary glands. The pituitary hormonal secretion then stimulates the appropriate target glands. The overall response is release of more hormones. Acute and chronic stress differ in their effect upon the endocrine system. The adrenal cortex and medulla are markedly affected by acute stress. Chronic stress has its primary effect upon the thyroid and adrenal cortex. The result is oversecretion which can result in the eventual exhaustion of the intact organ or adrenal gland.

When the chemical and neural inputs are unable to positively influence the endocrine glands and subsequently the hormone's influence upon target organs, then the system becomes disorganized. When disorganization begins, the individual becomes aware of his own ineffective responses.

Fourth Set of Relationships

A fourth set of relationships provides the transition between adaptive and maladaptive behavior. This set of relationships involves the body's response to external and internal stimuli and states that such stimuli will alter those external and internal stimuli. This is predicated on the propositions labeled 1.1 to 5.1 in Table 5.1.

External and internal stimuli will cause different responses in the hormonal system. Some hormones act on all cells or most cells whereas others have a limited effect. There may be receptor sites in certain cells that specifically respond to stimuli from certain hormones. This process of responding to hormones is the body's means of maintaining adequate adaptation. Thyroxin and growth hormone are examples of stimuli to which all cells respond. Insulin, on the other hand, is required by muscles and fat cells for utilization of glucose, but not by the brain and nerve cells. Therefore the release of some hormones is a response to feedback stimuli from the body on the appropriate target glands. The target glands include the thyroid, parathyroid, adrenal, pancreas, and sex glands.

The thyroid gland secretes the thyrotropic hormone. The internal stimuli produced by the thyroid releasing factor from the anterior pituitary gland can increase the output of thyrotropic hormone. Likewise stimuli from the external environment such as cold, heat, or emotional stress can alter stimuli from thyroid activity. Even during intake of external stimuli in the form of ingestion of thyroid hormone, the body is protected against thyroid excess. As the level of ingested thyroid hormone increases, the individual's own internal production of thyroid hormone decreases until balance is achieved. Because thyroxin regulates the rate of metabolism, alteration in its secretion can lead to hyperactivity or hypoactivity.

The parathyroid hormone or parthormone regulates the stability of the composition of the internal environment. It accomplishes this through regulation of blood concentration of calcium and phosphorus. Both ions are so controlled that an alteration in one causes the opposite alteration in the other. The parathyroid hormone acts upon the gastrointestinal tract, bones, and kidneys. It increases reabsorption of calcium in the gastrointestinal tract from intake of nutrients. It stimulates the bones to release calcium, and the kidneys to prevent calcium loss in the urine. All three processes contribute to the blood calcium level which then rises. The greater the level of calcium perfusing through the parathyroid gland, the greater will be the inhibitory response of hormone secretion (Langley 1965). Such a relationship is an example of negative feedback.

The pancreas secretes from the islets of Langerhans two significant endocrine hormones that are necessary for cell metabolism. The hormones secreted are insulin from the beta cells and glucogen from the alpha cells. Insulin serves the function of assisting the entry of glucose into the cells for cellular metabolism, carbohydrate metabolism, and the breakdown of fats and proteins into glucose. According to Milhorn (1966),

> The blood glucose level is regulated by the following mechanism: When the blood glucose concentration becomes elevated, the excess glucose acts directly on the islets of Langerhans of the pancreas to increase their secretion of insulin. This increased insulin secretion causes the cells of the body to become more permeable to glucose. Glucose is then transported into the interior of the cells and the blood glucose level falls. Consequently, a low blood glucose level acts through the same system to increase the blood glucose level.

The adrenal glands are divided into the adrenal cortex and the adrenal medulla. The adrenal cortex secretes chemical substances called steroids. The adrenocorticoid hormones enable the individual to respond to external or internal stimuli whether they be physical, chemical, or emotional stresses. The essential steroids include the following: glucocorticoids, which affect carbohydrate metabolism; mineralocorticoids, which affect metabolism of minerals; and adrenosterones, whose function is to stimulate growth of sex-related tissue.

The adrenal medulla secretes two hormones, namely, epinephrine and norepinephrine. Epinephrine and norepinephrine stimulate body processes and enhance the individual's capability for physical action. Epinephrine acts upon both the alpha and beta receptors. Its action is primarily inhibitory and metabolic. Norepinephrine acts mainly on the alpha receptor to increase diastolic and systolic blood pressure through enhanced peripheral resistance.

The sex glands produce female and male sex hormones. The female ovary produce two hormones, estrogen and progesterone. The hormones play a vital role in sexual development and function, including control of the menstrual cycle and breast development. The male sex hormones are referred to as androgens. There are two androgens, androsterone and testosterone. Both hormones serve the purpose of male sex organ development as well as the development of secondary sex characteristics.

The fourth set of relationships has an interadaptive quality signifying a linkage between adaptive and ineffective regulatory responses. There are times when the fourth set of relationships fails to successfully alter internal and external stimuli in an adaptive way. Instead the intact organ or system responds in a ineffective manner.

Fifth Set of Relationships

In the fifth set of relationships, the magnitude of the external and internal stimuli may be so great that the adaptive systems cannot return the body to a state of dynamic equilibrium. This includes propositions 1.1 to 5.1 in Table 5.1.

When the level of imbalance in the endocrine system or any one of its subsystems exceeds the body's internal ability to restore equilibrium, regulatory mechanisms cannot be depended upon to resist further imbalance. External and internal stimuli may be of a magnitude such that the body cannot return to equilibrium. Hyperfunction or hypofunction of endocrine glands can activate other systems which attempt to restore equilibrium. If regulatory mechanisms fail, the result ranges from the disorganization of illness or disease to death.

The ineffective responses to be covered will be discussed under the heading of hyperfunction and hypofunction of each endocrine gland. Each ineffective response will be discussed according to regulatory behaviors, focal stimuli, and manipulation of contextual and residual stimuli.

Endocrine glands

Thyroid Gland.   Imbalances confronting the thyroid gland consist of hyperfunction or hyperthyroidism and hypofunction or hypothyroidism. Hyperthyroidism, which represents an increase in the output of thyroid hormones, is associated with Grave's disease. Hypofunction or hypothyroidism is a decrease in the thyroid hormone. In children hypothyroidism is referred to as cretinism. Hypothyroidism in adults and older children is called myxedema. Hyperthyroidism and hypothyroidism each exhibit specific regulatory behaviors.

TABLE **13.1** Regulatory Behavior in Thyroid Imbalance

Hyperthyroidism: Grave's Disease	Hypothyroidism: Myxedema Disease
Speech: rapid and excited	Speech: swelling of tongue and slurred, hoarse speech
Skin: warm, moist, flushed and increased sweating	Skin: thick, puffy, and dry
Nervous system: hyperactive, hyperirritable, restless, and tremors in hand	Nervous system: apathetic, lethargic, slow cerebration, and can be hyperirritable
Muscles: weakness, twitching, and tremors	Muscles: weakness, and hypotonia
Circulatory status: tachycardia, palpitation, increased systolic pressure, CHF, arrhythmias, and dyspnea	Circulatory status: bruises easily, cardiomegaly, decreased cardiac output, decreased blood pressure, and weak heart beat
Gastrointestinal tract: anorexia, nausea, vomiting, and diarrhea	Gastrointestinal tract: constipation, hypophagia, and low glucose absorption rate
Eyes: protruding eyeballs, lid lag, and infrequent blinking	Hair: dry, brittle, and sparse

REGULATORY BEHAVIORS. In hyperthyroidism and hypothyroidism, the regulatory behaviors can be categorized as shown in Table 13.1.

The hypothyroid individual has an inadequate capacity to adapt to changes in his environment. He frequently complains when placed in a cold environment. Likewise the hyperthyroid individual makes inappropriate adjustments to his environment. He assesses the environment to be hot even when the temperature is cold.

FOCAL STIMULI. There may be several factors operative in the production of hyperthyrodism and hypothyroidism. The focal stimuli shown in Table 13.2 contribute to ineffective alterations in the thyroid gland.

TABLE **13.2** Focal Stimuli in Thyroid Imbalance

Hyperthyroidism	Hypothyroidism
Excessive secretion of TSH by anterior pituitary gland	Thyroidectomy
Prolonged stress	Inflammation of thyroid resulting in degeneration of the gland
Benign or malignant tumor	Decrease pituitary thyroid stimulating hormone

TABLE **13.3** Regulatory Behaviors in Parathyroid Imbalances

Hyperparathyroidism	Hypoparathyroidism
Bone pain in back Muscular weakness Anorexia Vomiting Depression of central and peripheral nervous system Stomach atony and constipation Polyuria and polydipsia	Tetany Laryngeal spasm Anxiety, depression, and irritability

Although there may be other focal stimuli contributing to hyperfunctioning or hypofunctioning thyroid gland, Table 13.2 includes the major maladaptive stimuli.

Parathyroid Gland.   The parathyroid glands are subject to both disease and injury. Furthermore, disturbances in their structure may also be accompanied by disordered function. In both hyerparathyroidism and hypoparathyroidism, the homeostasis of calcium and phosphorus is altered.

REGULATORY BEHAVIORS. In hypoparathyroidism, a reduced secretion of parathyroid hormone leads to inactivation of the bone's osteoclasts. The result is depression of bone reabsorption and subsequent reduction of calcium in body fluid. The bones nevertheless remain adaptively strong. On the other hand, hyperparathyroidism brings about extreme osteoclastic activity in the bones. The overall response is an elevation of calcium ions in the extracellular fluid. The regulatory behaviors summarized in Table 13.3 revolve around the alterations in calcium and phosphorus levels. Some of the ineffective responses are due to increased permeability of nervous and muscle membranes.

FOCAL STIMULI. The focal stimuli contributing to the ineffective response of hyperparathyroidism and hypoparathyroidism are shown in Table 13.4. Unlike other diseases or illnesses, the focal stimuli affecting thyroid and parathyroid alterations may be specific and well contained.

Adrenal Glands.   As discussed earlier, the adrenal glands are dual organs containing a medulla and cortex. The medulla portion is an extension of the sympathetic nervous system and produces epinephrine and

TABLE **13.4** Focal Stimuli in Parathyroid Imbalance

Hyperparathyroidism	Hypoparathyroidism
Adenomas	Accidental removal of parathyroidism
Hyperplasia	Ideopathic atrophy
Carcinoma	Trauma to parathyroid gland due to local hemorrhage

norepinephrine. The cortex is glandular in nature and produces the steroid hormones.

REGULATORY BEHAVIORS. The medulla and its hormones work together to stimulate body processes and enhance the capability for physical action through the following behaviors:

1. Increased blood pressure
2. Increased respiratory rate
3. Increased heart rate
4. Increased mental activity

The hormones themselves provide a short, lasting response to immediate and stressful life events. Hypersecretion of the medulla's hormones is caused by pheochromocytoma which is a secreting tumor of the sympathetic nervous tissue. Behaviors associated with pheochromocytoma are hypertension, hypermetabolism, and hyperglycemia.

The cortex produces the steroid hormones. Ineffective responses of the cortex leads to hypercorticism or Cushing's syndrome and hypocorticism or Addison's disease (see Table 13.5). Hypocorticism or Addison's disease because of its association with acute hypotension represents a medical emergency. The patient manifests many of the symptoms of shock.

FOCAL STIMULI. Focal stimuli associated with adrenal medulla consist primarily of pheochromocytoma. Ineffective responses of the adrenal glands are shown in Table 13.6. The regulatory behaviors and focal stimuli associated with Cushing's disease involve abnormally high levels of cortisol and to a lesser extent aldosterone.

Pancreas.   The pancreas produces two hormones, insulin and glucagon. Both hormones influence glucose metabolism; however, they produce opposite effects in relationship to blood sugar levels. Insulin's function is to promote utilization of glucose for the synthesis and storage of

TABLE **13.5** Regulatory Behaviors in Adrenal Imbalance

Hypercorticism: Cushing's Syndrome	Hypocorticism: Addison's Disease
Moonface due to increased tissue hydration and fat deposits in the cheeks	Fatigue, weakness, and restlessness
Buffalo hump	Anorexia, nausea, and vomiting
Hypertension	Weight loss
Weakness and petechial hemorrhages	Postural hypotension
Hyperglycemia and glycosuria	Hypoglycemia
Osteoporosis	Weak and irregular pulse
Irritability, euphoria, or frank psychosis	Headache and trembling
	Vitiligo

TABLE **13.6** Focal Stimuli in Adrenal Imbalance

Hypercorticism: Cushing's Disease	Hypocorticism: Addison's Disease
Prolonged stress	Primary atrophy
Hyperplasia	Tuberculosis
Neoplasia	Cancer
Cancer	

glycogen, fat, and production of energy in body cells. Insulin has a potent hypoglycemic effect. Glucagon on the other hand increases the blood sugar level.

REGULATORY BEHAVIORS. Ineffective alterations of the pancreas include hyperinsulinism or hypoglycemia and hypoinsulinism or diabetes mellitus. Both alterations have their own unique regulatory behaviors (see Table 13.7).

The stimulus for glucagon production is a reduction in blood sugar level which becomes the internal stimuli for neural stimulation of the gland by the central nervous system. Excessive stimulation of glucagon produces labile diabetes mellitus. Insulin serves as a stimulus to increase the movement of glucose from the blood to the intracellular compartment. It is at this level that glucose is utilized for energy production or storage and anabolic processes. Ineffective responses of either hormone is the result of specific pathological changes or focal stimuli.

TABLE **13.7** Regulatory Behaviors in Insulin Imbalance

Hyperinsulinism: Hypoglycemia	Hypoinsulinism: Diabetes Mellitus
Bizarre psychiatric symptoms	Fatigue
Seizures	Weight loss despite increased appetite
Hunger and weight gain	Polyuria
Loss of consciousness and eventual coma	Polydipsia
	Metabolic acidosis

FOCAL STIMULI. Focal stimuli responsible for hyperinsulinism and hypoinsulinism are shown in Table 13.8.

TABLE **13.8** Focal Stimuli in Insulin Imbalance

Hyperinsulinism	Hypoinsulinism
Hyperplasia	Insufficient production of insulin by islets of Langerhans
Beta cell tumor	Insulin inactivated by antibodies
Cortisol deficiency	Obesity
Retroperitoneal sarcoma	Excessive stress
Prolonged exercise	
Fasting or starvation	
Renal glycosuria	

Both ineffective responses of the pancreas lead to alteration in other body systems. Diabetes in particular causes systemic problems which range from cardiovascular alterations such as myocardial infarction to eventual blindness.

Gonads.   The gonads consist of the testes in the male and the ovaries in the female. Each sex gland secretes its own unique hormones. In the female, the hormones are estrogen and progesterone. The male secretes testosterone and androsterone. Only testosterone is to be discussed.

REGULATORY BEHAVIORS. The common regulatory behaviors associated with ineffective responses in the female and male sex glands are shown in Tables 13.9 and 13.10 respectively. Note that these tables are not all-inclusive—there may be other regulatory behaviors involved.

TABLE 13.9 Regulatory Behaviors in Ovarian Hormone Imbalance

Hyperfunction	Hypofunction
Edema due to retention of sodium and water	Delayed sexual development
Convulsive seizures	Absence of pubic and axillary hair
Increased coagulability of blood	Absence of menstruation
Nausea	

TABLE 13.10 Regulatory Behaviors in Testosterone Imbalance

Hypertestosterone	Hypotestosteronism
Precocious puberty	Impotence
(a) Penile growth	
(b) Pubic hair	
Increased libido	Infertility
Hostility and aggression	Decreased libido
Rapid growth of muscles and skeletal growth	Tendency toward feminization
	Sparse beard
	Decreased muscular strength
	Anemia
	Osteoporosis
	Atrophy of external genitalia

FOCAL STIMULI. There may be several factors operative in the production of hypergonadism and hypogonadism in females and males. The focal stimuli shown in Table 13.11 contribute to maladaptive changes in the female, with Table 13.12 indicates the focal stimuli which contribute to ineffective alterations in the male.

TABLE 13.11 Focal Stimuli in Imbalance of Ovarian Hormones

Hyperfunction	Hypofunction
Pregnancy	Ovarian failure
Oral contraceptive	Surgical removal of ovary
Ovarian tumor	Dysfunction of hypothalamo-pituitary system
Estrogen ingestion	

TABLE **13.12** Focal Stimuli in Testosterone Imbalance

Hyperfunction	Hypofunction
Interstitial cell tumor	Disease of testes
Hypothalamo-pituitary lesion	Castration
Tumor of testes	Inflammation or infection of gonads
Adrenal tumor	Decreased gonadotropic secretion
Androgen-secreting teratomas	
Pineal tumor	
Hypothyroidism	

Manipulating the stimuli

Given that the magnitude of the external and internal stimuli are so great that the adaptive systems cannot return the body to a state of dynamic equilibrium, the nurse intervenes by manipulating stimuli in an attempt to maintain or restore endocrine balance. In order to manipulate stimuli, the nurse assesses various influencing factors that contribute to the ineffective responses. The influencing factors consist of focal, contextual and residual stimuli. Focal stimuli were discussed in terms of pathophysiological ineffective responses. Contextual and residual stimuli will be discussed in relationship to nursing interventions.

Contextual stimuli

The nurse alters ineffective regulatory responses from external and internal stimuli through manipulation of the following contextual stimuli: fluid, activity, nutrition, communication, aeration, and pain.

Fluid. Fluid intake is balance with fluid loss. Some endocrine dysfunctions contribute to either a decrease or increase in fluid loss. The nurse's goal is to make accurate assessment of fluid loss in an attempt to prevent dehydration or volume deficit associated with specific endocrine problems. Fluid management involves assessment of sensible and insensible loss.

INTERSTITIAL EDEMA. The patient's edema may be the result of changes in capillary permeability, decreased tissue perfusion, or increased aldosterone. The latter contributes to sodium and water retention which further enhances an edematous state. For example, the edematous Cushing's disease patient may risk cerebral edema, pulmonary edema, and interstitial edema. Internal interstitial edema creates excessive stimuli in the form of tissue breakdown. Tissue breakdown can be a serious problem for the patient with diabetes or adrenal dysfunction. The diabetic patient has vascular insufficiency that slows the healing process. Such a patient has the potential for severe infection and gangrene. The patient with adrenal dysfunction has a lowered resistance to local and systemic infection.

INTAKE. Intake involves physiological intake of oral or parenteral fluids as well as environmental intake. Depending upon the specific endocrine maladaptive dysfunction, oral intake and parenteral intake may be either increased or decreased. For example patients with diabetes, Addison's disease, or hyperparathyroidism need to increase their fluid intake. The diabetic patient experiences rising levels of glucose. The increased glucose level causes additional problems. Glucose is osmotically active and increased levels in extracellular fluid serve to pull fluid across the cell membrane. The overall result is cellular dehydration. As the total body fluids are depleted, progressive dehydration causes secondary thirst and polydipsia. During an Addisonian crisis, the patient's volume status reaches critically low levels. Therefore the patient is given hydrocortisone together with adequate fluid therapy. An adequate fluid therapy may be a total of three to four liters over the first 24 hours. The hyperparathyroid patient is subject to renal calculi. Therefore fluid intake can be increased to at least 3000 cc daily. This will help prevent renal calculi. Oral fluid intake may include cranberry and prune juice. These juices lower the urinary pH thereby increasing the solubility of calcium in the urine.

Patients with volume excess need to have their fluid intake restricted. With Cushing's disease, the patient has a tendency to retain fluid. Hypercorticol leads to sodium retention with subsequent water retention. Therefore sodium intake and total fluid intake is limited according to the patient's output. Regardless of the particular endocrine dysfunction, the overall goal is to restore the patient's total body fluid and electrolytes to a normal level.

The nurse assesses the environmental stimuli in relationship to the patient's internal ability to cope metabolically. Excessive external stimuli in the form of temperature fluctuations or exposure to infection are problems. Hyperthyroid and hypothyroid patients are particularly sensitive to fluctuations in environmental temperature. A significant environmental hazard is infection. Patients with hypercorticism may experience reduced resistance to an infectious organism. Likewise they have reduced resistance to the spread of extant infection. The patient needs to be protected from infection and, when necessary, may need to be isolated.

OUTPUT. Output from the endocrine patient consists of sensible loss such as urine, stool, and emesis; diagnostic procedures including blood pressure, pulse, respirations, temperature, specific gravity, daily weight, and central venous pressure; and laboratory tests specific to a particular endocrine dysfunction.

Both sensible and insensible water losses are replaced according to the particular endocrine dysfunction. The amount of urinary output may be greatly increased for the patient with hypoinsulinism and Addison's disease. Likewise the Cushing's disease patient may have oliguria. Regardless of the ineffective response, the nurse can make hourly assessments of her patient's urinary output. The amount of urinary output in relationship to fluid intake may be a guide to the patient's overall fluid status. If the patient has hyperparathyroidism, his urine may be strained for stones. Furthermore such a patient may also experience abdominal pain and hematuria, both of which are symptoms of calculi in the renal system. The urine is also assessed for sugar and acetone. This is particularly significant to the diabetic patient receiving insulin. Furthermore glucose in the urine and in certain body fluids promotes the growth of fungi and other microorganisms. The result could be a predisposition to infection.

Other sensible losses consist of stool and emesis. The hyperthyroid may experience diarrhea. Therefore foods that enhance peristalsis can be eliminated and electrolytes maintained. Intestinal hypermobility leads to fluid loss and reduced reabsorption of both fluid and electrolytes. Therefore liquid stools can be measured and numbered. Patients with an endocrine dysfunction may experience nausea and vomiting. The amount can be measured and recorded. The patient with aldosteronism is prone to constipation due to potassium deficiency, which predisposes to atony of the smooth muscles of the intestine. All losses derived from stool and emesis should be recorded and incorporated into the total output.

Blood pressure variations are helpful in assessing body fluid disturbances. Without mineralocorticoids, the sodium and chloride levels decrease in extracellular fluid. Subsequently, the total extracellular fluid volume and blood volume are also reduced. At the same time, the effective action of the catecholamines in vasoconstriction also decreases because the synergestic effect of corticosteroid is lost. Therefore the patient with Addison's disease experiences an acute hypotensive crisis.

Endocrine disturbance associated with sodium and water retention causes edema and hypertension. Hypertension predisposes the patient to headaches, failing vision, irritability, left ventricular hypertrophy, congestive heart failure, and stroke. Therefore arterial blood pressure is taken frequently in order to evaluate whether there is a real or potential water and electrolyte balance problem.

The patient's pulse can be assessed for rate, volume, and regularity. The diabetic or Addison's disease patient may have a weak pulse. This is a reflection of volume deficit associated with dehydration. The hyperthyroid patient experiences tachycardia. The resulting tachycardia contributes to heat loss by circulating the patient's blood through the skin. Furthermore tachycardia increases the supply of oxygen and nutrients to the cells as well as removing the production of metabolism. The increased rate of metabolism and tachycardia place an extra burden upon the heart. Patients with certain endocrine disturbances can also experience arrhythmias. Therefore the patient's pulse can be assessed for regularity.

Respirations are also assessed for rate, rhythm, and regularity. The hyperglycemic patient demonstrates Kussmaul's breathing. Kussmaul's breathing consists of deep, regular, sighing respirations; the rate may be normal, slow, or fast. Changes in respiration reflect changes in the patient's metabolic status, such as onset of acidosis or alkalosis. Therefore the nurse assesses respirations along with the patient's pulse rate and temperature.

In the hyperthyroid patient, body temperature tends to be elevated. The patient is also unable to tolerate heat. Increased body temperature leads to tachycardia and increased metabolism. Both responses place an additional burden on the cardiovascular system. The nurse protects the patient from unnecessary heat. The hypothyroid patient tends to avoid cool environments. Such patients can be protected from cool environments which can cause chilling and shivering. Shivering increases metabolism which increases the workload of the myocardium. It should be remembered that a febrile state may not be assessed in the patient with hypercorticism. Therefore a normal body temperature is not always an indication that this patient is not infected. Temperature elevation may indicate excessive fluid loss or dehydration. The latter becomes significant for patients with diabetes and Addison's disease.

Specific gravity provides information regarding both the kidneys' ability to concentrate urine and the fluid status. The dehydrated diabetic or hypocorticism patient both have an elevated specific gravity.

Daily weights are necessary for determining the effectiveness of therapeutic measures that alter fluid volume. The Cushing's disease patient tends to show increased body weight whereas the Addison's disease patient shows body weight decreases. Both changes reflect alteration in fluid volume. The nurse should keep in mind that fluid can pool in the body even when the patient's weight reaches stability. Therefore a stable-appearing body weight may not be an accurate reflection of the internal instability of shifting fluid volume.

Assessment of central venous is another diagnostic tool designed to evaluate the endocrine patient's volume status. An increased central venous pressure might be expected with Cushing's disease. Likewise a decreased central venous pressure may occur in Addison's disease. An accurate assessment of intake and output becomes significant in determining the endocrine patient's volume status.

Laboratory tests of significance to the endocrine patient are those which measure serum electrolytes such as potassium, calcium, phosphorus, and soldium; protein-bound iodine level, radioiodine uptake and serum cholesterol; urinary vanillymandelic acid (VMA) test, and 17-hydroxycorticosteroids (17-OHCS) urinary test; hemoglobin and hemotocrit; glucose tolerance test (GTT), serum amylase, and Fashing blood sugar (FBS); arterial blood gases; and white blood count.

Several of these laboratory tests make specific diagnosis of endocrine dysfunction. Calcium and phosphorus levels are significant for the hypoparathyroid patient. Iodine studies are helpful in diagnosing thyroid maladaptive responses. VMA and 17-OHCS are 24-hour urine studies used to assess hypercorticism and hypocorticism. Pancreatic disturbances may be diagnosed through use of GTT, serum amylase, or FBS.

Activity.   The nurse in assessing her patient's activity must assess four major components: physical activity, cardiopulmonary activity, metabolic activity, and mental activity.

It may be difficult for the hyperthyroid patient to relax and rest. Such patients are nervous and irritable and have excessive energy. Disturbing external stimuli must be reduced to a minimum so that the patient can be encouraged to relax and sleep.

Physical activity may need to be closely monitored in patients with hyperparathyroidism and hypercorticism. Because the hyperparathyroid patient's bones have less than the normal mineral content, they are easily broken. Furthermore the patient is physically weakened, his joints are immobile, and he is mentally sluggish. Therefore when ambulating he needs to be protected from accidents. While in bed the patient should be comfortably positioned so that alteration in skeletal structure will be minimized.

The hypercorticism or Cushing's disease patient has weakened muscles and bones. In addition, his weakened muscles and bones must bear the burden of increased body weight due to excess fatty tissue and retained fluids. The patient is poorly coordinated, weak, and awkward. Therefore he needs the nurse's careful attention during ambulation. Kind, supportive assistance reduces fear of dependence and loss of personal dignity.

The Cushing's disease patient has a predisposition towards cardiovascular pathology with an increased tendency to thrombosis. Serum cholesteral level is elevated in patients with hypercorticism. This contributes to arteriosclerosis and subsequent coronary artery disease and hypertension. Likewise the diabetic patient has a tendency towards similar cardiovascular dysfunction associated with arteriosclerotic alterations.

Pulmonary status may vary depending upon the specific endocrine dysfunction. When calcium levels are altered the patient may experience tetany and laryngeal spasm. The Kussmaul's breathing of the diabetic patient is an attempt to compensate for metabolic acidosis.

Metabolic activity is greatly increased with hyperthyroidism. When the hypothyroid patient experiences shivering in response to a cool environment the result is also increased metabolic activity. Metabolic acidosis is associated with hypoinsulinism or diabetes. Regardless of the origin, increased metabolic activity or metabolic acidosis needs to be appropriately treated. Treatment may include the elimination of metabolic stimulating factors such as fever, hypotension, and tachycardia, and the administration of appropriate drugs.

The hypercorticism patient has a sluggish mental capacity. Likewise patients with volume depletion may experience psychological alterations. The nurse assesses lethargy, mental sluggishness, and the inability to concentrate. The confused endocrine patient needs to be environmentally protected.

Nutrition.   The hyperthyroid patient's diet should be high in vitamins, minerals, and protein. Furthermore his caloric level should be adequate enough to supply the increased needs of the body. Because the patient has a tendency towards diarrhea, foods that have a laxative effect may need to be avoided. Coffee and tea act as stimulants; consequently, they can also be avoided.

The hyperparathyroid patient needs to avoid food containing calcium and phosphorus. Milk and milk products may not be permitted in such patient's diet. The diet may need to contain potassium in amounts sufficient to oppose the effects of hypercalcemia in the myocardium. The hyperparathyroid patient is anorexic and sometimes experiences nausea and vomiting. Therefore nutritional intake may be limited due to the nausea or vomiting.

Patients experiencing endocrine dysfunction of hypercorticism maintain a diet low in calories, carbohydrates, and sodium. On the other hand the diet can contain potassium and protein. The diet is designed to promote weight loss, reduce edema, decrease hypertension, control hypokalemia, and rebuild wasted tissue.

Spiritual nutrition is a significant aspect of care for many patients. The endocrine patient whose physical appearance undergoes gross changes may need the supportive attention derived through the religious counsellor of their choice.

Communication.   The patient with endocrine imbalance needs to communicate his fears and apprehensions. The hypercorticism or Cushing's patient feels embarrassed because of his body image alterations. Physical changes are associated with acromegaly, hyperthyroidism, goiter, or excessive weight gain.

Depending upon the severity of the endocrine disturbance, the patient may experience behavioral changes. The behavioral changes communicate to the nurse alterations in fluid status, perfusion deficit, electrolyte changes, blood gases, or cerebral activity. The patient therefore needs to be protected, and his behaviors explained to the concerned family members. Metabolic changes in general may create psychological instability. The patient can be accepted and reassured that he is nevertheless an individual worthy of respect.

Aeration.   The nurse controls the patient's environmental aeration by reducing unnecessary external stimuli. The patient with Cushing's syndrome has reduced protective mechanism of inflammation and immune response. Therefore he is susceptible to various infections.

Pulmonary aeration is assessed according to the lungs' ability to compensate for metabolic acidosis. The pulmonary system helps to stabilize the body's fluctuating pH. The Kussmaul's breathing of the diabetic patient is an attempt to remove excess carbon dioxide. If the pulmonary system is ineffective in restoring the body's pH to a normal level, external stimuli such as medication or a volume respirator may be necessary.

Pain.   Psychological pain may be difficult to alleviate. The endocrine patient who experiences obvious alteration in his body image may feel insecure in his interaction with others. As stated earlier, the patient needs to regain his self-confidence and self-respect.

Physiological pain is characteristic of the hyperparathyroid patient. His pain is labeled as "bone" pain. The endocrine patient, whose level of metabolism is greatly altered, may be unable to metabolize narcotics. If narcotics or analgesics are absolutely necessary, the nurse assesses her patient's regulatory behaviors for any deviation from the normal.

Residual Stimuli

Residual stimuli include a history of endocrine disturbances; previous hospitalization for endocrine dysfunction or related subproblems; use of steroids, insulin or thyroxine; fluctuations in body weight; pain in joints or bones; and symptoms associated with hypertension or hypotension.

Example of Hypothesis for Practice

We have focused on the process of theorizing with the endocrine physiological mode. Based on our theorizing with the endocrine mode, we can postulate any number of hypotheses that can be tested. The theorizing encompasses the four sets of relationships and their related propositions. In addition the hypotheses can be used as a guide for practice. An example of a possible hypothesis will be discussed.

The hypothesis may be stated as follows: If the nurse helps the patient maintain an optimal level of hormonal secretion, the patient will achieve a higher level of hormonal or endocrine balance. The reason for this hypothesis is drawn from the set of relationships which are based on propositions stated earlier. The reasons are shown below.

General Statement: Chemical and neural inputs will influence normally responsive endocrine glands to hormonally influence target organs in a positive manner to maintain a state of dynamic equilibrium.

Specific Statement: The amount of hormonal input and control will positively influence hormonal balance.

The nurse utilizes the four sets of relationships to theorize regarding the endocrine mode. The theorizing permits hypothesis generation even when the nurse manipulates contextual stimuli. With each component of the contextual stimuli, the nurse can hypothesize regarding patient care. If the nurse finds evidence of significance for a hypothesis, the nursing activity specified in the research protocol can become a prescription for practice in situations where nursing diagnosis warrants this intervention. Hypotheses can also be generated around contextual stimuli. The nurse can formulate a different hypothesis for each aspect of the endocrine physiological mode.

Summary

The endocrine system is vital to life. Hormones secreted by the endocrine glands are distributed throughout the body and function to regulate responses of cells to changes in external and internal stimuli. The endocrine system has receptors and effectors that are sensitive to ineffective responses. A communication system transmits information obtained through the receptors to centers for interpretation and then to effector cells such as those of a muscle or gland.

The endocrine system and its various glands have been examined according to four sets of relationships that focus on adaptive regulatory responses. These responses take into consideration external and internal stimuli. The body through receptors and effectors attempts to adapt to chemical and neural inputs as they pertain to the endocrine glands. However ineffective responses occur when the magnitude of external and internal stimuli are greater than the body's ability to maintain a state of dynamic equilibrium. Because the endocrine glands are regulatory mechanisms, disequilibrium in the form of disease or injury causes changes in structure and function. The result is increased or decreased activity of the cells or structure regulated by a specific hormone.

When the external and internal stimuli exceeds the endocrine system's ability to adapt, the nurse assesses focal stimuli and regulatory behaviors, and manipulates contextual and residual stimuli. In doing so, the nurse hypothesizes based upon previous theorizing and propositions.

References and Additional Readings

Beland, Irene, and Joyce Passos. *Clinical Nursing Pathophysiological and Psychosocial Approaches.* New York: Macmillan, 1975.

Cataland, Samuel. "Hypoglycemia: A Spectrum of Problems," *Heart and Lung,* 7, no. 3 (May-June 1978): 455–62.

Cooperman, Diane. "Pituitary Apoplexy," *Heart and Lung,* 7, no. 3 (May-June 1978): 450–54.

Coughran, Edda, and Sonja Liggett. "Regulation of the Endocrine System." In *Introduction to Nursing: An Adaptation Model,* ed. Sr. Callista Roy. Englewood Cliffs, N.J.: Prentice-Hall, Inc., 1976.

Langley, L. L. *Homeostasis.* New York: Reinhold, 1965.

Lavine, Robert. "How to Recognize and What to Do about Hypoglycemia," *Nursing,* (April 1979): 52–55.

Luckmann, Joan, and Karen Sorensen. *Medical-Surgical Nursing: A Psychophysiological Approach.* Philadelphia: Saunders, 1974.

McCarthy, Joyce. "Somogy Effect: Managing Blood Glucose Rebound," *Nursing,* 9, no. 2 (February 1979): 39–41.

Milhorn, Howard. *The Application of Control Theory to Physiological Systems.* Philadelphia: Saunders, 1966.

Moore, Ward. "General Endocrinology: Hypophysis." In *Physiology,* ed. Ewald Selkurt. Boston: Little, Brown, 1966.

O'Dorisio, Thomas. "Hypercalcemic Crisis," *Heart and Lungs,* 7, no. 3 (May-June 1978): 425–34.

Oskins, Susan. "Identification of Situational Stressors and Coping Methods by Intensive Care Nurses," *Heart and Lung,* 8, no. 5 (September-October 1979): 953–60.

Read, Sharon. "Clinical Care In Hypophysectomy," *Nursing Clinics of North America,* 9, no. 4 (December 1974): 647–54.

Slater, Norma. "Insulin Reactions vs. Ketoacidosis: Guidelines for Diagnosis and Intervention," *American Journal of Nursing,* 78, no. 5 (May 1978): 875–77.

Smith, Gerard. "Neural Control of the Pituitary-Adrenocortical System." In *Physiological Controls and Regulations,* ed. William Yamamoto and John Brobeck. Philadelphia: Saunders, 1965.

Smith, Marcy, and Hans Selye. "Reducing the Negative Effects of Stress," *American Journal of Nursing,* 79, no. 11 (November 1979): 1953–55.

Sodeman, William, and William Sodeman Jr. *Pathologic Physiology: Mechanisms of Disease.* Philadelphia: Saunders, 1968.

Spencer, Roberta. *Patient Care in Endocrine Problems.* Philadelphia: Saunders, 1973.

Urbanic, Robert. "Thyrotoxic Crisis and Myxedema Coma," *Heart and Lung,* 7, no. 3 (May-June 1978): 435–49.

Walesky, Mary. "Diabetes Ketoacidosis," *American Journal of Nursing,* 78, no. 5 (May 1978): 872–74.

In Part 4 we shall focus on the three psychosocial modes described by Roy—self-concept, role function, and interdependence. Each mode is viewed as a system that forms part of the adaptive system. The modes act as effectors for the cognator-regulator processes. The system for each mode is described, then propositions are cited. Finally, each chapter closes with an hypothesis for nursing practice derived from relevant propositions.

Theory
of Adaptive Modes:
Psychosocial
Modes

PART **IV**

CHAPTER 14

Self-concept

The first of the psychosocial modes of adaptation is the self-concept. Self-concept has been defined as the composite of beliefs and feelings that one holds about oneself at a given time, formed from perceptions particularly of others' reactions, and directing one's behavior (Driever 1976). The vast literature related to self-concept supports the notion that self-concept may be viewed as a system. For example, Gergen (1971) states that the self is structurally "the *system* of concepts available to the person in attempting to define himself." Further, Spitzer, Couch, and Stratton (1970) note that certain methodologies are useful for "determining the degree to which different facets of the self-concept are being meaningfully differentiated and organized as a *system*."

In this chapter the self-concept adaptive mode will be explicated as a system through which the regulator and cognator subsystems act to promote adaptation. First the self system characteristics will be explored, including wholeness, subsystems, putting together of parts, inputs, outputs, and self-regulation and control. Then the self system functions will be discussed. Finally, the self system will be linked together with a series of propositions, and a specific hypothesis relevant to nursing practice will be derived.

System Characteristics

As we have noted, any system is characterized by wholeness, subsystems, parts related, inputs, outputs, and self-regulation and control. In viewing self-concept as a system[1] we shall examine each of these characteristics.

Wholeness

Gordon and Gergen (1968) find in the writing of numerous authors a strong commitment to view the self as a single entity, concept, gestalt, or collage of perceptions. Lecky (1969) especially emphasizes the unity of the organization of self. The self has a consistency regardless of the events of life. The 80-year-old person has no difficulty recognizing himself as the same person who was once a 3-year-old child, even though perhaps all his life circumstances (and all the cells in his body) have changed. Much of the research literature on self-concept reflects studies predicting behavior on the basis of single measures of self. These studies must assume that the self has wholeness. They accept the position that the person has a baseline manner of viewing himself, and that this basic view will influence his behavior over time and across situations. One related study was reported by Wylie in 1961. Diggory and Magazines had male college students rate themselves on five capacities and on their overall adequacy of functioning. Through experimental manipulation subjects "failed" tests in abilities they rated high and low. In spite of the effects on other aspects of the experiment, no change in global self-regard was noted after task failure. Thus we have support for the view of self as a unitary, consistent structure.[2]

From this point of view, then, self-concept as a system possesses the system characteristic of wholeness.

Subsystems

Even though the self is a unitary concept, when the self is viewed as a system, it is structurally composed of subsystems. Epstein (1973) proposes that in looking at self-concept, it is necessary to consider subsystems, or dif-

---

1. In this book we have referred to the person as an adaptive system. In analyzing the psychosocial adaptive modes, we again use the construct *system*. However, at this point, we are using a different level of analysis. Looked at individually, the modes are systems acting within the regulator and cognator subsystems of the overall person as an adaptive system.

2. The opposite view, the multidimensionality of self, is proposed in Gordon and Gergen (1968) and has also found support in symbolic interaction research.

ferent empirical selves, which retain a degree of independence despite being influenced by, as well as influencing, the generic self system.

There are many classifications of the self-concept subsystems. James (1918) uses the simple divisions of material me, social me, and spiritual me. In his article on self-concept methodologies, Gordon (1974) describes four levels of abstraction in sociocognitive content. The concrete level includes specific self-representations. The intermediate level involves four systemic senses of self—senses of competence, self-determination, unity, and moral worth. The next level is the sense of personal autonomy and last is self-esteem. The content of these four levels could be viewed as another description of the subsystems in self-concept system.

The componets of the self-concept system, as viewed by the Roy Adaptation Model, were originally described by Driever (1976). The major components are the physical self and the personal self. The personal self is further subdivided into the moral-ethical self, self-consistency, self-ideal, and self-esteem. These components form the subsystems of the self-concept system as we are looking at it.

Relations of parts

In describing a system, we need to know how the parts are put together, that is, how they are related. The parts of a system are put together by a basic mechanism that determines the output of the system. Just as the parts of a clock are organized around the mainspring which acts to determine the time told on the face of the clock, so the self-system must have an organizing force. In an earlier chapter we described how the cognator and regulator act to maintain the adaptation of the person. The internal processes of the coping mechanisms are activated in relation to the adaptive modes. We can first describe the basic self mechanism, then see that the cognator and regulator processes are activated in this mechanism.

Combs and Snygg (1959) have identified the basic self mechanism as a striving for adequacy. They note that the human person has a great driving, striving force within the self by which the person continually seeks to make himself even more adequate to cope with life. This need for adequacy provides the direction, drive, and organization for the behavior that is the output of the self system.

As the self mechanism of striving for adequacy is operating, it is obvious that certain cognator processes have been activated. It would seem that the major apparatuses involved are those dealing with perceptual information processing and emotion. When one seeks to see oneself as adequate, one is using selective attention, coding, and memory. At the same time, one also employs defenses to seek relief and effective appraisal and attachment.

The striving for adequacy is a particular way that the cognator effects its processes.

System inputs

The inputs of the self system may be described from two basic approaches, first, the processes of the suprasystem or system above the system, and, second, social experience. The processes of the suprasystem or cognator, will be internal stimuli coming from the person as an adaptive system. These include perception and social learning. Social experience reflects the external stimuli which surround the person.[3]

The person has been conceptualized as an adaptive system that functions by means of the regulator and cognator subsystems (see Chapter 5). These subsystems form the suprasystem of the self system. The sensations and cognitions processed by the regulator and cognator act as input to the self system. For example, the person who suddenly suffers a chill may receive this neural input in his body and process it through the regulator activity of perception where it also becomes a cognition. Through the process of coding and memory, the person comes up with the notion of impending illness. The person's self-concept receives this input and redefines his physical self from well to ill. If enough sensations and cognitions are thus processed, illness behavior may result such as going to bed, taking home remedies, or calling a physician.

The second major category of input for the self-concept is termed social experience. The outside world, including our role and interdependence relationships (as discussed later) forms our social experiences. It is proposed here that the particular ways this experience enters into the self system are through perception and social learning. For example, when a mother perceives that her child is well mannered, this social experience enters into her self-concept and she sees herself as an adequate mother. Likewise when a mother continually reinforces the well-mannered behavior of her child, this social learning forms the child's social experience which enters into the child's self-concept and he sees himself as the good child. It should be noted that the perceptions and social learning from the environment are also processed through the regulator and cognator subsystems so that all the input to the self-concept system actually comes from the suprasystem. And, in fact, as we simplify our conception of the self system to put it in diagramatic form, internal and external stimuli as inputs to the system will not be differentiated. In considering social experiences, the particular perceptions and social learning surrounding one's experience

---

3. For a more thorough treatment of the significance of social interaction in development of self-concept see Hardy and Conway (1978), Chapters 3—6.

of race, ethnicity, sex, and class will be significant input to the self-concept. Likewise the role-taking process will be a significant perception; that is, when the person assumes the role of the other, the person perceives how the other is seeing the person's self.

System output

In speaking of the organizing principle for the parts of the self-concept system we noted Combs's and Snygg's (1959) stress on the need for adequacy. They say that this striving for adequacy provides the direction, drive, and organization for human behavior. It is this behavior that is the output of the self system. Or more specifically, when considering the behavioral output of the self system, we may term this output the presentation of self—whatever the person does manifests what he thinks of himself. What he says about himself, how he dresses, how he approaches a problem—in all these acts he presents himself to himself and to the outside world. The presentation of self depends on the input to the system, but comes directly from the dynamism of level of adequacy.

Self regulation and control

Every system has regulating and control mechanisms that tend to keep the system in balance. The major regulatory mechanism for the self-concept may be termed self-consistency. Lecky (1969) proposes that through the mechanism of self-consistency the person strives to maintain a consistent self-organization, and thus to avoid disequilibrium. New experiences are incorporated into the self in such a way as to maintain a stable self-image. This tendency to reduce any dissonance in the self keeps the self system in balance.

Second, the self system has a feedback mechanism for control of output. This mechanism involves the person comparing his performance with his ideals. Deviation from the ideal will bring about a correction in the output or behavior to make the output correlate with the ideal. Thus, a runner whose ideal is to be the best runner will compare his performance with this ideal and continue efforts in the direction of running better until he reaches the ideal of being the best. The self system thus has its own regulation and control mechanisms that tend to keep the system in balance.

The view of the self-concept that we have been presenting here can be conceptualized as illustrated in Figure 14.1.

Perception and social learning, which includes social rewards, combine to form the input of social experience. The self-concept has an internal dynamic process of striving for adequacy. This process is regulated by the

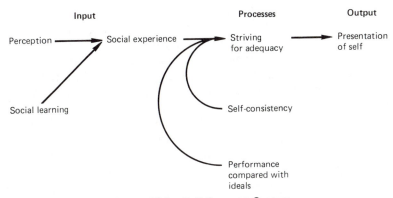

FIGURE **14.1.** Self Concept System.

tendency toward self-consistency. It is controlled by a comparison of performance with ideals. The output of the system is behavior in the form of the presentation of self.

These regulatory and control mechanisms can be related to the cognator processes. Once again it seems that the apparatuses for perceptual/information processing and for emotion are the most important. In striving for self-consistency one utilizes defenses to seek relief and affective appraisal and attachment. When comparing performance with ideals, the person uses selective attention, coding, and memory. This is not to say that other cognator processes are not involved, but that these seem to be the major ones activated by the regulatory and control mechanisms.

System Function

Now that we have described the self-concept system according to system characteristics, we may look at the functions served by this total system. The self-concept system serves two basic and interrelated function. First, it serves to meet the basic need for psychic integrity and, second, it promotes the adaptation of the total person.

It has been noted elsewhere (Driever 1976) that the Roy Adaptation Model assumes that the person has a need for psychic integrity. This need is met by the person knowing who he is and feeling that his self is an adequate self. The self-concept fulfills this function. In one of the two basic functions of self-concept listed by Epstein (1973) it is stated that the self-concept facilitates attempts to fulfill needs while avoiding disapproval and anxiety. Similarly, Sullivan (1953) notes that the self system is an organization of educative experience called into being by the necessity to avoid or to minimize incidents of anxiety. Thus self-concept fulfills the function of meeting the need for psychic integrity and thus minimizing anxiety.

In the conceptualization of the person being set forth in this book, the regulator and cognator subsystems act through the four adaptive modes to promote the person's adaptation. Adaptation, then, must be a function of the self-concept system. We can arrive at this same conclusion from the writings of the self-concept theorists. The second basic function of self-concept listed by Epstein (1973) is that it organizes data of experience. Adaptation has been defined as a positive response to environmental stimuli. To adapt, one must organize the data of experience. Self-concept thus fulfills a requirement, or serves the function of promoting adaptation. Gergen (1971) notes more specifically that the person's self-concept is important from the viewpoint of mental health and human happiness and that a significant degree of self-love seems a necessity. Positive mental health and human happiness would seem to be highly correlated with positive adaptation. If self-concept leads to these positive outcomes, it could be assumed to fulfill the function of leading to positive adaptation.

The self-concept system thus fulfills the twofold function of fulfilling human needs and promoting the person's adaptation.

Propositions Related to the Self-System

In the method of theorizing being followed in this book, the parts of each subsystem are related and linked together in general propositions. The linking of the parts of the self-concept system are shown in Figure 14.2 and the related propositions are given in Table 14.1.

In the vast literature of social psychology, we find theoretical and sometimes empirical support for the propositions related to the self-concept system.

Proposition 1.1 states that the quality of social experience in the form of others' appraisals positively influences the level of feelings of adequacy. In one inventory of scientific findings related to human behavior, Berelson and Steiner (1964) note the inverse of this proposition. They state that as a result of prejudice and discrimination, members of a minority group often suffer some deterioration of personality including self-doubt and self-hate. Studies by Goodman, Radke and Trager, and Davis are used by Berelson and Steiner, as evidence to support the generalization made. Thus it is reasonable to accept as true the proposition linking the quality of social experience with the level of feelings of adequacy.

The second proposition states that the adequacy of role taking positively influences the quality of input in the form of social experience.

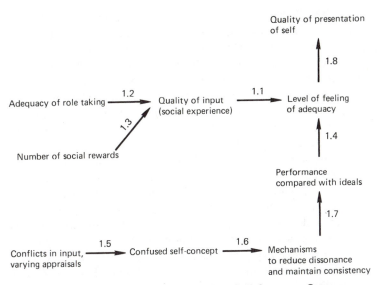

FIGURE **14.2** Linking of Parts of the Self-Concept System. Numbers refer to propositions in Table 14.1.

TABLE **14.1** Propositions Related to the Self-Concept System.

Proposition 1.1	The positive quality of social experience in the form of others' appraisals positively influences the level of feelings of adequacy.
Proposition 1.2	Adequacy of role taking positively influences the quality of input in the form of social experience.
Proposition 1.3	The number of social rewards positively influences the quality of social experience.
Proposition 1.4	Negative feedback in the form of performance compared with ideals leads to corrections in levels of feelings of adequacy.
Proposition 1.5	Conflicts in input in the form of varying appraisals positively influences the amount of self-concept confusion experienced.
Proposition 1.6	Confused self-concept leads to activation of mechanisms to reduce dissonance and maintain consistency.
Proposition 1.7	Activity of mechanisms for reducing dissonance and maintaining consistency (e.g. choice) tends to lead to feelings of adequacy.
Proposition 1.8	The level of feelings of adequacy positively influences the quality of presentation of self.[a]

[a]Adapted from Wylie, Ruth C. *The Self Concept: A Critical Survey of Pertinent Research Literature.* Lincoln: University of Nebraska Press, 1961.

This proposition is based on the early philosophical work of Mead (1934). Mead found the distinguishing trait of selfhood residing in the capacity of the person to be an object to himself. The mechanism involved is role taking through which the person takes the role of the other and looks back at himself from that perspective and so becomes an object to himself. Turner (1956) later expanded on the concept of role taking. He noted that when role taking involves identification and is reflexive, the self becomes specifically an object evaluated from the standpoint of the other. From this standpoint the individual begins to develop an estimate of his own adequacy and worth. Stryker's (1962) research added some qualifications to Mead's original conception but generally supported the notion that to engage in social activity, a person must take the role of the other implicated with him in the activity. If the activity can be carried out (output of the system) better with accurate role taking, then the quality of the input must also be more positive. We then accept our proposition linking adequacy of role taking with quality of social experience as a plausible statement.

The third proposition positively relates the number of social rewards with the quality of social experience. This proposition seems self-evident in that a positive social experience could be defined as one that is rewarding. However, we may cite the research related to the behavior of individuals in cohesive groups as evidence of the truth of our statement. For example, in studies of the United States Army in World War II, there is evidence that soldiers from cohesive (that is, rewarding) groups were more responsible in carrying out their soldierly duties, more confident of being able to perform well as soldiers, and less fearful in battle (Stouffer et al. 1949). Again we are arguing that if the output of the system behavior is more positive, then the input or social experience is also positive.

Proposition 1.4 states that negative feedback in the form of performance compared with ideals leads to corrections in levels of feelings of adequacy. In support of this general notion, Coopersmith (1959) studied self-esteem in fifth- and sixth-grade children. He obtained a partial $rpf + 0.30$ ($p < 0.01$) between Iowa Achievement Test scores and self-esteem, when sociometric status was held constant.

The next proposition relates conflicts in input in the form of varying appraisals to the positive influence on the amount of self-concept confusion experienced. This proposition is related to the generalization cited by Berelson and Steiner (1964) that the closer the correspondence between socializing agencies (home vis-à-vis school or parents vis-à-vis peers), the more securely and the more rapidly socialization takes place. The more conflicts between them, the slower and the more uncertain the process. To support this generalization, these authors report a study by Eisenstadt. In this study of Oriental Jews in Israel, the gulf between the parents and the school resulted in early school leaving on the part of the children, poor grades, and poor attendance.

In proposition 1.6 it is stated that confused self-concept leads to activation of mechanisms to reduce dissonance and maintain consistency. The proposition is well supported in the theoretical literature. (See Lecky 1969; Rogers 1951.) However, Wylie (1961) notes that little empirical work has been done on the characteristic of self-consistency since the theoretical propositions related to the characteristic tend to be vague and ambiguous. However, Wylie (1961) reports one study by Cartwright in which subjects were able to recall better the adjectives that they had previously identified as "like me." This may be an illustration of the existence of mechanisms to maintain consistency. In any case, our proposition seems reasonable based on the theoretical literature cited above.

The following proposition relates the activity of mechanisms for reducing dissonance and maintaining consistency with the tendency to lead to feelings of adequacy. Again, because empirical work on self-consistency is sparce, it is difficult to substantiate this particular proposition. However, Bill's (n.d.) study cited by Wylie (1961) found that greater satisfaction with the present period of life (possibly indicating successful mechanisms for reducing dissonance and maintaining consistency) was related to acceptance of self (possibly associated with feelings of adequacy.)

The last proposition states the major relationship of the theory of the self-concept system. That is, that the level of feelings of adequacy positively influences the quality of presentation of self. Wylie (1961) presents a series of studies that relate concepts such as self-regard with various measures of adjustment. For example, 11 studies show positive cross-sectional correlations between self-acceptance and acceptance by others. If we assume that the various measures of adjustment including acceptance by others are ways of describing the presentation of self, then it would seem that there is ample empirical support for proposition 1.8.

Example of Hypothesis for Practice

We have been demonstrating some theorizing concerning the self-concept mode of adaptation. One important function of theory is to generate testable hypotheses for research. Nursing needs to develop theories of nursing practice based on the overview of the theory of the person conceptualized. Nursing practice theory will give direction to nurses in intervening with patients. We may now ask what a nurse can do to help a patient based on our theorizing concerning the self-concept mode.

Literally hundreds of relationships between empirical indicators could be posited based upon the relationship between the concepts of the self-concept system theory. One particular relationship of two variables will be given as an example of the hypotheses that may be generated.

The hypothesis may be stated as follows: If the nurse helps the new mother to practice role taking, the mother will develop a higher level of feelings of adequacy. This hypothesis is based on the following reasoning.

Premise: Adequacy of role taking positively influences the quality of input in the form of social experience.

Premise: The positive quality of social experience positively influences the level of feelings of adequacy.

Conclusion: Adequacy of role taking positively influences the level of feelings of adequacy.

The nurse's guidance of practice sessions in role taking is seen as a special case of fostering adequacy in role taking. The mother's higher level of feelings of adequacy is seen as a special case of the level of feelings of adequacy. If the general concepts are related, then the concepts of the special case are hypothesized as having a relationship.

It is possible to specify the exact procedure a nurse will use in practicing role taking with the new mother. Further, we can specify empirical indicators for measuring the mother's level of adequacy. In this way we can design a study to test whether or not we have data to provide evidence that the proposed relationship exists. The particular activity of the nurse can then become a prescription for practice in a given diagnostic situation. Thus we are building nursing science and specifically nursing practice theory.

Summary

We have looked at the psychosocial mode of adaptation, the self-concept. Self-concept was described as a system involving wholeness, subsystems, relations of the parts, inputs, outputs, and self-regulation and control. The system functions of meeting needs and promoting adaptation were discussed. Finally, we did some theorizing with the self-concept system and derived a specific hypothesis for nursing practice.

References

Berelson, Bernard, and Gary A. Steiner. *Human Behavior: An Inventory of Scientific Findings.* New York: Harcourt, Brace & World, 1964.

Coombs, Arthur W., and Donald Snygg. *Individual Behavior: A Perceptual Approach to Behavior.* New York: Harper & Bros., 1959.

Coopersmith, S. "A Method for Determining Types of Self Esteem," *Journal of Abnormal and Social Psychology,* 59 (1959): 87–94.

Driever, Marie J. "Theory of Self Concept." In *Introduction to Nursing: An Adaptation Model,* ed. Sr. Callista Roy. Englewood Cliffs, N.J.: Prentice-Hall, Inc., 1976.

Epstein, Seymour. "The Self-Concept Revisited or a Theory of a Theory," *American Psychologist,* 28, no. 5 (May 1973): 404–16.

Gergen, Kenneth. *The Concept of Self.* New York: Holt, Rinehart & Winston, 1971.

Gordon, Chad. "Self Concept Methodologies," *Journal of Nervous and Mental Disease,* 148, no. 4 (July 1974): 328–64.

———, and Kenneth J. Gergen. *The Self in Social Interaction.* New York: John Wiley, 1968.

Hardy, Margaret E., and Mary E. Conway. *Role Theory: Perspectives for Health Professionals.* Englewood Cliffs, N.J.: Prentice-Hall, Inc., 1978.

James, William. *Introduction to Psychology.* New York: Henry Holt Co., 1918.

Lecky, Prescott. *Self-Consistency: A Theory of Personality.* New York: Doubleday, 1969.

Mead, George H. *Mind, Self and Society.* Chicago: University of Chicago Press, 1934.

Rogers, Carl R. *Client-Centered Therapy.* Boston: Houghton Mifflin, 1951.

Spitzer, Stephan, Carl Couch, and John Stratton. *The Assessment of Self.* Iowa City: Sernoll, Inc., 1970.

Stouffer, Samuel A., et al. *The American Soldier: Combat and Its Aftermath.* Studies in Social Psychology in World War II, vol. 2. Princeton, N.J.: Princeton University Press, 1949.

Stryker, Sheldon. "Conditions of Accurate Role-Taking: A Test of Mead's Theory." In *Human Behavior and Social Processes,* ed. Arnold Rose, pp. 42–60. Boston: Houghton Mifflin, 1962.

Sullivan, Henry Stack. *The Interpersonal Theory of Psychiatry.* New York: W. W. Norton & Co., Inc., 1953.

Turner, Ralph H. "Role-Taking, Role Standpoint, and Reference-Group Behavior," *American Journal of Sociology,* 61. no. 4 (January 1956): 316–28.

Wylie, Ruth C. *The Self Concept: A Critical Survey of Pertinent Research Literature.* Lincoln: University of Nebraska Press, 1961.

CHAPTER 15

Role function

Role function is the second of the psychosocial modes of adaptation. Role has been variously defined in the literature, but for the purposes of the Roy Adaptation Model, the definition used is as follows: A role is the functioning unit of our society; it defines the expected behaviors that a person should perform to maintain a title (Malaznik 1976). Although these role behaviors are those of the individual, they always occur in interaction with another person, that is, in a dyadic relationship.[1] As with the self-concept mode, role will be viewed as a system. References to the role *system* are common in the literature. For example, Znaniecki (1965) says that "social role is a dynamic *system* of actions"; Goode (1960) refers to viewing "one's total *role system* in perspective"; and Merton (1957) makes the observation that a frequent condition is *"role system* operating at considerably less than full efficiency."

In presenting the role function mode as a system through which the regulator and cognator subsystems act to promote adaptation we shall begin by looking at the system characteristics. Following this discussion, the role system functions will be explored. Then the role system will be linked

---

1. The focus of this chapter, however, will be on the individual as one side of that dyad.

together with a series of propositions and, finally, a specific hypothesis relevant to nursing practice will be derived.

System Characteristics

The first step in explicating the role system is to explore the system characteristics. These include wholeness, subsystems, parts related, inputs, output, and self regulation and control. Each of these characteristics will be discussed briefly.

Wholeness

The wholeness of the role system lies in its patterning of behavior. Turner (1956) refers to a role as the collection of patterns of behavior which are thought to constitute meaningful units and deemed appropriate to a person occupying a particular status in society. More simply stated is Merton's (1957) description of role as behavior oriented to the patterned expectations of others. Johnson's (1980) work in describing the person as a behavioral system is relevant here. She sees patterned behavior as characteristic of the behavioral system. In this way she is imputing wholeness to patterned behavior. The role system which involves patterned behavior is thus seen as possessing the characteristic of wholeness.

Subsystem

The subsystems of the role system can be easily conceptualized as the patterns of behavior related to each role set. Merton (1957) defines role set as the complement of the role relationships in which persons are involved by virtue of occupying a particular social status on position. If a person's position in society is variously defined, then he has as many role sets as there are ways of defining his position. Thus a mother, by virture of that position, interacts with her child, the child's teachers, the pediatrician, the P.T.A., and so forth. The role subsystems are the patterns of behavior related to all of these role sets.

Relation of parts

We have said that the parts of a system are put together by a basic mechanism that determines the output of the system. For the person viewed as an adaptive system, we have further postulated that the cognator and regulator are the basic coping mechanisms. These mechanisms have themselves been viewed as systems with internal processes. These internal processes will be activated in relation to the adaptive modes. How do the cognator/regulator processes form the basic mechanism of the role function mode?

Based on work by Mead and Turner, it is proposed that the basic mechanism of the role-taking process puts together the parts of the role system. This concept was introduced by Mead (1934) who observed that the individual works out the play of his own role by imaginatively "taking the role of the other." Turner (1956) extended this concept by specifying three standpoints from which the role-taking process takes place. First, ego may simply adopt the standpoint of the other. For example, he says, "If I were in his shoes, this is what I would do." In this case, the process is an automatic determinant of behavior. One simply acts from the standpoint of the other. Secondly, ego may adopt the standpoint of a third party. For example, he says, "I know what my mother would do in this case." This process indicates what behavior is expected of the actor depending upon the inferences made concerning the role of the other. Here the function of role-taking is to determine how he ought to act toward the other. Finally, ego may take the standpoint of a purpose or objective rather than a specific directive. For example, he says, "I want to impress this person and although I'm not sure what would work, I'll try this." Here the actor lacks a specific or detailed directive supplied by the standpoint of the third party and consequently must shape his own role behavior according to what he judges to be the probable effect of interaction between his own role and the inferred role of the other.

A later unpublished paper by Turner further described the characteristics of the role-taking process. It is first a reciprocal process; that is, viewed in this way, every role is a way of relating to other roles in a situation. Second, because role taking takes place in interaction, it is always a tentative process, a process of continuously testing the conception one has of the role of the other. Finally, role taking involves the grouping of behavior into units. That is, from this view, the role is a set or collection of possible actions that are regarded by the actor or viewer as belonging together.

The major mechanism of the role taking process draws upon and combines several cognator processes. The primary cognator processes involved seem to be those of perceptual information processing and of judgment. Surely as one sizes up the role of the other, one uses selective attention, coding, and memory. Then as one takes on the role of the other, one is likely to call upon problem-solving and decision-making processes. The parts of the role system are thus seen as being related by the basic mechanism of the role-taking process. This process is a particular way that the cognator effects its perceptual/information, and judgment processing.

System inputs

Just as the inputs to the self system come internally from the person and externally from the environment, so the role system inputs can be analyzed by discussing these two categories of input.

As implied earlier, the regulator and cognator subsystems form the suprasystem of the role system. One form of input to the role subsystem is the sensations and cognitions processed by the regulator and cognator. Any given role, for example that of the adult male, gets input from various neural and chemical activities from the regulator, such as the activity of jogging, as well as from the internal cognitions associated with these, for example the feeling of strength and power.

However, for the role function mode, the external inputs are probably the most significant. The vast array of external inputs to this system will be simplified by referring to them in the two categories of role cues and cultural norms. Based on Roy's (1967) research involving mothers of hospitalized children, role cues are seen as what another person does to allow the role-taker to focus on the other, recognize the other's position, and know the expected response to the other. Znaniecki (1965) explores the notion of cultural norms. He states that social roles are culturally patterned. There is a duty to act in accordance with definite norms. To him the task of the participant in collective life who performs a social role, together with those who cooperate with him, is first to apply certain moral standards, according to which human individuals are supposed to be evaluated by others. Second, the individuals are to conform with certain moral norms according to which their actions are expected to be satisfactory to others. Cultural norms, then, are significant input for the role system.

In noting how external input enters into the self system, the cognator processes of perception and learning were cited. In a similar way, role cues and cultural norms enter the role system primarily through perception and social learning. We perceive role cues and cultural norms in the here and now and we learn about them over time.

System output

The role system's organizing mechanism of role taking results in patterns of role behavior. This role behavior is the output of the role system and can be more generally termed role performance. Turner (1956) uses the term role performance for the complex of role behavior or the manner in which the role is actually enacted. Based on the inputs of role cues and cultural norms, the person goes through the role-taking process and comes up with his role performance. This includes all the behaviors resulting from his assuming the position of the other. It includes what the person says, what he does, and even how he dresses. Though it includes behaviors like the presentation of self behaviors, role behaviors are distinguished from self-concept behaviors in that they spring from a different basic mechanism. Self behaviors result from the striving for adequacy while role behaviors result from the role-taking process. In the actual analysis of human behavior it would be difficult to distinguish the two system outputs since the self and role mechanisms are acting and interacting simultaneously.

Self regulation and control

We have noted that every system has regulating and control mechanisms which tend to keep the system in balance. The major regulating mechanisms for the role system articulate role sets and reduce role strain. Merton (1957) describes six social mechanisms for articulating role sets. First, the person evaluates the relative importance of various statuses. For example, family and job obligations have priority over voluntary associations. Second, the differences of power of those in the role set gives the person a larger measure of autonomy. For example, if two members of the role set have competing power to impose their will, the individual may choose to whom he will respond. Third, Merton describes the situation of the insulation of role activities from observability by members of the role set. If one's activities in another role are not known to a member of one's role set, then the person is less subject to competing pressures. Fourth, observability of conflicting demands by members of the role set may serve to articulate the roles. When contradictions are plain, it becomes the task of members of the role set to resolve the contradictions. Compromise is usually the result. Merton's next consideration is that there is mutual social support among status occupants. Persons in certain statuses form supportive associations. Lastly, Merton says that one may abridge the role set. That is, the person may break off role relations, thus leaving a greater consensus of role expectations among those who remain.

Goode (1960) notes that in the role system, strain[2] is associated with mechanisms for reducing it. Two basic techniques are used. First, ego, or the self, manipulates its role structure in the following ways: compartmentalization, delegation, elimination of role relationships, extension, and barriers against intrusion. Secondly, ego responds by setting or carrying out the terms of the role relationship. Merton's and Goode's conceptualization can be used in understanding the major regulating mechanism for the role system, that is, the combination of mechanisms for articulating role sets and for reducing role strain.

In addition to these regulatory mechanisms, the role system has a feedback mechanism for control of output. When one perceives one's own

---

2. See Hardy and Conway (1978), Chapter 4, for a more recent development of the concepts of role stress and role strain.

behavior and the behavior of the other in an interaction, this perception acts as feedback to control further role behavior. Turner (1962) refers to internal validation of the interaction itself. This internal validation lies in the successful anticipation of the behavior of relevant others within the range necessary for the enactment of one's own role. External validation derives from the generalized other. It is based on ascertaining whether the behavior is judged to constitute a role by others whose judgments are felt to have some claim to correctness or legitimacy. If the role behavior is not validated, internally or externally, there will be corrections in the output of role performance. In this way the feedback controls the systems and maintains it in balance.

In relating the regulatory and control mechanisms to cognator processes, it seems that once again the apparatus involved in perceptual/information processing and in judgment are called into play. In internal and external validation selective attention, coding, and memory seem most important. When articulating role sets and reducing role strain is the problem, the mechanisms for accomplishing the appropriate solutions would utilize primarily the cognitive processes of problem solving and decision making.

We can summarize this section on the role system characteristics by showing the conceptualization of the system in Figure 15.1.

Perception and social learning provide the basis for role cues and cultural norms which act as input for the role-taking process. Mechanisms for articulating role sets and for reducing role strain act as self-regulation while internal and external validation provide feedback. All this leads to the system output of role performance.

System Function

Every system acts toward a purpose or end which is called the system function. Understanding the role system from the perspective of its six system

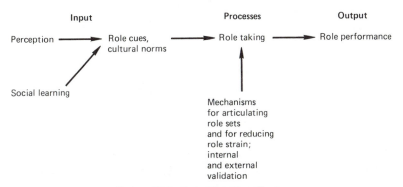

FIGURE 15.1 Role Function System.

characteristics, we may now describe the functions of this system. The role system functions primarily to meet the person's basic need for social integrity, and secondarily to promote the person's adapation to society and thus contribute to maintaining the social order.

Roy (1976) has noted that the person needs to know who he is in relation to others and what the expectations of society are regarding the positions he holds so that he can act appropriately. This need relates to role function. The operating of the role system fulfills this need and thus contributes to social integrity.

We have postulated that adaptation is the function of the person as an adaptive system. It must, then, be the function of the subsystems. We have seen that adaptation is the function, or goal, of the cognator and regulator subsystems. But in effecting their goal, the cognator and regulator act through the adaptive modes. We have seen how the cognator processes are called upon by the basic mechanism and the regulatory and control mechanisms of the role system. All of these cognator processes operate through the role mechanisms to promote the adaptation of the person as a total system. Support for the notion of a well-functioning role system promoting adaptation comes from sociological literature. Sarbin (1954) discusses the possible negative outcome of the role system. He says that if a person's locating of the position of the other is invalid, then his location of the position of self is likely to be invalid. His role enactment, therefore, will be inappropriate and *nonadaptive*. Cameron (1950) notes that any shift in role involves a shift in perspective; thus to have ease and skill in shifting perspectives (effective role taking) means to be capable of *adapting* to a wide range of shifting interpersonal relationships. This function of adaptation on the individual level is broadened by Merton (1957) and Parsons (1951) who imply that effective role function serves the goal of maintenance of the social order when considered in relation to society as a whole.

In general, then, the role system serves the functions of meeting the need for social integrity and of personal and social adaptation.

Propositions Related to the Role System

To develop propositions related to the role system, we must link together the concepts of the system. This is done in Figure 15.2. The related propositions are given in Table 15.1.

We may ask to what extent the propositions stated in Table 15.1 are supported in the theoretical and empirical literature. The following observations are offered relative to this question.

The first proposition states that the amount of clarity of input in the form of role cues and cultural norms positively influences the adequacy of

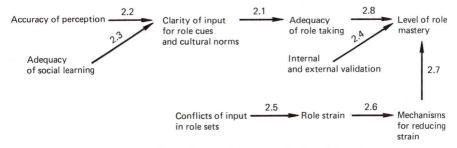

FIGURE **15.2** Linking of the Concepts of the Role System.
Numbers refer to propositions in Table 15.1.

role taking. Roy's (1967) role cue study demonstrated that introducton of
specific role cues by the nurse lead to greater role adequacy of the mother of
the hospitalized child. In this study, the author validated that the mothers
had in fact received the role cues. This may be seen as evidence supportive
of the statement that clarity of input in the form of role cues positively influences the adequacy of role taking.

Proposition 2.2 positively relates the accuracy of perception with the
clarity of input in the form of role cues and cultural norms. Empirical data
supporting this proposition seem to be lacking. However, some relevant notions come from Wright's (1960) analysis of the conditions underlying a
discrepancy between what a subject expects of the behavior of a person with
a disability and what at some later time he experiences of that behavior. One
of the conditions mentioned is the blurring of perception owing to anxiety.

TABLE **15.1** Propositions Related to the Role System

Proposition 2.1	The amount of clarity of input in the form of role cues and cultural norms positively influences the adequacy of role taking.
Proposition 2.2	Accuracy of perception positively influences the clarity of input in the form of role cues and cultural norms.
Proposition 2.3	Adequacy of social learning positively influences the clarity of input in the form of role cues and cultural norms.
Proposition 2.4	Negative feedback in the form of internal and external validations leads to corrections in adequacy of role taking.
Proposition 2.5	Conflicts in input in the form of conflicting role sets positively influences the amount of role strain experienced.
Proposition 2.6	Role strain leads to activation of mechanisms for reducing role strain and for articulating role sets.
Proposition 2.7	Activity of mechanisms for reducing role strain and for articulating role sets (e.g., choice) leads to adequacy of role taking.
Proposition 2.8	The level of adequacy of role taking positively influences the level of role mastery.

This blurring of perception leads to the obscuring of expectations and the apparent reality. Expectations are, as we have noted, part of role cues. The relationship between accuracy of perception and clarity of role cues seems reasonable, and by the same logic we may accept the relating of accuracy of perception and clarity of cultural norms.

The next proposition asserts that adequacy of social learning positively influences the clarity of input in the form of role cues and cultural norms. Burr's (1973) discussion of anticipatory guidance is applicable here. He defines anticipatory guidance as the *process of learning* the norms of a role before being in a social situation where it is appropriate to actually behave in that role. Burr makes the generalization that the amount of anticipatory socialization positively influences the ease of transitions into roles. He quotes a number of studies to support this generalization. For example, Dyer, as quoted by Burr, found that one factor that is inversely related to the severity of the crisis when parenthood occurs is whether one of the members of the couple had previously had a preparation for marriage course.

In proposition 2.4 we have the statement that negative feedback in the form of internal and external validations leads to corrections in adequacy of role taking. Again, empirical support seems lacking, but Wright (1960) describes this relationship in her analysis of reconciling the discrepency between what one expects of a disabled person and how he actually behaves. In describing the frequently occurring discrepancy where the performance of the disabled person is beyond the expectation of the observer or subject, she says:

> Assume that the subject in question is in the position of an outsider who, faced with the discrepancy, attempts to explain it. Because of this, he may cease ruminating about succumbing to the difficulties, i.e., emphasis on all the things the disability denies, and instead become concerned with the coping aspects, i.e., the ways in which the person has managed. In so doing, the subject begins to recognize the adjustment possibilities of a paraplegic, a blind girl, or an amputee. . . . not only will the coping aspects of difficulties have become dominant, but the subject will have also shifted his position to that of an insider.

The point being made here is that within an interaction, one corrects or adjusts the way one takes the role of the other such as becoming an insider rather than an outsider. This process was mentioned earlier in the discussion of Turner's three types of role taking, one "gets into the shoes of the other." Common experience thus supports this proposition.

The fifth proposition observes that conflicts in input in the form of conflicting role sets positively influence the amount of role strain experienced. In Gross, Mason, and McEachern's (1957) classic study, school superintendents perceived that their teachers expected them to recommend the highest salary increases possible. On the other hand, 75 percent of those superintendents with taxpayer's associations in their communities reported that these associations held opposite expectations. Similar conflicting expectations came from the city council and local politicans versus labor organizations, the P.T.A., personal friends, and individual schoolboard members. The strategies of compromise and avoidance described by the researchers clearly show the role strain resulting from these conflicting role sets.

This proposition is followed by one that states that role strain leads to activation of mechanisms for reducing role strain and for articulating role sets. The study just quoted (Gross, Mason, and McEachern 1957) described empirically and analyzed the activity stemming from the mechanisms activated by the conflict, namely, ignoring both demands, assuming the position of negotiator, substituting a new criteria, and trying to modify the conflicting expectations of one group. Based on this study, we have reason to accept these two propositions.

A further proposition in our theory submits that activity of mechanisms for reducing role strain and for articulating role sets leads to adequacy of role taking. Support for this proposition comes from Jacobson's (1952) study of conflict of attitudes toward the roles of the husband and wife in marriage. Differences in attitudes between divorced couples were on the average four times as great as those between married couples.

The final proposition relates positively the level of adequacy of role taking with the level of role mastery. Relevant here is Stryker's (1957) study to test the hypothesis that the adjustment of the individual is a function of the accuracy with which he can take the role of the other implicated with him in some social situation. Partial support was obtained with data from 46 family units showing that independent and high-agreement parents had higher mean adjustment when they were also accurate role takers than when they were inaccurate role takers. We have, then, some support for the validity of our last proposition.

Example of Hypothesis for Practice

We have dealt with the process of theorizing with the role function mode. In a practice-oriented discipline such as nursing, it is important that theory specify prescriptions for practice. That is, theory must meet the demand of giving direction for what nurses should do with patients. Based on our theorizing with the role function mode, we could postulate any number of hypotheses that could be tested, then used as guides for practice. One example of such an hypothesis will be discussed here.

The hypothesis may be stated as follows: If the nurse orients the patient to the sick role, the patient will perform at a higher level of role mastery in the sick role. The reasoning behind this hypothesis is drawn from the propositions stated earlier as shown below.

Premise: The amount of clarity of input in the form of role cues positively influences the adequacy of role taking.

Premise: The level of adequacy of role taking positively influences the level of role mastery.

Conclusion: The amount of clarity of input in the form of role cues positively influences the level of role mastery.

The nurse's specific, planned orientation of the patient to the sick role is seen as a specific type of clarity of input in the form of role cues. The level of role mastery in the sick role is a particular case of level of role mastery. We have given evidence for the truth of the premises in our discussion of the eight propositions for the role system. The conclusion based on the premises follows the rules of axiomatic logic. Thus, we may assume that the two concepts of the conclusion are in fact related, and by inference the relationship of the specific hypothesis is proposed as valid.

A given procedure may be specified for the nurse's orientation of the patient to the sick role. It would take into account the need for clarity and accuracy of perception as well as adequacy of social learning. In addition, in order to test this hypothesis, we must specify empirical indicators for level of role mastery in the sick role. If support is found for acceptance of the hypothesis, then the nursing activity specified in the research protocol can become a prescription for practice in situations where the nursing diagnosis warrants this intervention. In this way we are adding to the body of nursing knowledge and specifically testing nursing practice theory.

Summary

Our focus in this chapter has been on the process of theorizing with the role function mode. We described role function as a system with the characteristics of wholeness, subsystems, relations of parts, inputs, outputs, and self-regulation and control. Social integrity and individual and group adaptation were proposed as the system functions. In the last two sections of the chapter propositions and an hypothesis related to the role system were suggested.

References

Burr, Wesley. *Theory Construction and the Sociology of the Family.* New York: John Wiley, 1973.

Cameron, Norman. "Role Concepts in Behavior Pathology," *American Journal of Sociology,* 55 (March 1950): 464–67.

Goode, William J. "A Theory of Role Strain," *American Sociological Review,* 25 (1960): 483–96.

Gross, Neal; Ward S. Mason; and Alexander W. McEachern. *Explorations in Role Analysis: Studies of the School Superintendency Role.* New York: John Wiley, 1958.

Hardy, Margaret E., and Mary E. Conway. *Role Theory: Perspectives for Health Professions.* Englewood Cliffs, N.J.: Prentice-Hall, Inc., 1978.

Jacobson, Alver H. "Conflict of Attitudes Toward the Roles of the Husband and Wife in Marriage," *American Sociological Review* 17 (1952): 140–50.

Johnson, Dorothy E. "The Behavioral System Model for Nursing." In *Conceptual Models for Nursing Practice,* ed. Joan P. Riehl, and Sr. Callista Roy. 2 ed. Englewood Cliffs, N.J.: Prentice-Hall, Inc., 1980.

Malaznik, Nancy. "Theory of Role Function." In *Introduction to Nursing: An Adaptation Model,* ed. Sr. Callista Roy. Englewood Cliffs, N.J.: Prentice-Hall, Inc., 1976.

Mead, George H. *Mind, Self, and Society.* Chicago: University of Chicago Press, 1934.

Merton, Robert K., "The Role-Set: Problems in Sociological Theory," *British Journal of Sociology,* 8 (1957): 106–20.

Parsons, Talcott. *The Social System.* New York: Free Press, 1951.

Roy, Sr. Callista. "Role Cues and Mothers of Hospitalized Children," *Nursing Research,* (Spring 1967): 178–82.

———. *Introduction to Nursing: An Adaptation Model.* Englewood Cliffs, N.J.: Prentice-Hall, Inc., 1976.

Sarbin, Theodore. "Role Theory." In *Handbook of Social Psychology,* ed.Gardner Lindzey, pp. 223–58. Cambridge, Mass.: Addison-Wesley, 1954.

Stryker, Sheldon. "Role-Taking Accuracy and Adjustment," *Sociometry,* 20 (1957): 286–96.

Turner, Ralph. "Role-Taking, Role Standpoint and Reference Group Behavior," *American Journal of Sociology,* 61, no. 4 (January 1956): 316–28.

———. "Role-Taking Process Versus Conformity." In *Human Behavior and Social Processes,* ed. Arnold Rose. Boston: Houghton Mifflin, 1962.

———. "Role-Taking as Process." Unpublished paper, University of California, Los Angeles, n.d.

Wright, Beatrice A. *Physical Disability.* New York: Harper & Row, 1960.

Znaniecki, Florian. *Social Relations and Social Roles: The Unfinished Systematic Sociology.* San Francisco: Chandler Publishing Co., 1965.

CHAPTER **16**

Interdependence

The final psychosocial mode of adaptation is the interdependence mode.[1] In general, according to the Roy Adaptation Model, interdependence means a comfortable balance in relationships with others. The underlying need of this mode is to be loved and supported, to be nurtured and to nurture. According to Poush and Van Landingham (1977) the purpose of the mode is to be responded to by another and to establish an in-depth interaction with another person. This interaction has the characteristics of protecting, caring, proximity, physical contact, recognition, praise, and approval. When we visualize the person's interdependence mode, we move from a systems model to an intersystem model. Chin (1961) says that an intersystem model involves two open systems connected to each other. Connectives tie together or represent the lines of relationships of the two sytems. If we are looking at the relationship between persons, and persons have been viewed as systems, then it is appropriate to view the interdependence mode as an intersystem.

1. Significant work on this mode was carried out by a committee of Joyce Van Landingham, Mary Poush, Mary Hicks, and Dottie Clough at Mount St. Mary's College, Los Angeles, California during the years 1975–77 under a United States Public Health Service Grant.

As in the last two chapters, in examining this particular intersystem, we shall describe first the intersystem characteristics. This discussion will include wholeness, systems and subsystems, putting together of parts, inputs, and self-regulation and control. After this analysis, the interdependence intersystem functions will be investigated. Then the interdependence intersystem will be linked together with a series of propositions. Finally, a specific hypothesis relevant to nursing practice will be developed.

System Characteristics

We shall begin the explication of the interdependence intersystem with a brief discussion of system characteristics, as outlined earlier.

Wholeness

We have already argued that the parts of the intersystem—that is, the persons interacting—have wholeness. The person, as an adaptive system with regulator and cognator acting through the adaptive modes, functions as a unified whole. When two such systems are joined in an interrelatedness, this intersystem itself possesses a wholeness of its own. This notion of wholeness of the intersystem of interacting persons is supported by the symbolic interactionists literature (see, for example, Blumer 1969).

Systems and subsystems

The systems of the interdependence intersystem are the individual system relative to interdependence and the Other System. The subsystems of the interdependence individual system are the dependent response patterns and the independent response patterns. Just as the role subsystems are the patterns of behavior related to role sets, so in this mode relevant behavior patterns form the subsystems. The subsystems of the Other System have been identified by Poush and Van Landingham (1977) as significant others and support systems. They describe significant others as individuals or groups to whom significance is ascribed or inherent in the interaction. This category can include parents and other family members, social affiliations, God or a Supreme Being, animals, and objects. Caplan (1974) defines support systems as

> continuing social aggregates (namely, continuing interactions with another individual, a network, a group, or an organization) that provide individuals with opportunities for feedback about themselves and for validation of their expec-

tions about others, which may offset deficiencies in these communications within the larger community.

We thus have two systems, each with two subsystems.

Relation of parts

In this intersystem mode there will be two types of relation of parts. First we may ask about the basic mechanism that determines the output of the system. Second, we need to conceptualize the connectives that link the systems.

The central process of the individual system is seen as seeking to meet nurturance and nurturing needs. The cognator process that is activated in relation to this mode is primarily the process of learning. Through imitation, reinforcement, and insight the person seeks to meet nurturance and nurturing needs. The learning process relative to dependent-independent behaviors is well described by Gerwitz (1956).

The definition of support systems, quoted earlier from Caplan, gives us a view of the connectives between the individual and other systems. The feedback and validation of the significant others and support systems are seen as the connectives or relationship between the two systems. Poush and Van Landingham (1977) describe the content of this feedback and validation as being the needs, demands, and expectations of self and others. Again, these dimensions are exchanged in cognator learning processes.

System inputs

We have seen that the inputs for the self and role systems are both internal and external stimuli. McIntier (1976) describes the inputs for the interdependence individual system as being internal—the person's usual coping style—and external—an environmental change demanding a response. When environmental demands are so great that they are in conflict with the usual coping pattern, this input triggers the person's major adaptive mechanisms. Both internal and external stimuli are important as interdependence intersystem inputs.

System outputs

The process of seeking nurturance and nurturing, together with the control mechanism (to be discussed later) of balancing dependency and aggressive drives, leads to the output of the interdependence intersystem. Output is in the form of dependent and independent behavior. The classification of dependent behavior utilized by Sears, Maccoby, and Levin (1957) has been found useful in the development of the Roy Adaptation Model. It includes the following:

1. Help seeking: The purpose is to stimulate another to aid or assist the client to reach a goal.
2. Attention seeking: The purpose is to be noticed by others.
3. Affection seeking: The purpose is to be responded to by another and/or to establish an in-depth interaction with another person.

The classification of independent behaviors includes:

1. Initiative taking: The purpose is to begin and work on a task by oneself.
2. Obstacle mastery: The purpose is to complete a simple to difficult task by oneself.

Self-regulation and control

As with any system, the interdependence intersystem must have regulatory and control mechanisms. Poush and Van Landingham (1977) describe communication as the key to the interactional paradigm. Communication includes verbal and nonverbal exchanges. It is an effective regulator when it is direct, clear, specific, congruent, and honest. When Caplan (1976) discusses the relationship of the support system to the individual, he notes the importance of a common language and free communication. It is through communication that the systems regulate their interaction and the mutual meeting of nurturance and nurturing needs.

The control factor of the intersystem is the balancing of the dependency and aggressive drives. This balance is described by McIntier (1976) and Ellison (1976). The dependency drive is learned rather than innate. It emerges from the interactions of child and caretaker during infancy and early childhood. It is postulated that the drive behind the need to achieve is aggression. This drive and the patterns of control over it form the independent response tendencies. One eventually includes both kinds of behavior to maintain a balance in the intersystem.

When the regulatory and control mechanisms are related to the cognator processes, we have again a preponderance of the learning apparatus. Communication patterns are learned primarily through imitation and reinforcement. Similarly, one learns to balance dependency and ag-

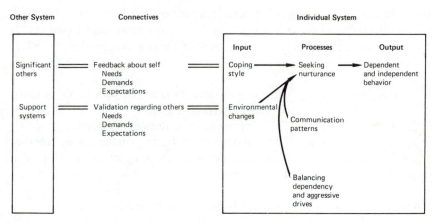

FIGURE **16.1** Interdependence Intersystem.

gressive drives in one's overt behavior. Heathers (1955) says that a central aspect of the process of becoming socialized is developing needs, perceptions, and response patterns having to do with dependence on others or with independence.

The conceptualization of the interdependence intersystem that we have presented can be represented as shown in Figure 16.1

The Other Systems with which the person is joined in this mode are significant others and support systems. The feedback and validation from the Other System are seen as the connectives or relationship between the two systems. We have described the content of the feedback and validation as the needs, demands, and expectations of self and others. The input to the system is external environmental changes and internal coping styles. The central process of this system is seeking to meet nurturance and nurturing needs. Regulating the system is communication patterns. The control factor of the intersystem is the balancing of dependency and aggressive drives in social situations. The output of the intersystem is in the categories of dependent and independent behaviors noted earlier.

System Function

The purpose or end toward which a system acts is the function of the system. Based on the system characteristics that have been discussed, we can describe the functions of the interdependence intersystem. We have noted that the purpose of the mode is to be responded to by another and to establish an in-depth interaction with another person. However, at the most basic level, this purpose serves the function of maintaining social integrity.

It gives one a feeling of being adequate and secure in relationships with other people. Thus this mode shares with the role function mode the function of social integrity.

Beyond the primary function of social integrity, this mode has the secondary function of promoting the person's adaptation. In discussing the child's dependent and independent behavior, Gerwitz (1956) says that the major problems raised may be considered a subclass of general behavior problems and hence continuous with questions characteristically raised about adaptive behaviors. The output of the system, dependent and independent behaviors, are adaptive or ineffective just as are the output of the systems of the other adaptive modes.

The general functions of the interdependence intersystem are thus social integrity and adaptation.

Propositions Related to Interdependence Intersystem

In the approach to theorizing being used in this book, we have been linking together the concepts of the various systems. This is done for the interdependence intersystem in Figure 16.2. The related propositions are stated in Table 16.1.

The body of literature on interdependence is more scattered and less fully developed than that on self-concept or role. Still it is possible to make a few observations on the theoretical and empirical support for the seven propositions.

The first proposition states that the balance and flexibility of coping

TABLE 16.1 Propositions Related to Interdependence Intersystem

Proposition 3.1	The balance and flexibility of coping style positively influences the adequacy of seeking nurturance and nurturing.
Proposition 3.2	The optimum amount of environmental changes positively influences the adequacy of seeking nurturance and nurturing.
Proposition 3.3	Clarity of feedback about self positively influences the balance and flexibility of coping style.
Proposition 3.4	Clarity of validation regarding others positively influences the balance and flexibility of coping style.
Proposition 3.5	Commonality and freedom of communication patterns positively influences the adequacy of seeking nurturance and nurturing.
Proposition 3.6	The balancing of dependency and aggressive drives positively influences the adequacy of seeking nurturance and nurturing.
Proposition 3.7	Adequacy of seeking nurturance and nurturing positively influences interdependence.

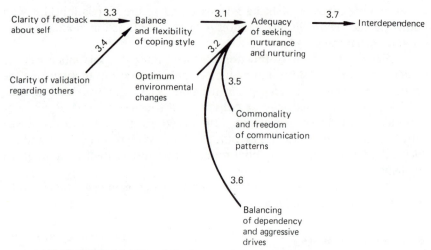

FIGURE 16.2 Linking of Concepts of the Interdependence Intersystem. Numbers refer to propositions in Table 16.1.

style positively influences the adequacy of seeking nurturance and nurturing. A relevant empirical finding is Hartup's (1958) study of nurturance and nurturance withdrawal in relation to the dependency behavior of preschool children. Boys who were less dependent (equated here with balance and flexibility of coping style) responded to withdrawal of nurturance with behavior not designed to gain the reassurance of adults. Thus, in a situation not appropriate to meeting their nurturing needs, they do not seek nurturance. It might be assumed that in appropriate circumstances their seeking of nurturance and nurturing would be adequate. Such a conclusion is implied in McIntier's (1976) definition of balanced coping as a pattern which exhibits an admixture of dependent and independent behaviors. The person is free to use whichever behavior is appropriate to the circumstances. In this way the person is more likely to get his needs met, or in other words, to have adequacy in seeking nurturance and nurturing.

Proposition 3.2 relates positively the optimum amount of environmental changes with adequacy of seeking nurturance and nurturing. Although empirical support for this proposition is not currently available, Helson's (1964) theoretical discussion of optimal levels and ranges of functions—the U-hypothesis—is relevant here. Helson notes that within the fairly wide limits under which animals are able to survive there are optimal zones, regions, or levels of functioning where demands of the environment are met with ease, accuracy, comfort, and with the least cost as gauged by long-term effects on the organism. Thus in this proposition we are assuming that there is an optimum amount of environmental change which will bring about an adequacy of seeking nurturance and nurturing. If, however, changes in the environment are outside that range, ineffectual, or overwhelming—for example, the sudden demand for total dependence produced by severe illness—then one will have difficulty in adequately meeting dependence-independence needs.

In the next two propositions we find a positive relationship postulated between clarity of feedback about self and clarity of validation regarding others and the balance and flexibility of coping style. Three generalizations cited by Berelson and Steiner (1964) are relevant here. They note that: (1) The more rejected the child feels the more dependent he is likely to be; (2) very little satisfaction or nurturance during the period of infantile and childhood dependency (as in institutional cases) leads to subsequent dependence in some, and exaggerated independence in others; and (3) very great nurturance during infantile and childhood dependency (as in the case of maternal overprotection and overpermissiveness) also seems to lead in opposite directions—continued need for dependency and hence lowered independence on the one hand, and rebellious and defiant behavior on the other. The series of studies done by Sears, Maccoby, and Levin (1957) are generally supportive of these conclusions. In other words, we have some evidence for asserting that the kind of feedback about self and validation about others communicated in childrearing approaches has a direct relationship to the kind of coping style the child develops.

Proposition 3.5 states that the commonality and freedom of communication patterns positively influence the adequacy of seeking nurturance and nurturing. The interactional model for nursing practice developed by Orlando (1961) is postulated upon just such an idea. She sees the adequate communication of perceptions, thoughts, and feelings as prerequisite to meeting the patient's need for help. Experimental evidence for the validity of this model comes from Bochnak's (1963) study which used the communication approach to obtain greater pain relief for patients.

The next proposition asserts that the balancing of dependency and aggressive drives positively influences the adequacy of seeking nurturance and nurturing. This proposition is based on the theoretical framework of the interdependence mode as presented by McIntier (1976). We have noted how she postulates that the energy for behavior in this mode comes, first, from a secondary dependency drive. Gerwirtz's (1956) discussion of the antecedents of emotional dependence support this notion. Second, energy is supplied by the aggressive drive. Ellison's (1976) interpretation of aggression as a problem of interdependence is supportive of this notion. Though empirical work has not been undertaken to validate this proposition, the theoretical writings support the claim that the balance in these two drives is related to adequacy in seeking nurturance and nurturing.

The final proposition relates positively the adequacy of seeking nurturance and nurturing with interdependence behavior. Again we have a generalization from Berelson and Steiner (1964) which is supportive of the stated relationship. These authors state that prolonged separation from the mother and a secure home environment (as in the case of hospitalized or institutionalized children) beyond the age of 3 months and up to about 5 years, but especially up to about age 30 months or so, seems to lead to serious emotional and intellectual retardation. Such retardation is shown by poor relations with people, inability to give or receive attention or affection for any prolonged periods, retarded speech, curtailment of intellectual development, apathy and inaccessibility, even some adverse effects on physical growth. Berelson and Steiner (1964) cite the work of Bowlby and Goldfarb as evidence in support of this generalization. Although this statement goes beyond our proposition, it is surely inclusive of it. Thus we have some substantiation for this major proposition of our theoretical system.

Example of Hypothesis for Practice

In this chapter we have gone through the process of doing some theorizing with the interdependence mode. Yet, because nursing is a practice discipline, we ask immediately about the relationship of this theorizing to the real world of nursing practice. What direction can theory give us for what nurses should do with patients? One way of linking theorizing to practice is to develop hypotheses that can be tested and, if found to be valid, can be prescribed for practice. Of the many possible hypotheses, one hypothesis will be used as an illustration here.

A relevant hypothesis can be stated as follows: If the nurse provides the time and space for private family visits, the patient will demonstrate more appropriate attention-seeking behavior. The following axiomatic reasoning, with the propositions stated earlier, is the basis of this hypothesis.

Premise: The optimum amount of environmental changes positively influences the adequacy of seeking nurturance and nurturing.

Premise: Adequacy of seeking nurturance and nurturing positively influences interdependence.

Conclusion: The optimum amount of environmental changes positively influences interdependence.

Since the family is accustomed to time and space for private visits in the home, the provision of these by the nurse within an institution is seen as an optimum environmental change within that setting. Use of appropriate attention-seeking behavior is seen as one form of positive interdependence. Again we have given evidence to support the premises used. By logic, then, the two concepts of the conclusion should be valid, as would be the hypothesis derived.

Procedures can be devised regarding private family visiting as in the case of the long-term rehabilitation patient or the patient in a nursing home. They would be based on an understanding of the functions of significant others and support systems. Empirical indications can be devised for the term *appropriate attention-seeking behavior.* We may then initiate a research project to test the hypothesis. If data point to the acceptance of the hypothesis, then the particular procedure that had been specified can become a prescription for practice. As with all the hypotheses that can be derived from our theorizing, this hypothesis has the potential of contributing to the body of nursing knowledge and specifically testing nursing practice theory.

Summary

Following the procedure established for Part 4, in this chapter we have focused on theorizing with the interdependence mode. This intersystem was described according to its characteristics of wholeness, systems and subsystems, relations of parts, inputs, outputs, and self-regulation and control. The intersystem functions of social integrity and adaptation were explored briefly. A series of propositions was proposed on the basis of the intersystem model. Finally, a hypothesis was derived based on logically linking two of the propositions.

References

Berelson, Bernard, and Gary A. Steiner. *Human Behavior: An Inventory of Scientific Findings.* New York: Harcourt, Brace and World, 1964.

Blumer, Herbert. *Symbolic Interactionism.* Englewood Cliffs, N.J.: Prentice-Hall, Inc., 1969.

Bochnak, Mary Ann. "The Effect of an Automatic and Deliberative Process of Nursing Activity on the Relief of Patient's Pain: A Clinical Experiment," *Nursing Research,* 12, no. 3 (Summer 1963): 191–92.

Caplan, Gerald. *Support Systems and Community Mental Health: Lectures on Concept Development.* New York: Behavioral Publications, 1974.

Chin, Robert. "The Utility of System Models and Development Models for Practitioners." In *The Planning of Change,* ed. Warren G. Bennis, Kenneth D. Bense, and Robert Chin. New York: Holt, Rinehart & Winston, 1961.

Ellison, Edythe. "Problem of Interdependence: Aggression." In *Introduction to Nursing: An Adaptation Model,* Sr. Callista Roy, ed. Englewood Cliffs, N.J.: Prentice Hall, 1976, pp. 330–341.

Gerwitz, Jacob L. "A Program of Research on the Dimensions and Antecedents of Emotional Dependence," *Child Development,* 27, no. 2 (June 1956): 205–21.

Hartup, Willard W. "Nurturance and Nurturance Withdrawal in Relation to the Dependency Behavior of Preschool Children," *Child Development,* 29 (1958): 191–201.

Heathers, Glen. "Acquiring Dependency and Independency: A Theoretical Orientation," *The Journal of Genetic Psychology*, 83, (1955): 277–91.

Helson, Harry. *Adaptation Level Theory.* New York: Harper & Row, 1964.

McIntier, Sr. Teresa Marie. "Theory of Interdependence," In *Introduction to Nursing: An Adaptation Model,* ed. Sr. Callista Roy, pp. 291–302. Englewood Cliffs, N.J.: Prentice-Hall, Inc., 1976.

Orlando, Ida Jean. *The Dynamic Nurse-Patient Relationship.* New York: Putnam's, 1961.

Poush, Mary, and Joyce Van Landingham. *Interdependence Mode Module.* Unpublished handout, Mount St. Mary's College, Los Angeles, 1977.

Sears, Robert R.; Eleanor E. Maccoby; and Harry Levin. *Patterns of Childrearing.* New York: Harper & Row, 1957.

Part 5 contains just one chapter, the conclusion of the book. In it some observations are made about the theory of the human person as an adaptive system. Then directions for nursing practice theory, based on the theory of the person, are indicated. Finally, some implications for further work are outlined.

Conclusion

CHAPTER 17

Conclusion

This book has focused on theory construction in nursing. After the introductory material on theory development in general, the major portion of the text was devoted to theorizing with the Roy Adaptation Model. What can be said about the theory that has been constructed? In Chapter 2 we noted that nursing needs theories of the human person and theories of the diagnoses and treatment of problems these persons have that are within the domain of nursing. In this chapter we shall draw some conclusions about these two types of theory based upon what has been developed earlier. Finally, some implications for further work will be outlined.

Theory of the Adapting Person

In Chapter 5 we put forth a theory of the adapting person. The person was viewed as an adaptive system with two main subsystems, termed *regulator* and *cognator*. The four adaptive modes were seen as the effectors of these subsystems (see Figure 5.3). The functioning of the cognator and regulator subsystems were described in a series of theoretical propositions.

When the physiological needs were developed theoretically in

Chapters 6 through 13, they were discussed in relation to major propositions of the regulator. Then in Chapters 14, 15, and 16 the theory of the psychosocial adaptive modes were developed. Self-concept, role function, and interdependence were developed as systems acting in conjunction with the cognator and the regulator.

Although the relationship between the subsystems and the adaptive modes has been referred to repeatedly, it seems appropriate to take a concluding look at it. How shall we speak of each kind of system? Is there some conceptual way of linking the systems that have been developed?

One appropriate way of distinguishing the two types of systems may be to call the cognator and regulator the primary or functional systems. The four adaptive modes, then, are the secondary or effector systems. In this way the two systems are identified by their roles and their use.

The intersystems model introduced in Chapter 16 provides one way of linking the primary and secondary systems. We noted that Chin (1961) says that an intersystem model involves two open systems connected to each other. Connectives tie together or represent the lines of relationships of the two systems.

Based on the beginning theoretical work in this book, it is proposed that the functions of the cognator and regulator be viewed as the connectives between the adaptive modes. This notion is illustrated in Figure 17.1.

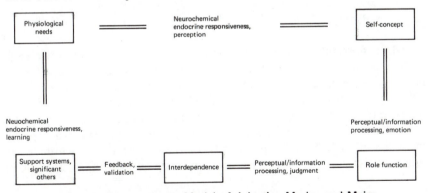

FIGURE 17.1 Intersystems Model of Adaptive Modes and Major Cognator-Regulator Connectives.

Each adaptive mode is linked to another adaptive mode by means of major cognator or regulator connectives. The view presented here capitalizes on specific ties between the primary and secondary systems noted in the earlier chapters. However, given these pieces of the whole, the picture could be shifted, as in a kaleidoscope,[1] and other arrangements of parts

---

1. We are indebted to **Patricia Whalen,** a graduate student at the University of San Diego, for the image of the kaleidoscope used in connection with the adaptation model.

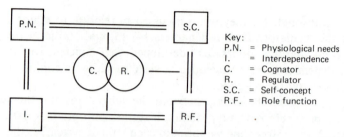

Figure 17.2 Abstract view of primary and secondary systems of the Roy Adaptation Model.

could be seen. For example, physiological needs might be related to role function through the cognator process of affective appraisal. An abstract view of these relationships is given in Figure 17.2.

The Roy Adaptation Model thus implies a theory of the person as an adaptive system that possesses the primary functional subsystems of cognator and regulator. The processes of these subsystems are the connectives which link together the systems of the adaptive modes, physiological needs, self-concept, role function, and interdependence. This text has developed interrelated propositions concerning each part of the person system.

Nursing Practice Theory

Based on nursing's view of the human person, nursing needs to develop theories of nursing practice. That is, nursing needs interrelated propositions denoting the nature of the problems and the concomitant treatment with which nurses are concerned. What direction does this text provide for nursing practice theory based on the Roy Adaptaion Model?

The Roy Adaptation Model has identified nursing diagnosis as a judgment about ineffective or potentially ineffective behaviors within each mode and identification of their most relevant influencing factors (Roy 1976).

As propositions were discussed relative to each adaptive mode, specific behaviors and stimuli were identified. This identification of behaviors and stimuli can guide the development of interrelated propositions relative to the occurrence of patient problems, or certain diagnostic categories. Furthermore, the theory of the adaptive person which was developed can lead to a new method of analyzing data to make a patient diagnosis. According to the view of the person given in Figure 17.2, ineffective behaviors in more than one mode can be summarized by ineffectiveness in the cognator or regulator which connects the modes. Thus cross-modal diagnoses can be made. This approach can be visualized as in Figure 17.3.

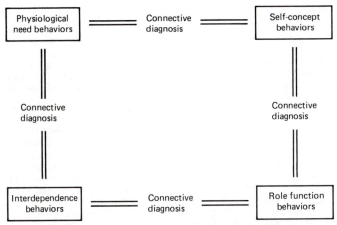

FIGURE **17.3** One View of Cross-Modal Diagnoses.

Note that this figure portrays only one of many possible views since once again the kaleidoscope may be turned to show a new arrangement of relationships between and among adaptive modes. The connective diagnoses are the statements made by the nurse based on judgments about the ineffective cognator and regulator processes. A clinical example may be helpful. Figure 17.4 gives the case study of Dr. Horace Ambrose. Figure 17.5 outlines the cross-modal diagnosis based on this data.

In Figure 17.5 we see the predominate behaviors in each mode listed in the boxes. A diagnostic label is given to that behavior and an ineffective cognator or regulator response is identified from among the processes acting as connectives between the modes. We still have four diagnoses, all of which are probably operating at some level with Dr. Ambrose. Which one is primary and which would be the entry level of choice for nursing intervention will be discussed below.

Thus far we have noted that our theorizing with the Roy Adaptation Model gives us some direction for developing nursing practice theory relative to diagnosis.

The treatment orientation of the Roy Adaptation Model follows from its diagnostic orientation. If the stimuli cause the behavior, then the stimuli must be changed to change behavior. The hypotheses at the end of Chapters 6 through 16 give examples of how stimuli may be changed to promote adaptation. This early work paves the way for developing a network of interrelated propositions concerning nursing intervention. Furthermore, since we have developed connective diagnoses based on cognator and regulator processes, this theory network can include process-oriented nursing interventions.

It is anticipated that some hierarchy of cognator/regulator processes

Dr. Horace Ambrose was admitted to the cardiac care unit five days ago, where the medical diagnosis of Acute Inferior Myocardial Infarction was established. Following an uncomplicated course with no chest pain past the initial episode, Dr. Ambrose was transferred on the sixth day to a private room on the medical unit.

Information from the chart and the nurse in the cardiac care unit revealed the following data. This was the first hospital admission for Dr. Ambrose, who presented himself at the hospital with the chief complaint of "crushing" severe substernal chest pain. Indeed, this 47-year-old man stated he had "never experienced such pain." The patient had no prior history of illness that had required hospitalization. Dr. Ambrose expressed pride in his state of "excellent health" and gave an account of having regular checkups, following a planned daily exercise schedule, participating in golf and tennis, watching his diet and weight, and abstaining from smoking. The nurse stated that on his last day in the unit he made comments during his bath as, "I'm not feeling any pain, I can do that," and talked about being transferred from the unit as meaning he could soon resume his successful practice as a head and neck surgeon. The nurse also related that his wife Janice, age 42; daughter Julie, age 18; and son Paul, age 16, were frequent visitors and overtly expressed their concern about the patient. His mother Martha, age 70, who also lives in the household, was unable to come to the hospital due to her arthritis, but she called frequently about her son. The nurse revealed that the patient was an American Jew and that some of the concerns and behavior of the family may be related to this fact.

Today an aide reported that she had seen the patient go to the bathroom and she wondered if there had been a change in the orders. The team leader confirmed that he was still on commode privileges only. An L.V.N. entered his room and found him standing at the sink shaving. She said, "I told him to get back to bed. He replied that he felt well enough and that his activity could be extended safely. He certainly isn't asking for assistance like he should." The team leader noted that the patient's son had brought his father a chili cheeseburger (at Dr. Ambrose's request). Another aide reported that the patient asked to have a phone connected as soon as he was transferred to the medical unit. He immediately made a call to his office, stating he would be leaving the hospital in the near future and to start arranging surgery for one of his patients.

The nurse who gave Dr. Ambrose morning care charted that he was holding a newspaper and not using the bedside table as all myocardial infarction patients were instructed. She had found the patient very talkative and her interview had validated his interest in sports and his concern about returning to his practice. He mentioned that he had noticed some weakness in his extremities which was new, but felt this might be due to his increased activity after five days of rest. During their conversation, Mrs. Ambrose entered the room. As the nurse was leaving she heard the patient ask his wife to keep him informed on all financial matters and decisions in the family, since he was feeling better now. Later, the wife told the nurse about her husband's interest in sports as a participant and expressed concern about how she was going to get him to slow down. "I keep telling him not to get out of bed and to take it easy. (pause) He just doesn't listen to me about such things."

FIGURE 17.4 The case of Dr. Ambrose. Reprinted with permission from Riehl, Joan B., and Sr. Callista Roy. *Conceptual Models for Nursing Practice*, 2 ed. Englewood Cliffs, N.J.: Prentice-Hall, Inc., 1980.

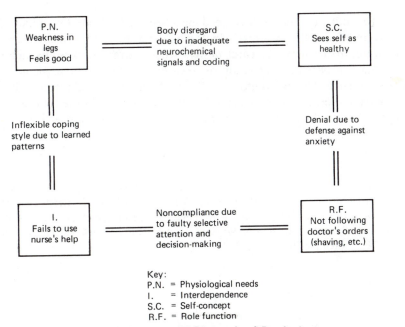

Key:
P.N. = Physiological needs
I.   = Interdependence
S.C. = Self-concept
R.F. = Role function

FIGURE **17.5** Cross-modal Diagnosis of Dr. Ambrose.

exists. Thus a nursing priority for intervention can be established. In the case of Dr. Ambrose, it may be necessary to deal with the underlying anxiety before one can deal with learned patterns, selective attention, and decision making. Considerable additional study will be needed to uncover such a hierarchy of processes.

In summary, although we have provided some promising leads for further development, the development of nursing practice theory based on the Roy Adaptation Model has barely begun.

Implications for Further Work

In what has been said regarding the theory of human person and nursing practice theory, we have implications for further work to be done in theorizing with the Roy Adaptation Model.

First, elaboration of the theory is needed. We must look at the theory of the adaptive person to further explain the interrelatedness of the adaptive modes. In this process we must also search for multivariable and nonlinear relationships. Cognator and regulator processes must be studied to discover the proposed hierarchy of processes. Furthermore, the whole nursing practice theory based on the model must be worked out according to the direction given here.

Secondly, the theory developed must be tested. This testing might take the form of a follow-up text which would review the pertinent research literature, then generate research designs where current work is unavailable. Eventually a systematic program of research will have to be implemented. Efforts such as these in programs of theory development and research, based on nursing models, can make significant contributions in the total process of establishing the science of nursing as a basis to nursing practice.

References

Chin, Robert. "The Utility of System Models and Developmental Models for Practitioners." In *The Planning of Change,* ed. Warren G. Bennis, Kenneth D. Benne, and Robert Chin. New York: Holt, Rinehart & Winston, 1961.

Roy, Sr. Callista. *Introduction to Nursing: An Adaptation Model.* Englewood Cliffs, N.J.: Prentice-Hall, Inc., 1976.

Author index

Subject index